Clausal Syntax of German

*Studies in Constraint-Based Lexicalism*



The aim of this series is to make work in various nonderivational, lexicalist approaches to grammar available to a wide audience of linguists. In approaches of this kind, grammar is seen as the interaction of constraints from multiple dimensions of linguistic substance, including information about syntactic category, grammatical relations, and semantic and pragmatic interpretation.

Studies in
Constraint-Based Lexicalism

# Clausal Syntax of German

Judith Berman

CSLI PUBLICATIONS
Center for the Study of
Language and Information
Stanford, California

Center for the Study of Language and Information
Leland Stanford Junior University
Printed in the United States
07 06 05 04 03 5 4 3 2 1

*Library of Congress Cataloging-in-Publication Data*

Berman, Judith, 1963-
Clausal syntax of German / Judith Berman.
p. cm. – (Studies in constraint-based lexicalism)
Includes bibliographical references and index.

ISBN 1-57586-361-8 (alk. paper)
ISBN 1-57586-362-6 (pbk. : alk. paper)

1. German language–Syntax. 2. German language–Clauses.
I. Title. II. Series.
PF3361.B46 2003
435–dc21 2002155641
CIP

∞ The acid-free paper used in this book meets the minimum requirements of the American National Standard for Information Sciences—Permanence of Paper for Printed Library Materials, ANSI Z39.48-1984.

CSLI was founded early in 1983 by researchers from Stanford University, SRI International, and Xerox PARC to further research and development of integrated theories of language, information, and computation. CSLI headquarters and CSLI Publications are located on the campus of Stanford University.

CSLI Publications reports new developments in the study of language, information, and computation. In addition to lecture notes, our publications include monographs, working papers, revised dissertations, and conference proceedings. Our aim is to make new results, ideas, and approaches available as quickly as possible. Please visit our web site at
http://cslipublications.stanford.edu/
for comments on this and other titles, as well as for changes and corrections by the author and publisher.

# Contents

**List of Abbreviations** ix

**Acknowledgments** xi

**1 Introduction** 1

1.1 German Syntax and LFG 1

1.2 Overview 4

**2 Lexical Functional Grammar** 7

2.1 C-Structure 8

2.2 F-Structure 10

2.3 The Correspondence between C- and F-structure 13

2.4 A-Structure 19

**3 Phrase Structure in German** 23

3.1 Essentials of German Sentence Structure 23

3.2 C-Structure of Sentential Phrases 29

3.2.1 The Functional Projection CP 29

3.2.2 No Evidence for $I^0$ 31

3.2.3 Function Specification in German 33

3.2.3.1 Choi's Approach 33

3.2.3.2 Haider's Approach 34

3.2.4 Verbal Complex 37

3.2.5 Extraposed Constituents 39

3.3 Verb Second and Extended Head 40

3.4 Summary 44

**4 Every Sentence in German has a Subject 45**

4.1 The Subject Condition 45

4.2 Clauses without a Structural Subject 47

4.2.1 Default vs. Lexical Case-Marking 49

4.2.2 Impersonal Passive 51

4.3 The Role of the Verbal Agreement Morphology 52

4.3.1 Pronoun Incorporation and Pro-Drop 54

4.3.2 Specifying Expletive Subjects 56

4.3.3 Predictions of the Analysis 59

4.4 German as a Semi-Pro-Drop Language 62

4.5 Is there an Expletive Subject DP in German? 63

4.5.1 Evidence for *Es* as a (Quasi)-Argument? 65

4.6 The Subject in Non-Finite Clauses 67

4.6.1 Functional vs. Anaphoric Control 68

4.6.2 Non-Representation of the Subject of Non-Finite Clauses on C-Structure 71

4.7 Summary 74

**5 Weak Crossover and Empty Categories 75**

5.1 The Analysis of Weak Crossover — Bresnan (1998) 77

5.2 Weak Crossover in German 79

5.2.1 Scrambling — Choi (1995) 79

5.2.2 Topicalization 80

5.2.3 Weak Crossover Involving Adjuncts 82

5.2.4 Weak Crossover between Objects 83

5.2.5 Weak Crossover and Complex Sentences 84

5.2.6 Weak Crossover Involving Long Distance Dependencies 86

5.2.7 Weak Crossover and Infinitives 89

5.3 A Traceless Account of Weak Crossover 90

5.3.1 Dalrymple *et al.* (2001) 90

5.3.2 Discussion 91

5.4 Summary 94

**6 Long Distance Dependencies 95**

6.1 Modeling Extraction with Functional Uncertainty 96

6.1.1 Outside-in Functional Uncertainty 97

6.1.2 Inside-out Functional Uncertainty 99

6.2 An Analysis of Long Distance Dependencies in

German Based on Inside-Out Functional Uncertainty 101
6.2.1 German Data Involving Extraction 101
6.2.2 Conditions on the Path — Kaplan and Zaenen (1989) 103
6.2.3 A Further Restriction on Long Distance Dependencies 106
6.2.4 Off-Path Constraints 107
6.3 Long Distance Dependencies as Locally Bounded Dependencies 111
6.4 A Comparison of the Two Accounts 115
6.5 Summary 120

**7 Distribution of Sentential Arguments 123**
7.1 Topicalization of Sentential Arguments in English 123
7.2 German Data 126
7.3 Previous Analyses 128
7.3.1 Webelhuth (1992) 128
7.3.2 Büring (1995b) 131
7.3.3 Dalrymple and Lodrup (2000) 133
7.4 Topicalization vs. Left Dislocation of Sentential Arguments 137
7.5 Distribution of Nominal vs. Sentential Arguments 140
7.6 Extraposition of Sentential Arguments 141
7.7 Summary 145

**8 Cooccurrence of *Es* with a Finite Clause 147**
8.1 Data 148
8.2 Correlative *Es* as an Argument 151
8.3 LFG-Analysis 151
8.3.1 Theoretical Preliminaries 151
8.3.2 *Es* as a Thematic Argument 153
8.3.2.1 OBJ-Clauses (*Sagen* Verbs) 153
8.3.2.2 SUBJ Clauses (*Beweisen* Verbs) 156
8.3.3 Psych-Verbs (*Stören* Class) 157
8.3.3.1 A-Structure 157
8.3.3.2 Non-Thematic *Es* 159
8.3.4 Passive of *sagen* 162
8.4 Summary 164

**9 Conclusion 167**

9.1 Summary 167

9.2 Further research 169

**References 173**

**Index 183**

# Abbreviations

## Syntactic Functions

| | |
|---|---|
| ADJ | adjunct |
| AF | argument function |
| $\overline{\text{AF}}$ | non-argument function |
| APP | apposition |
| CF | complement function |
| COMP | sentential complement |
| COMPL | complement (COMP or XCOMP) |
| DF | discourse function |
| FOC | focus |
| GF | grammatical function |
| POSS | possessive |
| OBJ | object |
| $\text{OBJ}_\theta$ | thematically restricted object |
| $\text{OBL}_\theta$ | thematically restricted oblique |
| TOP | topic |
| SUBJ | subject |
| XCOMP | functionally controlled complement |

## Syntactic Categories

• **Lexical**

| | |
|---|---|
| C | complementizer |
| D | determiner |
| I | inflection |
| N | noun |
| V | verb |

- **Phrasal**

| | |
|---|---|
| ADVP | adverb phrase |
| CP | complementizer phrase |
| DP | determiner phrase |
| FP | functional projection |
| IP | inflection phrase |
| NP | noun phrase |
| S | (exocentric) sentence |
| VP | verb phrase |

## Attributes and Values

| | |
|---|---|
| ACC | accusative case |
| AGR | agreement |
| CASE | case |
| DAT | dative case |
| DECL | declarative |
| DEF | definite |
| FEM | feminine |
| FIN | finite |
| GEND | gender |
| GEN | genitive case |
| MASC | masculine |
| NEUT | neuter |
| NOM | nominative case |
| NUM | number |
| PERS | person |
| PL | plural |
| REFL | reflexive |
| SG | singular |

# Acknowledgments

This book is based on my doctoral dissertation, completed in June 2000 at the University of Stuttgart.

First, I would like to express my gratitude to my two thesis advisors, Christian Rohrer and Hubert Haider. Christian Rohrer is responsible for my initial acquaintance with LFG and he made my doctoral research possible by admitting me into the Graduiertenkolleg "Linguistische Grundlagen für die Sprachverarbeitung" at the University of Stuttgart. I have benefitted from his advice and help while working on my dissertation as well as since completing it. Hubert Haider's teaching and work on German syntax showed me how fascinating theoretical syntax can be. I am very grateful to him for many helpful discussions and comments during his time in Stuttgart.

I am especially indebted to Joan Bresnan for much encouragement and continued support of my work. In particular, she kindly invited me to come to Stanford in November 1997 and the discussions we had then were very fruitful for my work.

I also would like to thank Hans Altmann, my linguistics teacher at the University of Munich, who has been very important for my linguistic understanding in general.

A large number of linguists have helped me by discussing questions and commenting on previous versions of the analyses. Thanks to Steve Berman, Miriam Butt, Mary Dalrymple, Stefanie Dipper, Christian Fortmann, Anette Frank, Werner Frey, Jonas Kuhn, Tracy King, Uwe Reyle, Sten Vikner, Gert Webelhuth and Heike Zinsmeister. Special thanks go to Jonas who made detailed comments on a preliminary version of the dissertation and helped me with numerous technical points of LFG; to Christian who always found time to to discuss questions; and to my husband Steve who not only helped in clarifying the presentation and formatting and editing the manuscript, but without whom

I probably wouldn't have written this work (and in fact this sentence) in English in the first place.

My friends and collegues at the University of Stuttgart created a very enjoyable and productive atmosphere; thanks especially to my former officemates Matthias Jilka and Erika de Lima.

I want to thank Karin Pittner, my new "boss" at the University of Bochum, for giving me the opportunity to finish this book.

Finally, my deepest gratitude goes to my parents, my husband and my daughters Milena and Elisabeth.

# 1

# Introduction

## 1.1 German Syntax and LFG

This book analyses a number of central interrelated aspects of the clausal syntax of German in the framework of Lexical-Functional Grammar (LFG). It addresses both empirical and theoretical concerns by dealing with phenomena which, on the one hand, have long been discussed in the literature yet remain controversial, and on the other hand, pose specific challenges for the theory of LFG. I attempt to address these challenges by providing consistent analyses of the phenomena and, where appropriate, comparing them with alternative approaches in the literature. Hence my goal is not only to provide a detailed examination of German syntax in LFG, but also to highlight and discuss matters of concern for LFG in general.

LFG is a framework well-suited to a language like German, which has relatively free word order and a relatively rich morphology that can serve, among other uses, to indicate syntactic function. LFG reflects these properties by separating information about syntactic functions from information about phrase structure. Syntactic functions are not universally derived from phrase-structure configurations but may be identified morphologically. This is so because syntactic representations in LFG are distributed over three independent but interacting structures: phrase structure (c-structure), functional structure (f-structure) and argument structure (a-structure). Mapping principles which relate c-structure to f-structure can therefore refer not only to phrase structure configurations but also to the morphology.

Within generative grammar, relatively little work has been done on German in LFG compared to transformational analyses.[1] Transforma-

[1]For LFG treatments see, e.g., Netter and Rohrer (1987), Netter (1988), Berman and Frank (1996), Berman, Dipper, Fortmann, and Kuhn (1998), Choi (1999), Kuhn (2001). Among the many transformational analyses, see, e.g. Fanselow (1987),

tional grammar and LFG have in common that they both postulate phrase structure as a level of representation. However, phrase structure serves quite different purposes and has different properties in these frameworks. In transformational grammar phrase structure is the only type of representation and distinct phrase structures are related by transformation operations. In LFG c-structure (phrase structure) is only one of three types of structures. Precedence and dominance relations are represented in c-structure, functional information is represented on f-structure and thematic roles are represented in a-structure. Hence, c-structure does not have to contain all syntactic properties of a constituent. And instead of employing movement operations as in classical transformational grammar, LFG relies on unification, morphological function identification, and lexical rules (e.g. with passive in configurational languages). Although in earlier work in LFG, f-structure was the primary focus of interest, increasing attention has been paid to the wellformedness conditions and restrictions on phrase structure. Withn the last decade, various principles have been proposed to constrain the possible organization of c-structures and the mapping from c-structure to f-structure.[2] The present work pursues this line of research.[3]

The main phenomena treated in this book are: verb-second constructions, so-called 'subjectless' clauses, expletives and agreement, weak crossover, long distance dependencies, the distribution of subordinated clauses, and the cooccurrence of correlative pronouns and embedded clauses. These topics are especially interesting, since on the one hand their analysis is still controversial, and on the other hand they also raise some general questions for the theory of LFG. Of particular concern are the status of the subject, the necessity or dispensability of traces, and the syntactic function of complement clauses.

So-called 'subjectless' clauses in German pose a challenge for LFG because of the *Subject Condition*, which has been postulated as a gram-

---

Fanselow (1991), Grewendorf (1989), Haider (1993a), Müller (1995a), Stechow and Sternefeld (1988), Webelhuth (1992).

[2]See, e.g., Kroeger (1993), King (1995), and especially Bresnan (2001).

[3]In addition to LFG and transformational grammar, generative grammar analyses of German syntax have also been done in the framework of HPSG (see, e.g., Kiss 1995, Kathol 2000, Meurers 1999, Müller 2001). HPSG is similar to LFG in that both are constraint-based theories, i.e. the grammaticality of a sentence is determined by the satisfaction of simultaneous constraints. However, while LFG postulates parallel representations of information with different formal properties, HPSG claims that all linguistic structure is of the same kind, represented by attribute-value matrices (similar to f-structures). Since the present book is concerned especially with differences between c-structure and f-structure, and how their respective wellformedness principles interact, I have refrained from making comparisons to corresponding HPSG treatments.

matical universal. This condition requires that every sentence must have a subject (Baker 1983). In contradiction to the Subject Condition, traditional descriptions of German grammar have assumed that certain types of finite clauses can or must occur without a subject. The most frequent type is the so-called impersonal passive as in

(1) Vielleicht wird getanzt.
Perhaps becomes danced
'Maybe there will be dancing.'

In this construction the occurrence of a subject, even the expletive subject *es*, leads to ungrammaticality:

(2) *Vielleicht wird es getanzt.

Hence, it seems that either we have to abandon the Subject Condition as a universal or we have to show how German satisfies the Subject Condition even in the absence of a lexical subject. In this book I provide an analysis that does the latter.

The question of whether traces or empty categories are required in LFG has recently received much attention. In early LFG work (Kaplan and Bresnan 1982) gaps were assumed in order to account for long distance dependencies as in

(3) Who does Mary like _?

More recently, Kaplan and Zaenen (1989) proposed an account in terms of *functional uncertainty*, which identifies the f-structure of the extracted element in the higher clause (*who* in (3)) and the f-structure of the clause internal grammatical function (direct object in (3)). It does this by using regular expressions over functional equations, without making use of traces. Kaplan and Zaenen note that this is possible because subcategorization in LFG is defined on f-structure and is independent of phrase-structure configurations. In addition, Bresnan (2001) proposes wellformedness conditions on the c-structure that require it to be as simple as possible, i.e., roughly to have as few nodes as necessary. Empty categories seem to go against this approach, since they make the c-structure more complex. Nevertheless, Bresnan (2001) postulates that traces are sometimes needed in LFG, for instance in the analysis of topicalization in English, in order to identify the function of the topicalized phrase. In this book I examine several constructions in German which bear on the status of traces in LFG: scrambling, local and non-local topicalization, cyclic extraction, verb-second, finite and non-finite clauses without lexical subject. I will show that, in view of the role of morphological function specification in German, only non-local topicalizations involve an antecendent-gap configuration. In all the other cases an empty category violates the wellformedness conditions of c-structure.

A final topic of concern is the grammatical function of complement clauses. Since the earliest work in LFG, complement clauses have been associated with the function COMP. Yet it remains controversial whether all sentential complements have this function, and proposals have been made that assign different functions to different kinds of complement clauses (e.g., Dalrymple and Lodrup 2000). There has also been much discussion about whether clausal complements should have a different function than their nominal counterparts (cf. Berman and Frank 1996 and a 1996 exhange on the LFG list (see <`http://listserv.linguistlist.org/cgi-bin/wa?A2=ind96&L=lfg&P=11516`> and followups)). I examine the function of the complement clauses and provide an analysis of their distribution in German. I also provide a treatment of the cooccurrence of the correlative pronoun *es* and complement clauses. These analyses do not rely on the function COMP but are based on the assumption that embedded clauses have the same grammatical function as their nominal or prepositional counterparts.

## 1.2 Overview

This book proceeds as follows:

Chapters 2 and 3 set the theoretical and descriptive stage for the subsequent chapters. Chapter 2 presents a basic overview of the LFG framework, illustrating its overall structure and the key theoretical assumptions and principles used in this book. In chapter 3 I first describe the basic properties of German sentence structure and then motivate a particular c-structure representation for sentential phrases in German. I will conclude that German has no distinct subject or object positions, but the syntactic functions are identified by morphological function specification, namely by case and agreement.

Chapters 4 through 8 are detailed case studies of central areas of German clausal syntax. While these chapters can be read independent of each other (assuming the background provided by chapters 2 and 3), there is a logical development in that each chapter raises issues that are dealt with at length in the following chapter. The final case study in chapter 8 relies most extensively on the theoretical assumptions presented and argued for in the preceding chapters.

Chapter 4 concerns the status of the Subject Condition, which requires that the f-structure representation of clauses must have a subject. I provide an analysis on which German satisfies the Subject Condition, although it has clauses without a (c-structure) subject-constituent. In particular, I argue that expletive subjects are provided by the verbal agreement morphology; from this it follows that the insertion of either a lexical or an empty subject expletive in c-structure is not necessary to satisfy the Subject Condition and therefore, by the wellformedness principle Economy of Expression, is prohibited. The chapter concludes with a discussion of non-finite clauses, which are another case where the subject is represented only on f-structure, but not on c-structure.

In chapter 5 I address the questions of whether empty categories are needed in the analysis of scrambling, clause-internal and clause-external topicalization and, if so, how they are motivated. On the basis of weak-crossover data and the role morphological of function specification in German, I will show that empty categories are required only with non-local topicalization. I will also compare this trace-based analysis to a recent traceless account.

Chapter 6 discusses two alternative ways to capture long distance dependencies involving an empty category and shows how restrictions on extraction can be accounted for on these analyses. The chapter closes with a comparison of the two approaches.

In chapter 7 I provide an analysis of the distribution of sentential arguments. First I will argue that sentential arguments have the same grammatical function as their nominal or prepositional counterparts, rather than a distinct clausal function, as traditionally assumed in LFG. Then I will claim that the apparent topicalization of sentential arguments can't be accounted for in functional terms. Instead I will argue that sentential arguments in German cannot be topicalized at all: rather, what we find is an instance of left dislocation.

In chapter 8 I examine the cooccurrence of correlative *es* and CP and show how the mapping principles from a-structure to f-structure account for the cooccurrence pattern, given a plausible assumption about the thematic status of *es*.

The concluding chapter 9 briefly summarizes the main results of this research and notes various open problems and unresolved issues.

2

# Lexical Functional Grammar

In this chapter I lay out the principles and hypotheses of LFG that provide the foundations for my investigation of German clausal syntax. These are largely based on Bresnan (2001).[1]

The syntactic representation in LFG consists of three independent but interacting structures: c(onstituent)-structure[2], f(unctional)-structure and a(rgument)-structure. Each of the structures encodes a different aspect of syntactic information, namely syntactic category, grammatical function and thematic role, respectively. Thus, unlike some other syntactic theories, in LFG syntactic information is not all located in one representation but is distributed across different structures. Each structure has a different formal representation and has to satisfy specific constraints.

The organisation of syntactic information in LFG can be schematized as follows:

a-structure
$\Updownarrow$ Lexical Mapping Theory
f-structure
$\Updownarrow$ functional annotations
c-structure

The three structures are related to each other by distinct mapping principles. The mapping from c-structure to f-structure is mediated by functional annotations (see section 2.3). The mapping principles formulated in the Lexical Mapping Theory relate the a-structure and the

[1]Other recent comprehensive treatments of LFG are Dalrymple (2001) and Falk (2001). For brief introductions see, e.g., Neidle (1994), Sadler (1996). The classical texts of early LFG, which still contain much relevant material, are Bresnan (1982) and Kaplan and Bresnan (1982).

[2]Also called categorial structure in Bresnan (2001, p. 19).

f-structure (see section 2.4). C-structure and a-structure are related to each other through f-structure. While c-structure is meant to be a variable structure, with different realizations across languages, f-structure is a more invariable structure which reflects universal syntactic principles.

In the following we will look at the different structures in more detail.

## 2.1 C-Structure

C-structure is represented as a phrase structure tree and encodes precedence and dominance relations. Thus, c-structure reflects word order and represents the hierarchical organization of phrases.

C-structure observes either of two modes of organization, namely, endocentricity or exocentricity. Endocentric phrases follow the X-bar schema (Bresnan 1977, Bresnan 2001):

(1) a. $X' \rightarrow X^0$, YP
   b. XP $\rightarrow$ ZP, $X'$

In this schema, the maximal projection YP is called the complement, the maximal projection ZP is called the specifier (henceforth denoted XP-Spec for brevity).

Categories are classified as lexical or functional. The lexical categories are V(erbs), P(repositions), N(ouns) and A(djectives). Functional categories are a subclass of lexical categories which determine features like definiteness, clause type or finiteness; they are designated D(eterminers), C(omplementizers) and I(nflection). C-structure categories can be decomposed into type of category and level of structure. The type of the category is represented by the binary categorial features 'predicative' (must have a subject of predication) and 'transitive' (may take a direct object).[3] The level of the structure distinguishes between lexical categories ($X^0$), projections ($X^1$) and maximal projections ($X^2$). Following common practice, I will frequently write these as X, $X'$, and XP, respectively. The projected categories ($X'$ and XP) are collectively referred to as *syntactic phrase structure nodes* (Bresnan 2001, p. 91), to distinguish them from preterminal (i.e., $X^0$) and terminal nodes (i.e., morphological words). Tables 1 and 2 summarize the properties of c-structure categories.

Endocentric phrases are characteristic of configurational languages and result in highly hierarchial c-structures. For example, the English

[3] Bresnan (2001, p.100f.) introduces a third privative feature to distinguish lexical and functional categories. Since this feature plays no role in this book, I omit it here for simplicity.

| | + transitive | – transitive |
|---|---|---|
| + predicative | V, I , C | A |
| – predicative | P | N, D |

TABLE 1 Types of Categories

| 0 | 1 | 2 |
|---|---|---|
| V | V′ | V″ (VP) |
| N | N′ | N″ (NP) |
| A | A′ | A″ (AP) |
| P | P′ | P″ (PP) |

TABLE 2 Levels of Structure

sentence *John will buy the house* has the structure in (2).[4]

(2)

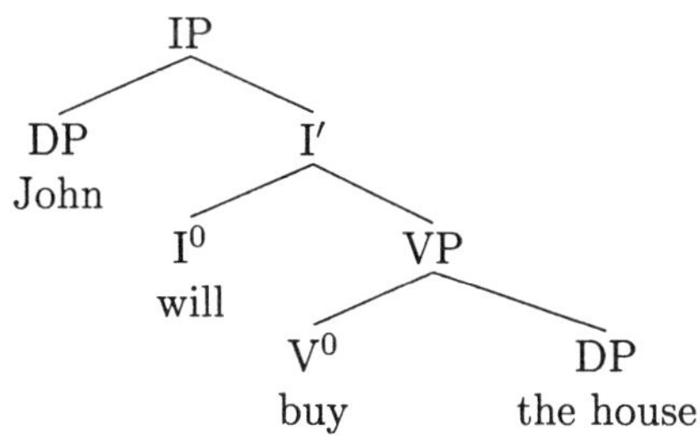


The exocentric organization of c-structure is characteristic of non-configurational languages, such as Walpiri; it makes use of the nonprojecting exocentric category S. S may expand as a totally flat stucture:

(3) $S \rightarrow C^*$

This is illustrated by the sentence *The two small children are chasing that dog* in Walpiri (cf. Bresnan 2001, p. 6):

(4)

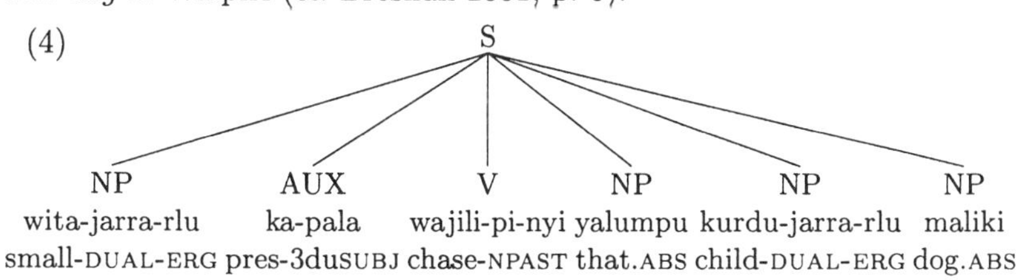


A claim of LFG is that there is no strict division between configu-

[4] I follow most current work in assuming that nominal constituents in German and English are determiner phrases (DPs). However, I will use the notation NP when citing other analyses that use this notation, and also when it occurs in commonly accepted terminology, such as the split NP construction.

rational and non-configurational languages (cf. Nordlinger 1998, ch.2). Hence the exocentric category S may dominate a configurational structure (i.e., a VP):

(5) S → NP VP

C-structure has to satisfy the wellformedness conditions Economy of Expression and Lexical Integrity:

(6) **Economy of Expression** (Bresnan 2001, p. 91, (1))
All syntactic phrase structure nodes are optional and are not used unless required by independent principles (completeness, coherence, semantic expressivity[5]).

(7) **Lexical Integrity** (Bresnan 2001, p. 92, (4))
Morphologically complete words are leaves of the c-structure tree and each leaf corresponds to one and only one c-structure node.

Roughly speaking, the effect of Economy of Expression is to avoid structural complexity as far as possible. Lexical Integrity requires that word formation is done in the lexicon and that only fully inflected words are inserted in the syntax.

## 2.2 F-Structure

Grammatical functions are represented on f-structure. F-structures are composed of attribute-value pairs. Attributes are symbols like SUBJ, OBJ, TENSE, NUM, CASE, PRED. A value can be a symbol, such as SG (singular), a semantic form, an f-structure or a set of f-structures. The following f-structures illustrates the different values:

[5] These principles are discussed and illustrated in the following section.

(8) John will buy the ring secretly tomorrow.

$$\begin{bmatrix} \text{SUBJ} & \begin{bmatrix} \text{PRED} & \text{'John'} \\ \text{NUM} & \text{SG} \\ \text{PERS} & 3 \end{bmatrix} \\ \text{TENSE} & \text{FUTURE} \\ \text{PRED} & \text{'buy } \langle(\uparrow \text{SUBJ})(\uparrow \text{OBJ})\rangle\text{'} \\ \text{OBJ} & \begin{bmatrix} \text{PRED} & \text{'ring'} \\ \text{NUM} & \text{SG} \\ \text{PERS} & 3 \\ \text{DEF} & + \end{bmatrix} \\ \text{ADJ} & \left\{ \begin{matrix} \begin{bmatrix} \text{PRED} & \text{'secretly'} \end{bmatrix} \\ \begin{bmatrix} \text{PRED} & \text{'tomorrow'} \end{bmatrix} \end{matrix} \right\} \end{bmatrix}$$

Grammatical functions are grouped into several subclasses, which are partly complementary and partly overlapping. There are **argument functions**, **non-argument functions**, **discourse functions**, and **non-discourse functions**. Further, the non-discourse argument functions constitute the **complement functions**, while the non-discourse non-argument functions are the **adjuncts**. The following table displays the classes of functions:

| | | | | | | | | |
|---|---|---|---|---|---|---|---|---|
| Non-argument functions | TOP | FOC | | | | | | ADJ |
| Discourse functions | TOP | FOC | SUBJ | | | | | |
| Argument functions | | | SUBJ | OBJ | OBJ$\theta$ | OBL$\theta$ | COMPL | |
| Non-discourse functions | | | | OBJ | OBJ$\theta$ | OBL$\theta$ | COMPL | ADJ |
| Complement functions | | | | OBJ | OBJ$\theta$ | OBL$\theta$ | COMPL | |
| Adjuncts | | | | | | | | ADJ |

TABLE 3 Classes of Grammatical Functions

F-structure has to satisfy a number of wellformedness conditions, namely COHERENCE, COMPLETENESS, EXTENDED COHERENCE and UNIQUENESS.

(9) **Completeness** requires that every function designated by a PRED be present in the f-structure of that PRED. (Bresnan 2001, p. 63)

The functions designated by a PRED are the functions which are listed in the PRED-feature. For example, the PRED-feature of *define* designates a SUBJ and a OBJ. In the f-structure of the following example, the OBJ is missing, in violation of COMPLETENESS. Therefore, the sentence is ruled out.

(10) *John will define.

$$\left[\begin{array}{ll} \text{SUBJ} & \left[\begin{array}{ll}\text{PRED} & \text{`John'}\\ \text{NUM} & \text{SG}\\ \text{PERS} & 3\end{array}\right] \\ \text{TENSE} & \text{FUTURE}\\ \text{PRED} & \text{`define } \langle(\uparrow \text{SUBJ})(\uparrow \text{OBJ})\rangle\text{'}\end{array}\right]$$

(11) **Coherence** requires that every argument function in an f-structure be designated by a PRED (Bresnan 2001, p. 63).

COHERENCE is the converse of completeness. COHERENCE rules out an f-structure which contains an argument function that is not listed in the PRED-attribute, for instance $\text{OBJ}_\theta$ in the following example:

(12) *John will define Anna the word.

$$\left[\begin{array}{ll} \text{SUBJ} & \left[\begin{array}{ll}\text{PRED} & \text{`John'}\\ \text{NUM} & \text{SG}\\ \text{PERS} & 3\end{array}\right] \\ \text{TENSE} & \text{FUTURE}\\ \text{PRED} & \text{`define } \langle(\uparrow \text{SUBJ})(\uparrow \text{OBJ})\rangle\text{'} \\ \text{OBJ} & \left[\begin{array}{ll}\text{PRED} & \text{`word'}\\ \text{NUM} & \text{SG}\\ \text{PERS} & 3\\ \text{DEF} & +\end{array}\right] \\ \text{OBJ}_\theta & \left[\begin{array}{ll}\text{PRED} & \text{`Anna'}\\ \text{NUM} & \text{SG}\\ \text{PERS} & 3\end{array}\right]\end{array}\right]$$

EXTENDED COHERENCE is an extension of the coherence condition to all grammatical functions, not only argument functions:

(13) **Extended Coherence**:
All syntactic functions (including adjuncts and grammaticalized discourse functions) must be appropriately integrated into the f-structure (Bresnan and Mchombo 1987, Bresnan 2001, p. 63).

Argument functions are appropriately integrated if they are designated by a PRED, ADJ functions are appropriately integrated if their immediate f-structure contains a PRED, and for the functions TOP and FOC to be appropriately integrated, they must be identified with, or anaphorically linked to, an integrated function.

The UNIQUENESS CONDITION prohibits a single attribute from having two or more non-identical values.

(14) **Uniqueness Condition:**
Every attribute has a unique value.

The following constellation is therefore disallowed:

*attribute < value$_1$ / value$_2$

Note, however, that this does not prevent an attribute from receiving its value from different sources, as long as the source values can be unified, as is the case, for example, with subject-verb agreement (see chapter 4, section 4.3 for discussion of this process).

Further aspects of f-structure, such as **f-precedence** and **functional uncertainty**, will be discussed later in the relevant chapters.

## 2.3 The Correspondence between C- and F-structure

C-structure and f-structure are related to each other by the mapping function $\phi$, which maps each c-structure node to a unique f-structure. $\phi$ is a many-to-one function, i.e., different c-structure nodes may be mapped onto the same f-structure. In addition, $\phi$ is not onto, i.e., an f-structure may have no corresponding c-structure node (for a more precise description of $\phi$ see Kaplan 1995).

The mapping from c- to f-structure is mediated by functional annotations on c-structure. Consider the annotated c-structure of *John will buy the house* in (15), which is augmented with the assumed lexical entries:

(15) John will buy the house.

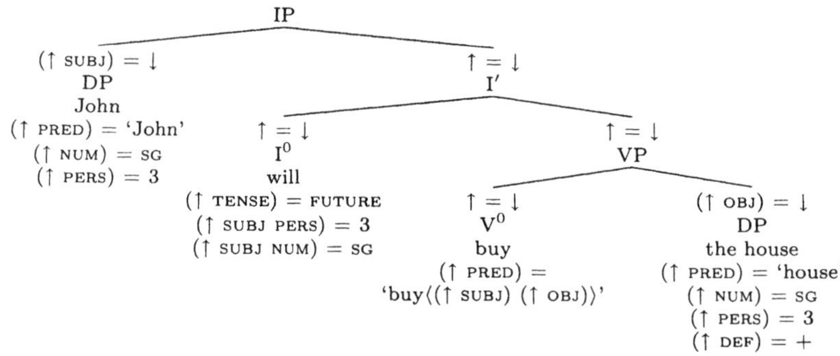


The annotations determine how the information is mapped onto the f-structure. The up and down arrows are metavariables for f-structures. The down arrow ↓ denotes the f-structure corresponding to the node annotated by it, while the up arrow ↑ denotes the f-structure corresponding to the immediately dominating node, the mother node. Via these metavariables every c-structure node is related to its corresponding f-structure. The annotation ↑ = ↓ indicates that two f-structure are identified: the f-structure of the node annotated by the down arrow is identified with the f-structure of its mother node. The annotation ↑ = ↓ on I′, $\mathrm{I}^0$, VP, $\mathrm{V}^0$ consequently means that all these nodes are all mapped to the same f-structure.

Annotations can also provide f-structure attributes. The annotation (↑ SUBJ) = ↓ states that the f-structure of the mother (in (15) the f-structure corresponding to IP) has a SUBJ attribute whose value is the f-structure of the node which bears the annotation (in (15) the DP in IP-Spec). Likewise, (↑ OBJ) = ↓ indicates that the f-structure of the mother (in (15) the f-structure corresponding to VP) has an OBJ attribute whose value is the f-structure of the node which bears the annotation (the DP which is the sister of $\mathrm{V}^0$).

In the following illustration each c-structure node is subscripted with a label which denotes the corresponding f-structure. After instantiation of the metavariables ↑ and ↓ we get the following c-structure and the corresponding f-structure:

(16)

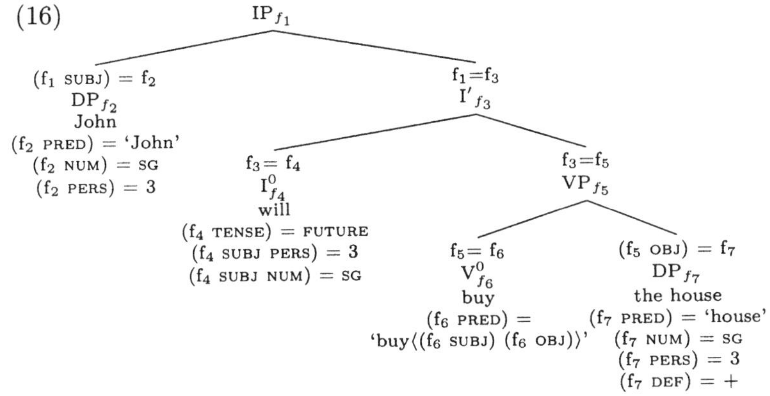


(17)

$$f_1, f_3, f_4, f_5, f_6 \left[\begin{array}{lll} \text{SUBJ} & f_2 & \left[\begin{array}{ll} \text{PRED} & \text{`John'} \\ \text{NUM} & \text{SG} \\ \text{PERS} & 3 \end{array}\right] \\ \text{TENSE} & \text{FUTURE} & \\ \text{PRED} & \multicolumn{2}{l}{\text{`buy } \langle (f_6 \text{ SUBJ})(f_6 \text{ OBJ})\rangle\text{'}} \\ \text{OBJ} & f_7 & \left[\begin{array}{ll} \text{PRED} & \text{`house'} \\ \text{NUM} & \text{SG} \\ \text{PERS} & 3 \\ \text{DEF} & + \end{array}\right] \end{array}\right]$$

In the preceding examples we have seen how the mapping from c- to f-structure works. Now we turn to the question of how the c- to f-structure mapping is constrained, i.e., the principles that determine the annotations at c-structure. These questions are discussed at length by Bresnan (2001), where the mapping principles are proposed which are briefly summarized below.

In section 2.1 we saw that the c-structure categories can be organized endocentrically or exocentrically. The mapping principles differ according to the organization of c-structure. In endocentric phrases c-structure positions are associated with specific grammatical functions. The correspondence between structure and function is formulated in the Endocentric Mapping Principles:

(18) **Endocentric Mapping Principles:** (Bresnan 2001, p. 119)

a. **Heads:** Annotate a projecting node in a projection of the same kind with $\uparrow = \downarrow$.

b. **Specifiers:** Annotate a non-projecting node in F$''$ with $(\uparrow \text{DF}) = \downarrow$.

c. **Coheads:** Annotate a non-projecting complement node (cf. (19)) dominated by any functional category $F^n$ with $\uparrow = \downarrow$.

d. **Complements:** Annotate a non-projecting complement node dominated by any lexical category $L^n$ with $(\uparrow \text{CF}) = \downarrow$.

e. **Adjuncts:** Optionally annotate a nonprojectiong node and its adjoined-to sister node with $(\uparrow \overline{\text{AF}}) = \downarrow$ and $\uparrow = \downarrow$, respectively.[6]

(19) **Flexible Definition of an Endocentric Complement:** (Bresnan 2001, p. 118)[7]

A c-structure complement is a nonprojecting node which is the sister of no non-projecting node.

$X^0$ and $X'$ are defined as projecting nodes. A projection is any $X^n$ category for $n > 0$. A projection of the same kind as another node *N* matches the categorial features of *N*'s category label. Non-projecting nodes are maximal projections $X''$. A node in *X* refers to a node immediately dominated by a node labelled *X*. Nodes to which constituents are adjoined are called adjoined-to nodes. Adjoined-to nodes are syntactic phrase structure nodes immediately dominated by a node having the same label.

Applying the endocentric mapping principles to the structure proposed in (2) results in the following annotated c-structure (which was stipulated in (15) and (16)):

---

[6] The optional annotation allows lexocentric specification of argument functions in adjoined positions (see page 17).

[7] This definition assumes that endocentric phrases are strictly binary branching; cf. Bresnan (2001, p. 124, fn.36).

(20) 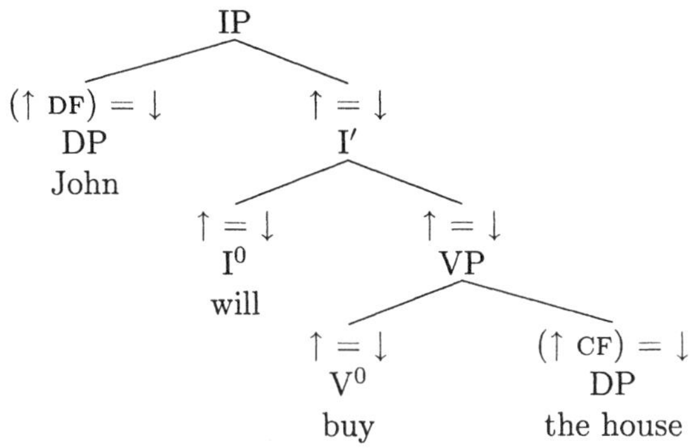


The realization of the discourse functions associated with each FP-Spec varies depending on the language. For English IP-Spec is associated with SUBJ. The complement function is specified as OBJ. Notice that in accordance with (18c) a functional head and its complement (in (20) $I^0$ and VP) arc always mapped onto the same f-structure, i.e., they are f-structure co-heads. This implies that a functional category can't have a semantic feature which would conflict with the semantic feature of its complement.

In exocentric phrases grammatical functions are not associated with specific phrase structure positions. It is assumed that in the radically non-configurational structure type

(21) $S \rightarrow C^*$

the various constituents $C$ are freely annotated with $\uparrow = \downarrow$ and non-argument functions, but not with argument functions. Instead, it is assumed that the argument functions are identified by means of the morphological features borne by words themselves, e.g., case and agreement. This morphology-driven mode of identification is called *lexocentricity*

Based on Nichols (1986), Bresnan (2001, p. 111) formulates two general types of lexocentric or morphological function specification, namely dependent-marking and head-marking, for which she provides the following schematizations:[8]

[8]Cf. Nordlinger (1998), who proposes that case markers themselves construct the grammatical function in a sentence by making use of inside-out function application (see chapter 6 for an explanation of inside-out function application).

(22) **Types of Morphological Function Specification:**

a. dependent-marking:

$(\downarrow \text{CASE}) = \kappa \Rightarrow (\uparrow \text{GF}) = \downarrow$

b. head-marking:

$(\downarrow \text{AGR}) = (\uparrow \text{AF AGR}) \Rightarrow (\uparrow \text{AF}) = \downarrow$

When these schemata are instantiated, the annotations appear on non-projecting nodes. This results in schematic c-structures like the following:

(23) a. dependent-marking:

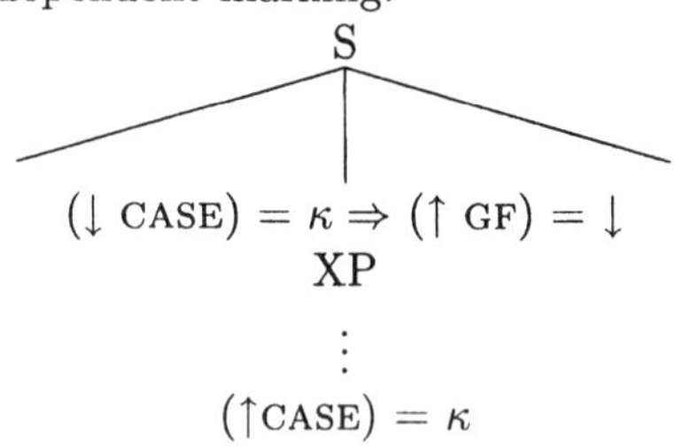


b. head-marking:

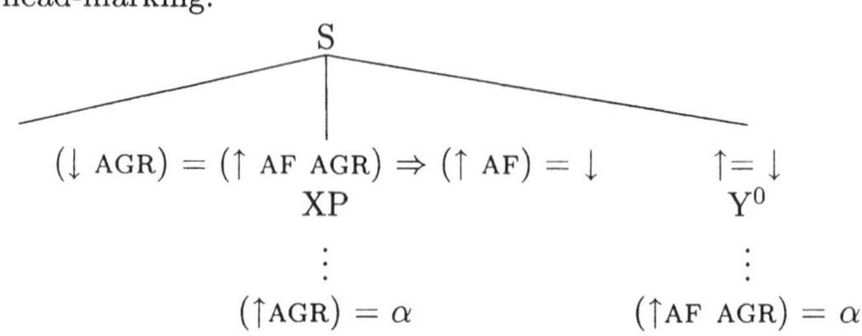


With dependent-marking, the grammatical function of a dependent, i.e. non-head, constituent is identified by morphological information borne by the dependent itself. For example, according to (23a), due to the dependent's particular case feature $\kappa$, it is associated with the function GF. Conversely, with head-marking, the grammatical function of a dependent constituent is identified by morphological information borne by the head which it is a dependent of. For example, according to (23b), if the head's morphology specifies that the function AF has certain agreement features, and a dependent is marked for these features, then that dependent is associated with the function AF. Thus, in a flat structure like (21), each of the constituents will be associated with its grammatical function, due to the morphology of the dependent itself, if the language is dependent-marking, or to the morphology of the head, if the language is head-marking. A language may also realize both types of function specification; German is such a language, as will be shown in chapter 4.

We have seen that the exocentric category S may also dominate configurational structures like the following:

(24) S $\rightarrow$ NP VP

In order to obtain the necessary annotations, an additional structure-function association principle is needed (Bresnan 2001, p. 112):

(25) The daughters of S may be subject and predicate.

Thus we get the following well-formed annotated c-structure rule:

(26) $\begin{array}{lcc} \text{S} \rightarrow & \text{NP} & \text{VP} \\ & (\uparrow \text{SUBJ}) = \downarrow & \uparrow = \downarrow \end{array}$

## 2.4 A-Structure

The arguments (thematic roles) of a predicate are represented on a-structure. The linking from a-structure to f-structure is formulated in the Lexical Mapping Theory (LMT). I will the formulation of LMT developed in Bresnan and Zaenen (1990) and Alsina and Mchombo (1993, p. 24–31).[9]

Linking principles are formulated in terms of the thematic hierarchy (27) and the features [±o(bject)] and [±r(estricted)].

(27) **Thematic Hierarchy**:
agent > beneficiary > experiencer/goal >instrument > patient/theme > locative

Grammatical functions are not primitive notions, but defined by the features [±o] and [±r].

(28)

| Grammatical Function | Features |
|---|---|
| SUBJ | [−r, −o] |
| OBJ | [−r, +o] |
| $\text{OBJ}_\theta$ | [+r, +o] |
| $\text{OBL}_\theta$ | [+r, −o] |

This classification yields the following natural classes of grammatical functions:

(29) [ −o] = SUBJ, $\text{OBL}_\theta$ [ −r] = SUBJ, OBJ
[ +o] = OBJ, $\text{OBJ}_\theta$ [ +r] = $\text{OBL}_\theta$, $\text{OBJ}_\theta$

[9] For a similar account see also Bresnan and Kanerva (1989), Bresnan and Moshi (1990). For alternative formulations see Alsina (1996), Butt, Dalrymple, and Frank (1997), Butt (1998).

This functional underspecification allows generalizations over different functions, which is used in the mapping from thematic roles to grammatical functions.

On the a-structure of a predicate the thematic roles are ordered according to the thematic hierarchy. For example the verb *pound* has the following representation:

(30) pound < agent patient >

According to Alsina and Mchombo (1993) intrinsic properties of the thematic role determine one of its feature values (this is called *intrinsic classification*). Internal arguments (prototypical internal arguments are the patient and the theme) are intrinsically marked [−r] or [+o], other roles have the intrinsic classification [−o], e.g.

| (31) pound | < agent | patient > |
|---|---|---|
| | [−o] | [−r] |

The other feature value is determined by the hierarchical position of the thematic role relative to the other roles (this is called *default classification*). Specifically, the highest role gets the default classification [−r], the others [+r]. Since intrinsic values cannot be changed (principle of *preservation of information*), the patient, which is intrinsically marked [−r], can't get the default classification [+r] and remains underspecified. Since the agent is mapped onto the SUBJ, the underspecified patient has to be mapped onto the OBJ (*Function-Argument Biuniqueness*).

| (32) pound | < agent | patient > |
|---|---|---|
| | [−o] | [−r] |
| | [−r] | |
| | SUBJ | OBJ |

According to Bresnan and Zaenen (1990), the basic principles for determining the syntactic feature in the a-structure are based on the underlying lexical semantics of the roles:

- Patientlike roles get the intrinsic classification [−r]
- secondary patientlike roles get [+o]
- other roles get [−o].

Mapping Principles associate the underspecified thematic roles with the grammatical functions (Bresnan and Zaenen 1990, p. 51):

(33) **Mapping Principles:**

a. Subject roles:

(i) $\hat{\theta}$ is mapped onto SUBJ; otherwise:
$[-o]$

(ii) $\theta$ is mapped onto the SUBJ.
$[-r]$

b. Other roles are mapped onto the lowest compatible function on the markedness hierarchy (SUBJ < OBJ, $\text{OBL}_\theta$ < $\text{OBJ}_\theta$).

Both formulations of the LMT make use of the Subject Condition, which requires that every sentence must have a subject (cf. chapter 4).

This completes the overview of the basic theoretical assumptions and formal machinery of LFG that will be made use of in the following chapters.

# 3

# Phrase Structure in German

In this chapter I describe the syntax of sentential phrases in German and provide an LFG formalization of these structures. I start with a general descriptive presentation using traditional German grammatical terminology and concepts (section 3.1). Then in section 3.2 I present a specific implementation of German sentence structure in LFG, based on work on German sentence structure done in the generative framework especially by Hubert Haider. In section 3.3 I present an analysis of verb-second constructions using the LFG notion of extended head.

The main concern of this chapter is not to review and compare the major competing theoretical analyses but to have a carefully argued sentence structure of German as basis for the analyses I will present in the subsequent chapters.

## 3.1 Essentials of German Sentence Structure

German sentence structure exhibits two basic word-orders, depending on whether the clause is syntactically embedded or not. In an unembedded declarative or wh-interrogative clause only one constituent can and must precede the finite verb, irrespective of whether the finite verb is an auxiliary, a modal or a main verb:

(1) a. Annie **lobt** das Kind.
Annie praises the child

b. Annie **will** das Kind loben.
Annie wants the child praise
'Annie wants to praise the child.'

c. Annie **hat** das Kind gelobt.
Annie has the child praised
'Annie has praised the child.'

This property of matrix clauses is characteristic of so-called verb-second (V2) languages.

In contrast, in embedded clauses which are introduced by a complementizer or a wh-phrase, the finite verb has to be at the end of the clause:[1]

(2) a. ... dass Annie das Kind gelobt **hat**.
that Annie the child praised has

b. ... warum Annie das Kind gelobt **hat**.
why Annie the child praised has

c. *... dass Annie **hat** das Kind gelobt.
that Annie has the child praised

d. *... warum Annie **hat** das Kind gelobt.
why Annie has the child praised

German also has embedded V2 clauses. With some verbs the complement clauses can occur without a complementizer. In this situation the finite verb has to occupy the second position; for example:

(3) a. Er glaubt, dass sie zugesagt **hat**.
he thinks that she accepted has

b. Er glaubt, sie **hat** zugesagt.
he thinks she has accepted

c. *Er glaubt, sie zugesagt **hat**.
he thinks she accepted has

d. *Er glaubt, dass sie **hat** zugesagt.
he thinks that she has accepted

On the basis of such evidence we may conclude that the complementizer and the finite verb are in complementary distribution, i.e., they occupy the same structural position.[2]

Note that only finite verbs can be in second position, non-finite verbs always have to be in sentence-final position (cf. (1b) and (1c)).

While verbs and complementizers have fixed positions in the sentence structure, all other constituents can essentially be freely ordered.

---

[1] After the finite verb in sentence final position extraposed constituents may occur, see examples (12) and (13) below and chapter 7, section 7.6 for further examples and discussion.

[2] There is dialectal evidence that in embedded clauses the (dislocated) wh-phrase and the complementizer do not occupy the same position, since they can cooccur. For example, in Bavarian sentences like the following are grammatical:

(i) Ich weiß nicht, **wer dass** es gesagt hat.
I know not who that it said has
'I don't know who said it.'

See also chapter 6, section 6.4.

Practically any order is grammatical, regardless of whether the clause is verb-final (4) or verb-second (5):[3]

(4) a. ... dass der Vater dem Kind den Roman
that the father-NOM the child-DAT the novel-ACC
vorgelesen hat.
read has
'... that the father read the novel to the child.'

b. ... dass dem Kind der Vater den Roman vorgelesen hat.

c. ... dass den Roman der Vater dem Kind vorgelesen hat.

d. ... dass den Roman dem Kind der Vater vorgelesen hat.

e. ... dass dem Kind den Roman der Vater vorgelesen hat.

f. ... dass der Vater den Roman dem Kind vorgelesen hat.

(5) a. Heute hat der Vater dem Kind den Roman
today has the father-NOM the child-DAT the novel-ACC
vorgelesen.
read
'Today the father read the novel to the child.'

b. Heute hat dem Kind der Vater den Roman vorgelesen.

c. Heute hat den Roman der Vater dem Kind vorgelesen.

d. Heute hat den Roman dem Kind der Vater vorgelesen.

e. Heute hat dem Kind den Roman der Vater vorgelesen.

f. Heute hat der Vater den Roman dem Kind vorgelesen.

Similarly, adverbials can generally occupy almost any position, though particular types may have a more restricted distribution:

(6) ... dass (heute/?gerne) der Vater (heute/gerne) dem
that (today/willingly) the father (today/willingly) the
Kind (heute/gerne) den Roman (heute/gerne) vorgelesen
child (today/willingly) the novel (today/willingly) read
hat
has

The constituent preceding the finite verb is also not restricted to a particular type. Almost any constituent can precede the finite verb, e.g. in (7a) the subject, in (7b) an adjunct, in (7c) a VP:

(7) a. Der Hans hat im Garten getanzt.
the Hans has in-the garden danced
'Hans danced in the garden.'

[3]The actual acceptability of particular word orders depends on lexical and pragmatic factors.

b. Im Garten hat der Hans getanzt.
c. Getanzt hat der Hans im Garten.

In yes/no-questions the finite verb must occur clause initially:

(8) Tanzt der Hans im Garten?
dances the Hans in-the garden
'Is Hans dancing in the garden?'

In an embedded clause introduced by a complementizer, the complementizer must be the first constituent of the embedded clause:[4]

(9) a. Ich glaube nicht, dass der Hans im Garten tanzt.
ich believe not that the Hans in-the garden dances
'I don't think Hans is dancing in the garden.'
b. *Ich glaube nicht, der Hans dass im Garten tanzt.

A sequence of verbs in sentence final position forms a verb cluster. In general, the non-finite verb forms precede the finite verb[5] and no constituent can intervene in the verb cluster:

(10) a. ... dass der Hans im Garten getanzt hat.
that the Hans in-the garden danced has
'... that Hans has danced in the garden.'
b. ... dass der Hans im Garten getanzt haben mag.
that the Hans in-the garden danced have may
'... that Hans may have danced in the garden.'

(11) a. *... dass der Hans im Garten getanzt gestern hat.
that the Hans in-the garden danced yesterday has

Following clause-final verbs there may occur right dislocated phrases and extraposed clauses, namely relative clauses and argument and adjunct clauses. Relative clauses have to come first, argument and adjunct clauses may occur in any order (cf. Berman and Frank 1996, p. 48; Haider 1995a; see also chapter 7):

[4]In Standard German; in some German dialects it is also possible for a constituent to precede the complementizer in certain constructions:

(i) Der Hans dass im Garten tanzt, das glaube ich nicht.
the Hans that in-the garden dances, that believe I not
'That Hans is dancing in the garden, that I don't believe.'

[5]An exception to this generalization are constructions involving the so-called *Ersatzinfinitiv*, where the infinitive verb form is used instead of the participle form; in this case, the finite verb precedes both infinitive forms:

(i) ... dass der Hans im Garten hat tanzen können.
that the Hans in-the garden has dance can
'... that Hans could dance in the garden.'

(12) a. Maria hat die Bücher bestellt, die sie interessieren,
Maria has the books ordered, which her interest,
obwohl sie kein Geld mehr hat.
although she no money more has
'Maria ordered the books that interest her, although she has no more money.'

b. *Maria hat die Bücher bestellt, obwohl sie kein Geld mehr hat, die sie interessieren.

(13) a. Er hat geglaubt, dass Schweine fliegen können, als er
He has believed that pigs fly can, when he
vier Jahre alt war.
four years old was
'He believed that pigs could fly when he was four years old.'

b. Er hat geglaubt, als er vier Jahre alt war, dass Schweine fliegen können.

These basic properties of German sentence structure are described in the so-called topological model of traditional German grammar.[6] In this model the sentence is divided into three fields, the *Vorfeld* (prefield), the *Mittelfeld* (middle field) and the *Nachfeld* (postfield), which are separated from each other by the *Satzklammer* (the sentential bracket, which surrounds the *Mittelfeld*).

The constituent in the left *Satzklammer* is either a finite verb, in the case of a verb-second clause, or a complementizer, in the case of a verb-final clause. In front of the left *Satzklammer* is the *Vorfeld*. Only one constituent can occupy the *Vorfeld*. Arbitrarily many constituents can occupy the *Mittelfeld*. What the right *Satzklammer* consists of depends on whether the sentence is verb-final or verb-second: in the former case, it contains a finite verb (possibly preceded by sequence of non-finite verbs); in the latter case, it contains either a non-finite verb, a sequence of non-finite verbs, or a separable verbal prefix. The *Nachfeld* is occupied by various types of right-dislocated constituents, as well as extraposed sentences. In front of the *Vorfeld* is the *Vorvorfeld*, where left-dislocated phrases occur. The topological model is displayed and illustrated in Table 4.

[6] This model was proposed as early as Erdmann (1886). Cf. Höhle (1986) for a contemporay discussion, also Kathol (2000) for an implementation in the HPSG framework.

| Sentence type | **VVF** | **VF** | **LSK** | **MF** | **RSK** | **NF** |
|---|---|---|---|---|---|---|
| V2-declarative clause | | Hans | kann | im Internet | nachprüfen | ob Plätze frei sind. |
| | | | (*can*) | (*on the web*) | (*check*) | (*if there are seats*) |
| V2-declarative clause | | Hans | prüft | im Internet | nach | ob Plätze frei sind. |
| V2-interrogative clause | | Wann | kann | Hans im Internet | nachprüfen | ob Plätze frei sind? |
| | | (*when*) | | | | |
| V2-declarative clause | | | | | | |
| with left-dislocated DP | Hans | der | kann | im Internet | nachprüfen | ob Plätze frei sind. |
| | | (*he*) | | | | |
| V2-declarative clause | Ob Plätze | | | | | |
| with left-dislocated clause | frei sind | das | kann | Hans im Internet | nachprüfen. | |
| | | (*that*) | | | | |
| V1-interrogative clause | | | Kann | Hans im Internet | nachprüfen | ob Plätze frei sind? |
| VL-Satz | | | Ob | Plätze frei | sind? | |

TABLE 4 The Topological Model of Traditional German Grammar

Abbreviations:
LSK: left Satzklammer
MF: Mittelfeld
NF: Nachfeld
RSK: right Satzklammer
VF: Vorfeld
VVF: Vorvorfeld

## 3.2 C-Structure of Sentential Phrases

### 3.2.1 The Functional Projection CP

In analyses of German phrase structure it is commonly assumed that the complementizer as well as the finite verb in a matrix clause are generated in $C^0$, which is the head of the endocentric phrase CP (cf. Grewendorf 1988, Vikner 1995, Schwarz and Vikner 1996, Choi 1999 and many others).[7] This approach accounts for the complementary distribution of the finite verb and the complementizer and also explains why only one constituent can precede the finite verb, since there is only one specifier of the CP. Left-dislocated phrases are adjoined to CP. Hence we get the following structure:

(14)

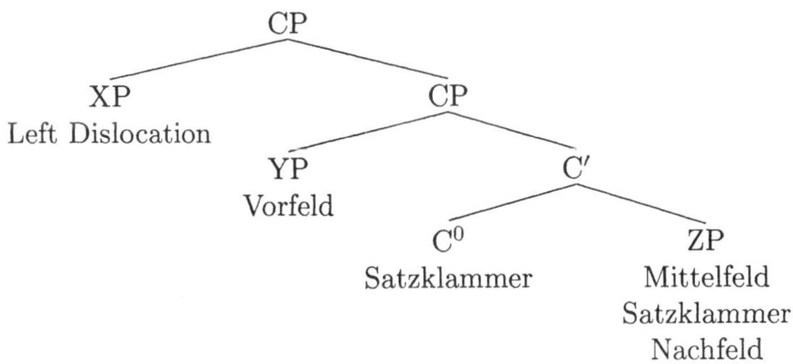


Applying the Endocentric Mapping Principles formulated in Bresnan (2001) (cf. (18) in chapter 1), we have the following annotated c-structure:

(15)

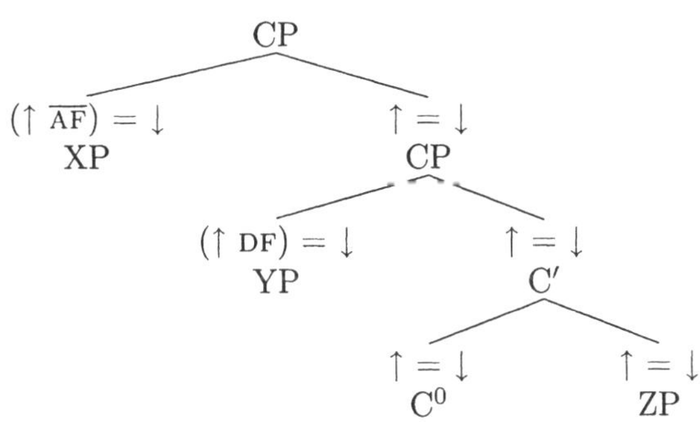


The adjoined XP and its adjoined-to sister are associated with the non-argument functions $(\uparrow \overline{\text{AF}}) = \downarrow$ and with $\uparrow = \downarrow$, respectively. The specifier of the functional categroy CP is associated with a discourse

[7] For alternative analyses cf. e.g. Travis (1984), Brandt, Reis, Rosengren, and Zimmermann (1992), Frey (1993).

function, ($\uparrow$ DF) = $\downarrow$. The functional head $C^0$ and the projection $C'$ are the c-structure heads, being annotated with $\uparrow = \downarrow$. The complement of the functional head $C^0$ is the f-structure co-head[8] and is likewise annotated with $\uparrow = \downarrow$.

Consider the specifier of CP. Is there any evidence in German that the constituent preceding the verb in verb-second position is annotated with a discourse function? Remember that the discourse functions include TOP, FOC and SUBJ.

If the *Vorfeld* is annotated with a discourse function, it follows that all grammatical functions in CP-Spec except the SUBJ must be marked as TOP or FOC.[9] Evidence for this conclusion comes from the distribution of the personal pronoun *es*[10]. This pronoun realizes the third person singular neuter in both the nominative and the accusative. As a nominative pronoun, it can occur in the *Vorfeld*, but as an accusative pronoun it cannot:

(16) Es (das Brot) ist gut.
it-NOM (the bread) is good

(17) *Es (das Brot) mag ich.
it-ACC (the bread) like I

An idiosyncratic property of *es* is that, unique among the pronouns of German, it is not capable of bearing phonological accent. Now, in the function of an OBJ, *es* in the *Vorfeld* would, according to the present analysis, have to be marked either as TOP or as FOC; but this is incompatible with its being necessarily deaccented. In contrast, since SUBJ is itself a discourse function, *es* as subject can occur in the *Vorfeld* despite its lack of accent.

The complement of $C^0$ contains the *Mittelfeld*, the right *Satzklammer* and the *Vorfeld*. Via the $\uparrow = \downarrow$ annotation the complement of $C^0$ is mapped to the same f-structure as the c-structure head $C^0$ itself. Concerning the structure of the German *Mittelfeld* and the right

[8] An "f-structure head is a category... whose f-structure will be identified with that of its mother category (Bresnan 2001, p. 52–53)." An f-structure head is not necessarily a c-structure head; in particular, two sister categories may be f-structure co-heads.

[9] Cf. Höhle (1982, p. 127), Travis (1984, p. 123f.) and Büring (1997, p. 63), who observe that the subject can occur in clause-initial position without being topic or focus. On the realization of topic and focus accents in German, see Féry (1992, p. 39), Féry (1993). It should be mentioned that this does not hold for adverbials: sentential adverbs in particular, and occasionally other adverbials, can also occur unaccented—i.e., not marked as topic or focus—in the *Vorfeld*, e.g.:
(i) Glücklicherweise hat er gelacht. (Fortunately has he laughed.)

[10] This diagnostic is often used in the literature, e.g., by Travis (1984) (who, however, argues for a different structure than I am adopting).

*Satzklammer*, two questions arise:

- Is there evidence for structurally distinct subject and object positions? More generally, how are the syntactic functions identified?
- Is there evidence for another functional head which can host a verb in addition to $C^0$—namely, the inflectional head $I^0$? This would mean that German would have three verbal head positions: $C^0$, $I^0$ and $V^0$.

These questions are briefly addressed in sections 3.2.2 and 3.2.3.

### 3.2.2 No Evidence for $I^0$

There is a longstanding debate in the literature about whether German has an IP constituent (see e.g. Grewendorf 1989, Haider 1993a, Haider 1997, Vikner 1995, Choi 1999 among others), which I will not review here. Although there are proponents for both assumptions, the general consensus is that there is no theory-external evidence for an IP constituent in addition to CP and VP.

Consider for example the following argument. If German does have $I^0$, it may either precede or follow the complement, and in fact both structures have been proposed (cf. Vikner 1995, p.153 for discussion and references therein):

(18) a. b.

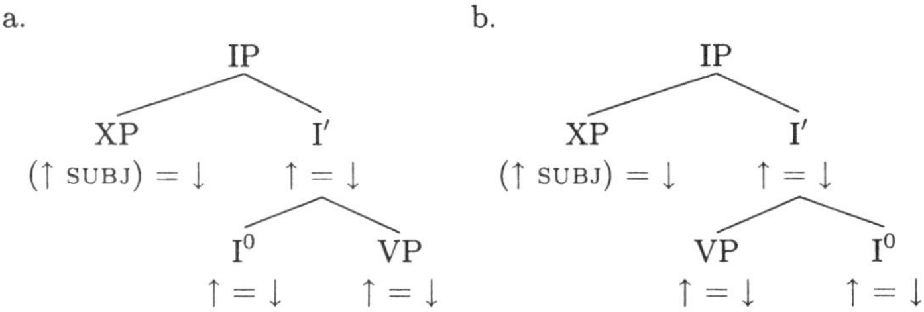


Convincing evidence for the presence of $I^0$ would be presented by a construction where the verb occupies a position which is demonstrably neither $V^0$ nor $C^0$.

According to Vikner (1995), Icelandic and Yiddish do have such constructions, involving so-called obligatory V-to-I-movement, as exemplified by the following data (cf. Vikner 1995, p. 139, (15b-c)/(16b-c)):

(19) a. *… af hverju Helgi [$_{VP}$ oft **hefði** lesið þessa bók ]
why Helgi often had read this book

b. af hverju Helgi **hefði** [$_{VP}$ oft lesið þessa bók ]
why Helgi had often read this book

(20) a. *... ven Avrom [$_{VP}$ deriber **hot** geleyent dos dozike bukh ]
when Avrom therefore has read this book

b. ... ven Avrom **hot** [$_{VP}$ deriber geleyent dos dozike bukh ]
when Avrom has therefore read this book

The adverbs *oft* and *deriber* mark the VP boundary in Icelandic and Yiddish, respectively. In (19) and (20) the finite verb (*hefði* and *hot*, respectively) must precede the adverb. Since $C^0$ is already occupied by a wh-word, there must be another verbal head between $C^0$ and $V^0$, namely $I^0$.

In contrast to Icelandic and Yiddish, in German there is no such evidence for the existence of an IP, as Choi (1999) points out. Assuming that $I^0$ is the category of finite verbs, the principle of LEXICAL INTEGRITY (see (18) in chapter 1) requires the insertion of the complete morphological word in $I^0$. But if the IP is head-initial, as in (18a), this results in an ungrammatical sentence:

(21) *[$_{CP}$ ... weil [$_{IP}$ die Annie hat [$_{VP}$ das Kind gelobt ] ] ]
because the Annie has the child praises

On the other hand, if we assume that the IP is, like the VP, head-final in German (cf. (18b)), then the two verbal positions are empirically indistinguishable, since nothing can occur between the V- and the I-head:

(22) [$_{CP}$ ... weil [$_{IP}$ die Annie [$_{VP}$ das Kind gelobt] hat ] ]

(23) *[$_{CP}$ ... weil [$_{IP}$ die Annie [$_{VP}$ das Kind gelobt] gestern hat ] ]

Moreover, as Choi (1999) notes, an additional projection would violate the economy principles of LFG (cf. Haider 1995b, Haider 1997, who argues against an IP in German with reference to economy principles in the transformational grammar framework).

If German does have an inflectional head position distinct from $C^0$ and $V^0$, and this head projects to a maximal projection IP, this would imply a distinct subject position in IP-Spec. However, even though we reject the idea that German has an $I^0$, and hence an IP, this still does not definitively answer the question whether there is a distinct subject position in German. This question will be discussed in the next section.

### 3.2.3 Function Specification in German

#### 3.2.3.1 Choi's Approach

Choi assumes that German is configurational, i.e., German has a VP which includes the object but excludes the subject. Hence although Choi does not assume that German has the functional projection IP, she does claim it has a distinct subject and object position and that the subject and the object in canonical, unmarked word order[11] are identified by structural positions.

She bases her assumption of configurationality on grammaticality contrasts involving topicalization, like the following (Choi 1999, p. 24 (12a–b)):

(24) a. Dem Mann geholfen hat der Junge.
the man-DAT helped has the boy
'The boy helped the man.'

b. *Der Junge geholfen hat dem Mann.
the boy-NOM helped has the man

The elements preceding the finite verb in (24a) have to form a constituent, otherwise the verb-second constraint would be violated. And since this constituent contains a verb and its object, it is clearly a VP. Hence, the grammaticality of (24a) constitutes evidence for the claim that German has a VP. However, (24b), where the topicalized VP contains the subject, is ungrammatical. This contrast leads Choi to suggest that the German sentence structure makes use of the exocentric category S which dominates a configurational structure, namely a subject and a predicate. While the subject is immediately dominated by S, the objects are inside the VP.

The sentence structure proposed by Choi is thus the following:[12]

[11] Roughly speaking the canonical order is the order which occurs without special requirements on the preceding utterance context. The marked order can occur only in restricted discourse conditions, cf. e.g. Choi (1999, p. 29), Bader (1996, p. 112ff.).

[12] To be consistent with the preceding analysis, I continue to assume that German has DPs instead of NPs, although Choi's analysis contains NPs.

(25)

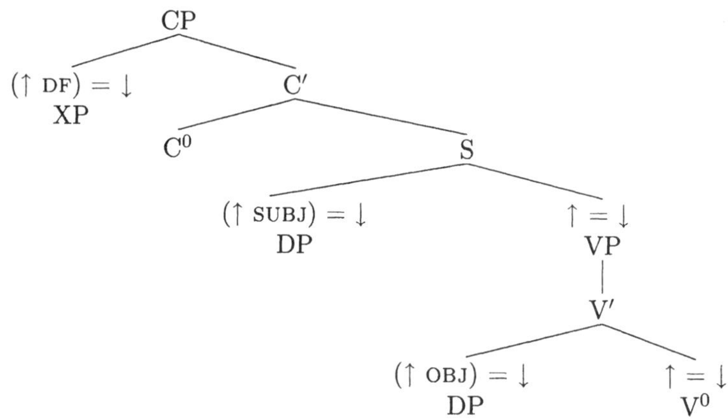


The free word order in the *Mittelfeld* is captured by the assumption that non-verbal constituents can scramble. Choi assumes that scrambled phrases are adjoined to S or VP.[13] Adjoined arguments cannot be identified via structural position but only by the morphology.

#### 3.2.3.2 Haider's Approach

Haider also argues, in numerous works (see especially Haider 1990a, Haider 1993a, Haider 1997), that the German sentence structure has only one functional projection.[14]

But in contrast to Choi, Haider argues that German displays no

[13] Choi proposes an analysis of word order in the German *Mittelfeld* in the optimality theoretic framework of LFG-OT. She argues that scrambling is motivated and constrained by interactions among syntactic, semantic and discourse principles.

[14] Haider (1995b) and (Haider 1997) mention an additional argument against the occurrence of an I-head in German. Based on the observation of Höhle that there are some finite verbs in German that can only occur sentence-finally, e.g. *uraufführen* ('to premiere'), Haider, assuming head-movement, argues that if German had a sentence-final functional category $I^0$ to which finite verbs move, there would be no independent principle excluding their further moving to the verb-second position. *Uraufführen* consists of a stem with a separable prefix (*auf-*), preceded by an inseparable prefix (*ur-*). Now, if a verb with a separable prefix occurs in V2-position, the separable prefix has to be in final position:

(i) $[_{CP}[_{C^0}$ Führten] sie die Oper $[_{V^0}$ auf]]?
put they the opera on
'Did they perform the opera?'

The combination of a separable and an inseparable prefix leads to a conflict. The inner prefix (*auf-*) must be in final position and the outer prefix (*ur-*) must not. The only way to avoid this conflict is to avoid movement (for details see Haider 1995b, Haider 1997, p. 86 (4a,c)):

(ii)a. ... dass sie es uraufführten.
that they it premiered
'... that they premiered it.'

b. *Führen sie es urauf?

syntactically conditioned subject/object asymmetries. One piece of evidence is that in German the subject of an ergative or a passivized verb is the argument which is the linearly closest to the verb in canonical order.[15]

(26) a. (Es heißt,) dass dem Buben das Geschenk versprochen
(it means) that the boy-DAT the present-NOM promised
wurde.
was
'(They say) that the boy was promised a present.'

b. (Es heißt,) dass dem Buben der Fehler aufgefallen
(it means) that the boy-DAT the mistake-NOM noticed
ist.
is
'(They say) that the boy noticed the mistake.'

Secondly, VP-topicalization containing the subject of an ergative or a passivized verb is in fact grammatical (the examples are from Haider 1993a, p. 151 (54a–b)):[16]

(27) a. Ein Fehler unterlaufen ist dabei schon manchem.
a mistake-NOM happened is thereby already many-DAT
'Many people have made a mistake with this.'

b. Ein Zug entgleist ist hier erst kürzlich.
a train-NOM derailed is here only recently
'A train derailed here only recently.'

Furthermore, Haider observed that VP-topicalization is also possible with subjects of unergative verbs (Haider 1990a, p. 97 (12g) and (12a)):

LFG does not, however, assume head-movement (cf. section 3.3). If German had an IP, finite verbs should be of the category I and base-generated in $I^0$ (cf. the analysis of Russian in King 1995). But then the ungrammaticality in V2 position can't be derived from movement restrictions and thus does not constitute an argument against the existence of the category $I^0$.

[15]That (26) is the canonical word order and does not result from scrambling is supported by the fact that it is the natural answer to the question like *Was ist los?* ('What's the matter?') *Was hast du gesagt?* ('What did you say?'), i.e., the unmarked word order allows maximal focus projection (cf. Höhle 1982).

[16]Choi (1999, p. 24f.) mentions that VP-internal topicalization of the subject is possible with a subject of an unaccusative or passivized verb and she proposes that the VP in German may be a boundary for agent and non-agents but not for subject and non-subject. However, she does not pursue this idea. But notice that even if we restrict the VP to certain thematic roles, the functional annotations on the c-structure must allow a subject to occur inside the VP.

(28) a. Kinder gespielt haben hier noch nie.
children-NOM played have hier still never
'Children have never played here.'

b. Ein Außenseiter gewonnen hat da noch nie.
An outsider-NOM won has there still never
'An outsider has never won there.'

Such data imply that the VP in German is neither a boundary for certain grammatical functions nor for certain thematic roles, but that subjects, regardless of there thematic role, may occur inside the VP.[17]

Therefore, Haider proposes (Haider 1991a, p. 32 and Haider 1993a), in agreement with the analysis of the German *Mittelfeld* proposed by Frey and Tappe (1991), Frey (1993) that arguments as well as adjuncts are adjoined to VP.[18,19]

Thus, the sentence structure proposed by Haider for German contains only one functional projection, which directly embeds a VP. Arguments as well as adjuncts are adjoined to VP. This is illustrated by the following example:

(29) ... weil der Vater den Jungen lobt.
because the father the boy praises
'... because the father praises the boy.'

[17]There are, however, some restrictions on the occurrence of the subject in these constructions; for example, it has to be indefinite (cf. e.g. Kratzer 1984).

[18]Instead of VP to denote the maximal projection of V, Haider uses $V^n$ and Frey amd Tappe use $V^{max}$.

[19]Frey and Tappe (1991, p. 3 (3)) also observe that in sentences with unmarked word order, like the following, the object may precede the adjunct:

(i) ... weil Paul jede Frau auf mannigfaltige Weise umwirbt.
because Paul each woman on manifold way woos
'... because Paul woos each woman in a variety of ways.'

This shows that it is problematic to restrict the complement function to the sister of $V^0$. Instead Frey and Tappe (1991) assume that the traditional complement position—i.e., sister of $V^0$—is occupied by phrases which can't be freely ordered in the *Mittelfeld*, such as resultive predicates. They give the following contrast (Frey and Tappe 1991, p.9 (14)/(15)):

(ii) Paul hat den Tisch mit dem Lappen trocken gewischt.
Paul has the table with the rag dry wiped
'Paul wiped the table dry with the rag.'

(iii) *Paul hat den Tisch trocken mit dem Lappen gewischt.

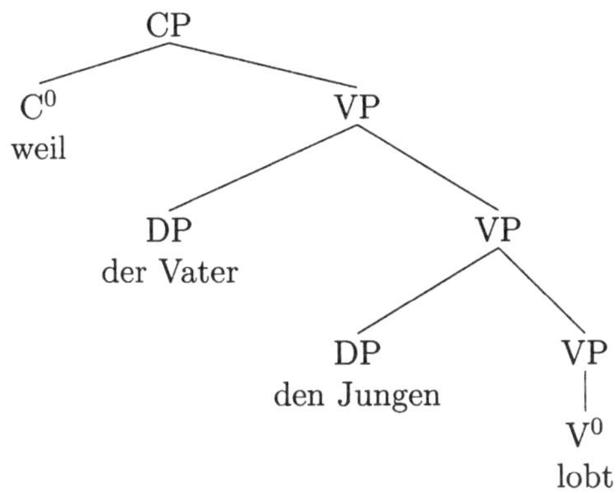


This analysis, on which arguments as well as adjuncts are adjoined to VP, entails that the grammatical functions can't be identified by different structural position but must be identified exclusively by the morphology.

In this book I adopt Haider's analysis. It lends itself well to LFG because it is consistent with the endocentric mapping principles. Recall that annotating adjoined positions with non-argument functions is optional (cf. (18e) in chapter 2); thus, lexocentric function specification is possible in adjoined positions. Hence we get the following annotated c-structure for (29) (simplified for present purposes; see chapter 4, section 4.2 for a more detailed discussion of these annotations):

(30)

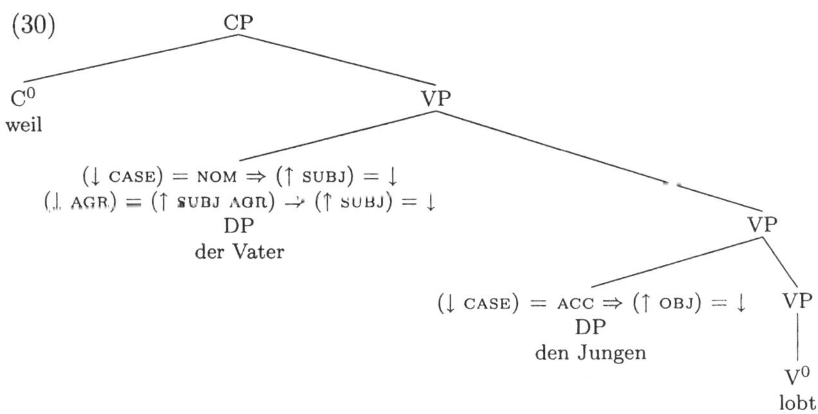


### 3.2.4 Verbal Complex

In the right *Satzklammer* (sentential bracket, cf. page 28) only verbal elements can occur, e.g.:

(31) a. . . . weil er den Sohn **lobt**.
because he the son praises
'. . . because he praises the son.'

b. . . . weil er den Sohn **gelobt hat**.
praised has
'. . . because he praised the son.'

c. . . . weil der Sohn **gelobt worden ist**.
praised been is
'. . . because the son has been praised.'

On the assumption that German has no IP there are two different proposals for the structure of the verbal complex in sentence final position. On the one hand, Haider (1991a) argues that coherent verbs (i.e., verbs that take a nonfinite verbal complement in a syntactically monoclausal construction) as in (31) form a verbal cluster, that is, they are head-adjoined and form a complex projection base, as in the following structure:[20]

(32)

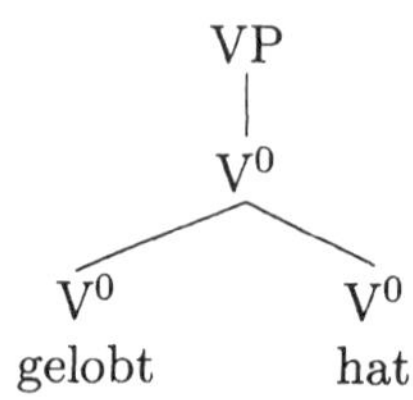


On the other hand, Frey and Tappe (1991) and Choi (1999) claim that every verb projects its own VP, e.g.:

(33)

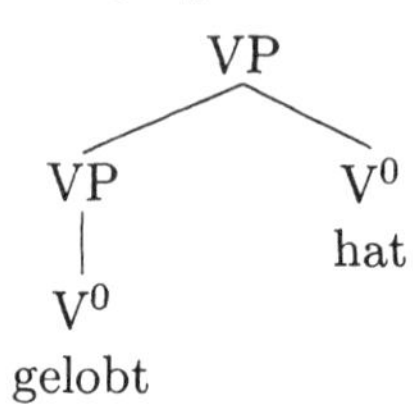


Recall that Economy of Expression applies only to syntactic phrase structure nodes; terminal nodes (i.e., the word itself) and preterminal nodes (i.e., nodes which immediately dominate words) do not fall under this principle. Now the analysis of the verbal complex proposed by Haider contains only one syntactic phrase structure node, while the analysis proposed by Frey and Tappe (1991) and Choi (1999) contains two phrase structure nodes. Hence the structure in (33) violates Econ-

[20] $X^0$-adjunction in LFG was also proposed e.g. by Sells (1998) for Japanese and Korean and by Sadler (1997) for Welsh.

omy of Expression, since the additional phrasal node it contains is not required, given the possibility of the structure in (32).

Haider's analysis also immediately captures the fact, exemplified in (11a) (repeated in (34a) below), that no constituent can intervene between the verbs in sentence-final position, while this restriction has to be stipulated in the account of Frey/Tappe and Choi.[21]

(34) a. *... dass der Hans im Garten getanzt gestern hat.
that the Hans in-the garden danced yesterday has

Further, notice that on Haider's analysis there is a structural difference between a topicalized and a non-topicalized verb: in (35a) the non-finite verb *lesen* is immediately dominated by a maximal projection, while in (35b) it is part of a verbal cluster:

(35) a. [$_{VP}$ [$_{V^0}$ Lesen]] hat er den Brief dürfen.
read hat he the letter be-allowed
'He was allowed to read the letter.'
b. ... weil er [$_{VP}$ den Brief [$_{VP}$ [$_{V^0}$ hat lesen dürfen]]]

This structural distinction is consistent with certain grammaticality differences between topicalized and non-topicalized VP. For example, in (36a) with VP-topicalization an extraposed clause can follow the non-finite verb, while this order is ungrammatical in non-topicalized position (36b) (cf. Haider 1990b, p. 95; (36a) is his example (5)):

(36) a. Fragen, ob wir einverstanden sind, wird er wohl
ask, whether we agreed are, will he well
müssen.
have-to
'He'll probably have to ask if we agree.'
b. *Er wird doch wohl fragen, ob wir einverstanden sind, müssen.
c. Er wird doch wohl fragen müssen, ob wir einverstanden sind.

For further empirical differences between the topicalized and not topicalized VP, see Haider (1990b, 94ff.) and also chapter 7, section 7.6.

### 3.2.5 Extraposed Constituents

As we have seen, extraposed arguments as well as adjunct clauses can appear in the *Nachfeld* in any order. I therefore propose that extraposed clauses are also adjoined to VP,[22] but in contrast to nominal arguments,

[21] For a detailed comparison of the analysis of the verbal complex in Haider (1991a) and Frey and Tappe (1991) see Meier (1994).

[22] An alternative analysis is proposed by Haider (1995a), who assumes that it is a universal property of phrase structure that they are always right-branching (Basic Branching Conjecture (BBC)). According to Haider, extraposed clauses are

adjoined to the right, as illustrated in the following c-structure for (13b), repeated here:[23]

(37) Er hat geglaubt, als er vier Jahre alt war, dass Schweine
He has believed when he four years old was that pigs
fliegen können.
fly can
'He believed that pigs could fly when he was four years old.'

(38)

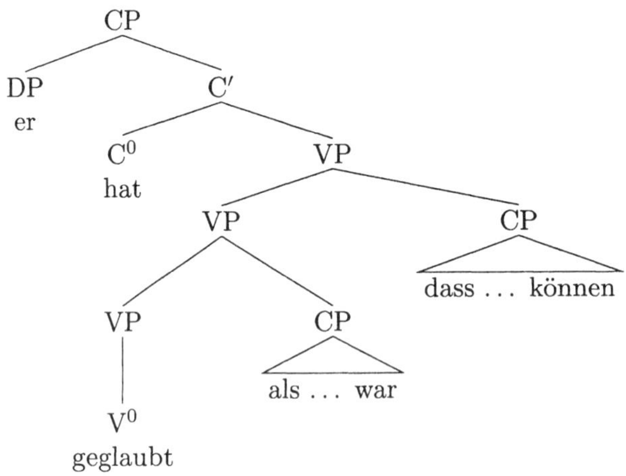


## 3.3 Verb Second and Extended Head

Haider and Frey & Tappe, working in the GB framework, have to assume that the verb in a verb second clause is coindexed with a trace in $V^0$. This is necessary to ensure that the endocentric phrase VP has a head. Thus, on Haider's analysis the sentence

(39) Anna strickt einen Pullover.
Anna knits a sweater
'Anna is knitting a sweater.'

has the following structure:

therefore more deeply embedded than nominal arguments. Büring and Hartmann (1995) assume that CPs are base-generated in the *Mittelfeld* and adjoined to the right.

[23]The obligatory occurrence of embedded clauses at the periphery of the matrix clause might be connected to parsing strategies.

(40)

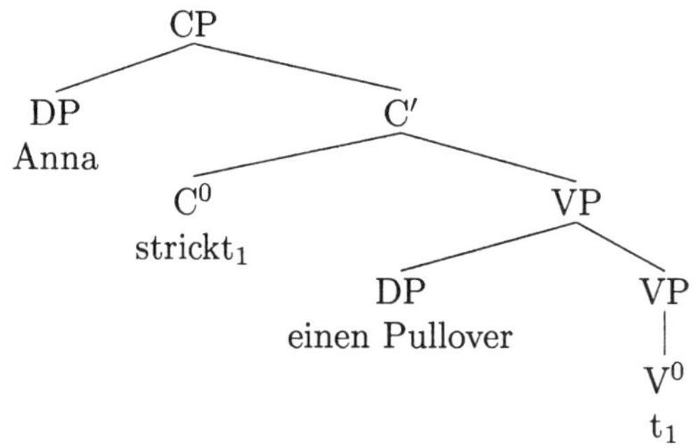


In LFG, however, the different head-positions are not captured by head-movement. In LFG (39) has the following (well-formed) structure:

(41)

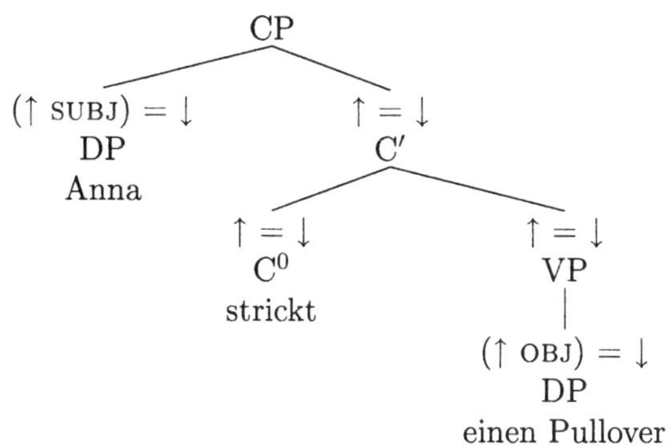


The head of the VP appears outside the VP, namely in $C^0$. However, notice that $C^0$ and VP are mapped to the same f-structure, since according to the Endocentric Mapping Principles $C^0$ and VP are both annotated with $\uparrow = \downarrow$, i.e., they are f-structure co-heads. The concept of endocentricity suggested in Bresnan (2001) takes c- and f-structure correspondence into consideration and is thus formulated as the following principle: (42) (Bresnan 2001, p. 134, (17)):

(42) **Endocentricity:**
Every lexical category has an extended head.

As will be shown in the following, the extended head of a lexical category is the internal c-structure head if it is present. But if the internal c-structure head is missing, Endocentricity is satisfied by the c-commanding head of its extended projection.

Extended head is defined as follows (Bresnan 2001, p. 132, (13)):

(43) Given a c-structure containing nodes $N$, $C$, and c- to f-structure correspondence mapping $\phi$, $N$ is an **extended head** of $C$ if $N$ is the minimal node in $\phi^{-1}(\phi(C))$ that c-commands $C$ without

dominating $C$.

(44) **c-command**
$A$ c-commands $B$ if every node properly dominating $A$ also dominates $B$.

(45) **dominance**
Every node dominates itself and its daughters, its daughters' daughters, etc., but it properly dominates only its daughters, its daughters' daughters, etc.

(46) Of all the nodes in $\phi^{-1}(\phi(C))$ that c-command $C$ without dominating $C$, $N$ is the **minimal node**, if there is no node $B$ which c-commands $C$ and is c-commanded by $N$.

Let us apply these definitions to our example in (41). To see what the extended head of the VP is, we have to look at the inverse mapping of VP, $\phi^{-1}(\phi(VP))$. The following figure shows the resulting correspondences:

(47) Anna strickt einen Pullover.

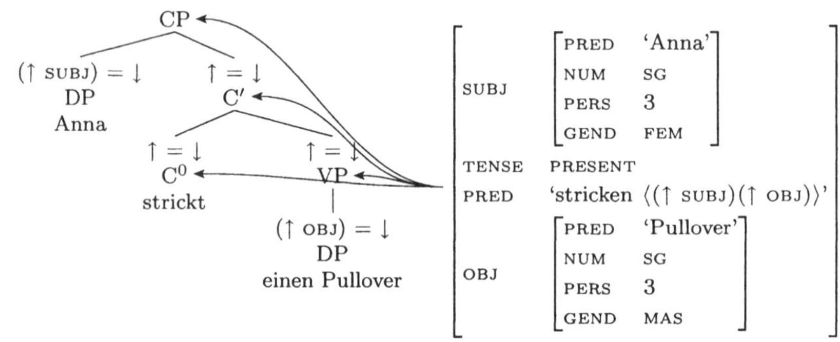


The inverse mapping $\phi^{-1}(\phi(VP))$ contains all the nodes which are mapped onto the same f-structure as VP: $\phi^{-1}(\phi(VP))$ = { CP, C′, C, VP }. CP, C′ and C$^0$ c-command VP, but of these nodes only C$^0$ c-commands VP without dominating it. C$^0$ is therefore the extended head of the VP and the Endocentricity principle (42) is satisfied.[24]

In short, structures for V2-sentences like (41) do not violate Endocentricity and hence are wellformed. Moreover, (41) is less complex than and maps to the same f-structure as a corresponding structure that contains an empty V-head inside the VP (as in (39)). Therefore, by Economy of Expression, (41) is the only admissible structure for (39).

[24]Notice that if VP dominates V′ and V′ dominates the OBJ-DP, then V′ is the extended head of the VP and C$^0$ the extended head of V′.

Contrast this with an embedded clause, which has verb-final word order:

(48) ... weil Anna einen Pullover strickt.

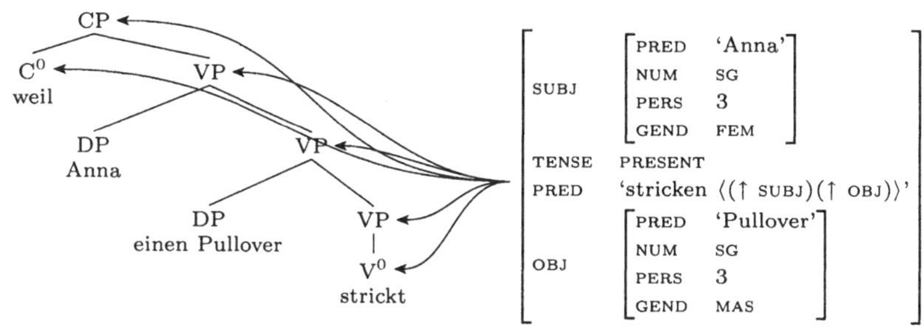


Here, $V^0$ (and not $C^0$) is the extended head of VP. Both $C^0$ and $V^0$ c-commands VP according to (44) and (45) (since every node dominates itself) but $V^0$ is the minimal c-commanding node, since $C^0$ c-commands VP and $V^0$.

The notion of extended head also explains the following grammaticality contrast:

(49) a. [$_{\text{VP}}$ Auf die Kinder aufgepasst] hat er ungern.
to the children attended has he unwillingly
'He didn't like taking care of the children.'

b. *[$_{\text{VP}}$ Auf die Kinder auf] passte er ungern.

The claim is that VP-topicalization is only grammatical if the topicalized VP is headed by an extended head. This is obviously the case in (49a). The ungrammaticality of (49b) shows the separable prefix, though part of the verbal projection, cannot function as the head. The only other possibility is the finite verb *passte* in $C^0$. However, according to the definition of c-command in (44), $C^0$ does not c-command the topicalized VP, as can be calculated from the following schematic c-structure:

(50)

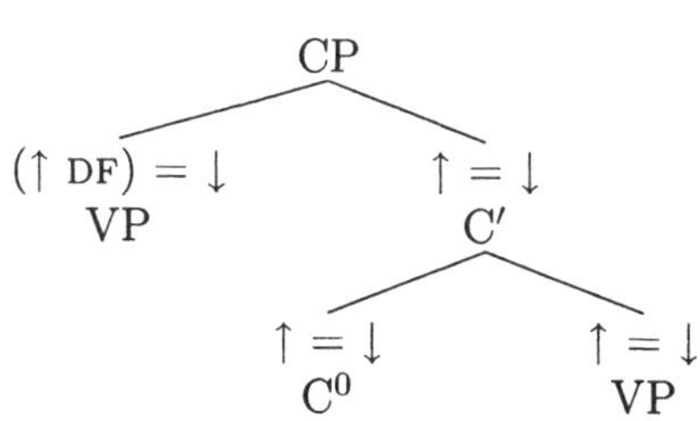


Hence by (43) $C^0$ can't be the extended head of the topicalized VP, which thus remains without a head and violates Endocentricity. Therefore (49b) is ruled out.

## 3.4 Summary

The distribution of the subject in German shows that an analysis on which the subject must occur outside the VP and objects inside the VP is problematic. Therefore I follow the analysis by Frey and Tappe (1991) and Haider (1993a, 1997), according to which German sentence structure consists of one functional projection that directly embeds a VP. The arguments—the objects as well as the subject—are adjoined to VP. This implies that there are no structurally distinct subject and object positions in German, but rather, the grammatical functions are identified by the morphology. This analysis is compatible with the Endocentric Mapping Principle proposed by Bresnan (2001), which allows lexocentric function specification in adjoined positions. The verb-second property of German is not accounted for by head-movement. 'Variable head-positioning' (Bresnan 2001, p. 126) is possible since, according to the definition of extended head, a verb in $C^0$ is the extended head of the VP (in the *Mittelfeld*, though not, as we have seen, in the *Vorfeld*) and hence satisfies the Endocentricity principle. Thus we do not need to stipulate an empty V-head inside the VP. The question still remains, however, whether there are empty categories in the case of scrambling, topicalization or extraction. This will be discussed in chapter (5).

The conclusion that German has no distinct subject position might suggest that there can be sentences in German that lack a subject altogether, which would mean that German is a language which fails to satisfy the Subject Condition. Whether this is so is the topic of the next chapter.

# 4

# Every Sentence in German has a Subject

## 4.1 The Subject Condition

In this chapter I will address the question whether German is a language that satisfies the Subject Condition, i.e., put informally, whether every sentence in German has a subject.[1] This is particularly interesting since, as we have seen, German has no distinct subject position. Moreover, in LFG the *Subject Condition* is postulated as a universal. It is therefore important to carefully examine data which may call this universal status into question.

The Subject Condition was originally proposed by Baker (1983); the following definition of it is given in Alsina (1996, p. 20):

(1) **Subject Condition**
An f-structure with propositional content must include a subject (as one of its grammatical functions) and no f-structure may include more than one subject.

Grammatical functions are represented on f-structure; hence, the Subject Condition is a condition on f-structures. Consequently, the Subject Condition does not itself regulate the representation of the subject constituent in c-structure, and is compatible with subjectless c-structures. As we will see, in German there are in fact clauses without a representation of the subject in c-structure. Given that the f-structure is constructed from c-structure by the mapping function $\phi$ (cf. chapter 2, section 2.3), this fact appears to lead to the conclusion that the Subject Condition does not hold in German, which would mean that it is not an unconditional linguistic universal. Recall, however, that $\phi$ is not onto, i.e., there may be f-structures that are not the image under $\phi$ of

[1]This chapter is a elaborated version of Berman (1999).

any c-structure. Thus, the following question arises: Does the Subject Condition hold in German even when there is no structurally realized subject? If so, then German does not provide evidence against its being a universal. Furthermore, if subjectless c-structures in German do not lead to violations of the Subject Condition, then it must be clarified precisely how it is satisfied, i.e., precisely how the subject is introduced in f-structure.

It is still controversial whether the Subject Condition in LFG should be a universal or not. According to Alsina (1996, p. 20, fn. 6) the Subject Condition is "if not an absolute universal, at least the unmarked parameter setting". Mohanan (1994, p. 191) concludes: "The status of the Subject Condition (...) as an inviolable universal is thereby called into question by this construction [the Hindi accusative logical subject construction/ J.B.]. Given that the motivation for the Subject Condition is cross-linguistically robust, the condition can by no means be abandoned. The only conclusion open to us then is that the Subject Condition may be violated under certain special circumstances." Bresnan and Zaenen (1990, p. 51, fn.10) remark that "this condition may need to be parameterized so as to hold only for some types of languages".

Note, however, that, although the status of the Subject Condition is not clear, it is used as a wellformedness condition in the Lexical Mapping Theory as formulated, e.g., in Bresnan and Zaenen (1990) and Alsina and Mchombo (1993) (cf. chapter 2, section 2.4). According to the formulation of Alsina and Mchombo, in German, the Subject Condition is necessary to capture the mapping from a-structure to f-structure with passive and ergative constructions, since in these cases the theme argument, which is intrinsically marked [−r], must be mapped on the SUBJ, although the mapping to the OBJ would in principle be possible. *Kommen* ('come') is an example of an ergative verb, and *gelobt* ('praised') is an example of a passivized transitive verb:

(2) kommen < theme >
[−r]
SUBJ

(3) gelobt < agent theme >
[−o] [−r]
∅ SUBJ

In the following, an analysis will be presented which shows that German is consistent with the universal status of the Subject Condition, although there are clauses without a structurally represented subject. It will be shown that this follows without further stipulation from the analysis of agreement in LFG. Some interesting predictions of this analysis will also be discussed.

## 4.2 Clauses without a Structural Subject

Before demonstrating that there are clauses in German without a structurally represented subject, it is useful to recapitulate how the grammatical functions are identified in German. We have seen that there are two types of morphological function specifications, dependent-marking and head-marking:

(4) **Types of Morphological Function Specification:**
a. dependent-marking:
$(\downarrow \text{CASE}) = \kappa \Rightarrow (\uparrow \text{GF}) = \downarrow$
b. head-marking:
$(\downarrow \text{AGR}) = (\uparrow \text{AF AGR}) \Rightarrow (\uparrow \text{AF}) = \downarrow$

In German both types of morphological function specification can be observed simultaneously with the subject: it is marked nominative (which is an instance of dependent-marking) and it has to agree in number and person with the finite verb (which is an instance of head-marking). The sentences in (5) illustrate this:

(5) a. Der Junge lacht.
The boy-NOM laugh (3.pers.sg/2.pers.pl)
b. *Den/dem/des Jungen/s lacht.
The boy-ACC/DAT/GEN laugh (3.pers.sg/2.pers.pl)
c. *Der Junge lachst.
The boy-NOM laugh (2.pers.sg)
d. *Der Junge lachen.
The boy-NOM laugh (1./3.pers.pl)

In (5a) the DP is marked nominative and has the same person and number features as the finite verb. (5b) shows that the subject must be marked nominative, no other case-marking is possible. In (5c) there is number agreement but no person agreement, in (5d) there is person agreement but no number agreement. Hence, the morphological function specification for the subject in German can be formalized as in (6):

(6) $(\downarrow \text{CASE}) = \text{NOM} \wedge (\downarrow \text{NUM}) = (\uparrow \text{SUBJ NUM}) \wedge (\downarrow \text{PERS}) = (\uparrow \text{SUBJ PERS}) \Rightarrow (\uparrow \text{SUBJ}) = \downarrow$

In contrast to the subject, there is no object-verb agreement in German. An object is identified only by accusative case-marking:

(7) … weil der Junge **den Mann** auslacht.
because the boy the man-ACC laughed-at
'… because the boy is laughing at the man.'

(8) $(\downarrow \text{CASE}) = \text{ACC} \Rightarrow (\uparrow \text{OBJ}) = \downarrow$

It follows from (6) that the Subject Condition is always satisfied in German if there is a nominative marked DP in c-structure that agrees with the verb in person and number, regardless of whether such a DP is the argument of an unergative, as in (9a), an ergative (9b,d), a transitive (9c) or a passivized verb (9e).[2]

(9) a. … weil **der Junge** tanzt.
because the boy-NOM dances
'… because the boy is dancing.'

b. … weil **der Junge** kommt.
because the boy-NOM comes
'… because the boy is coming.'

c. … weil **der Junge** den Roller gestohlen hat.
because the boy-NOM the scooter stolen has
'… because the boy stole the scooter.'

d. … weil dem Jungen **der Zaubertrick** gelungen
because the boy-DAT the magic trick-NOM succeeded
ist.
is
'… because the boy managed to do the magic trick.'

e. … weil dem Jungen **der Roller** gestohlen wurde.
because the boy-DAT the scooter-NOM stolen was
'… because the boy's scooter was stolen.'

There are, however, certain types of sentences in German which lack a nominative-marked, agreeing DP, e.g. ((10b) and (10c) are based on examples from Reis 1982, p.185):

(10) a. … weil getanzt wird.
because danced is
'… because people are dancing/because there is dancing.'

[2]One might object that the subject of an ACI-construction is marked accusative and does not agree with the finite verb, as in (i):

(i) Ich sehe ihn kommen.
I see him-ACC come-INF

However according to the analysis proposed in Bresnan (1982) for ECM-verbs the accusative marked DP in (i) is a non-thematic object of the verb *sehen* which is unified on f-structure with the subject of *kommen*.

b. ... weil mir an einer schnellen Lösung liegt.
because me-DAT on a quick solution lies
'... because a quick solution is important to me.'

c. ... weil dem Kind komisch zumute ist.
because the child-DAT funny in-mood is
'... because the child feels funny.'

d. ... weil mich friert.
because me-ACC freezes
'... because I'm cold.'

Such sentences are consistent with one of two conclusions: either the Subject Condition is violated by these constructions, or the subject, though not structurally expressed, is provided by another component of the grammar, thus satisfying the Subject Condition.

Another question is under what conditions these 'subjectless' constructions occur. Notice that, while the passive sentence in (10a) lacks any argument, the active sentences in (10b)–(10d) have dative or accusative marked arguments. There is in fact a restriction in German that every verb in the active voice has to subcategorize for at least for one function (cf. e.g. Reis 1982, p. 206, fn. 41). But this descriptive generalization leaves unanswered the question of why the argument of predicates like those in (10b)–(10d) does not have to be mapped onto the subject, as e.g. with passivized transitive verbs, but is mapped onto an accusative or dative marked object. In the following it will be argued that this pattern results from the interaction of case-marking and verbal agreement morphology in German; and I claim that even in these cases the Subject Condition is satisfied. First let us look at case-marking.

### 4.2.1 Default vs. Lexical Case-Marking

As was shown by Zaenen, Maling, and Thrainsson (1985, p. 465) there is a distinction between default case-marking (which is similar to structural case-marking in GB) and lexical case-marking (which is similar to inherent case-marking in GB). While default case marking is sensitive to surface grammatical relations and results in nominative subjects and accusative objects, lexical case-marking is an idiosyncratic property of the lexical item and is associated with a particular thematic role. In German lexically case-marked arguments are obligatorily mapped onto $\text{OBJ}_\theta$ (Zaenen, Maling, and Thrainsson 1985, p, 479).

Consider the contrast between the verbs *loben* ('to praise') and *helfen* ('to help'): *loben* is a verb which has no lexically case-marked argument. According to the mapping principles formulated in Alsina and

Mchombo, the agent, which is intrinsically marked [−o], gets the default classification [−r] and is mapped onto the SUBJ. Hence the theme, which is intrinsically marked [−r], has to be mapped onto the OBJ:

(11) loben $<$ agent theme $>$

| | agent | theme |
|---|---|---|
| | [−o] | [−r] |
| | [−r] | |
| | SUBJ | OBJ |

The SUBJ is assigned nominative case by default; the OBJ is assigned per default accusative case:[3]

(12) ... weil **der** Vater **den** Jungen lobt.
because the father-NOM the boy-ACC praises

In the passive construction the agent is suppressed, so the theme argument, being intrinsically marked [−r], is mapped onto the subject and satisfies the Subject Condition, as shown in (13):

(13) gelobt $<$ agent theme $>$

| | agent | theme |
|---|---|---|
| | [−o] | [−r] |
| | ∅ | SUBJ |

Notice that the mapping rules require that the underspecified theme-argument must be mapped onto the SUBJ (hence assigned nominative case), although the intrinsic feature specification [−r] of the theme would permit it to be mapped onto the OBJ (hence assigned accusative case):

(14) ... weil **der** Junge/ ***den** Jungen gelobt wird.
because the boy-NOM/ the boy-ACC praised is

In contrast to default case-assignment, lexical case is associated with specific thematic roles. In German such thematic roles are obligatorily mapped onto $\text{OBJ}_\theta$.[4] So if we assume that *helfen* has a lexically case-marked argument, we can explain why in the passive voice *helfen* does not subcategorize for a SUBJ but for an $\text{OBJ}_\theta$. We can assume that

[3] In chapter 8 it will be argued that default case (see Bresnan, p.143, footnote 24 for default feature specification) influences the mapping to grammatical functions. It is therefore assumed that default-case is assigned after all relation changes but before the mapping to grammatical functions. With default case-assignment the highest available (not lexically case-marked) thematic role is assigned nominative case, the next highest accusative; i.e. the highest not lexically case-marked thematic role must be mapped onto the SUBJ.

[4] There are no 'quirky' subjects in German; see Zaenen, Maling, and Thrainsson (1985) for a comparison of Icelandic non-nominative marked subjects and German dative marked DPs, which cannot function as a subject (e.g. dative marked DPs can't be controlled: *(*Mir) geholfen zu werden ist angenehm* '(for me) to be helped is agreeable').

the feature values of the case-marked thematic role are already fully specified:

(15)

| geholfen | < agent | beneficiary > |
|---|---|---|
| | [−o] | [+o]/DAT |
| | | [+r] |
| | ∅ | $\text{OBJ}_\theta$ |

Lexical case does not change when the clause is passivized. In (16) we see that the dative is also retained in the passive voice:

(16) a. ... weil der Vater **dem Mädchen** hilft.
because the father-NOM the girl-DAT helps

b. ... weil **dem Mädchen** geholfen wird.
because the girl-DAT helped is

Hence, in sentences like (16b) there is no nominative marked DP.

The same thing can be observed with certain verbs in the active voice which have only one lexically case-marked argument and oblique functions. Here are some examples:

(17) a. ... weil mir schlecht ist.
because me-DAT ill ist
'... because I feel ill.'

b. ... weil mir (davor) graut.
because me-DAT (before-that) dreads.
'... because I dread that.'

c. ... weil mich ekelt.
because me-ACC disgusts
'... because I'm disgusted/feel disgusted.'

Again, due to lexical case-marking these verbs do not subcategorize for a SUBJ, but an $\text{OBJ}_\theta$. Therefore sentences with such verbs, as in (16b) and (17), violate the Subject Condition, unless there is an alternative way to provide a SUBJ.

### 4.2.2 Impersonal Passive

A similar case where the Subject Condition seems to be violated is the impersonal passive of intransitive verbs, where no argument is left, as in (18).

(18) ... weil (gestern) (im Wald) getanzt wurde.
because yesterday in the woods danced was
'... because there was dancing (in the woods) (yesterday).'

When intransitive verbs are passivized, the only argument is suppressed and the verb does not subcategorize for any function at all:

(19) getanzt < agent >
[−o]
———
∅

This results in sentences containing only the predicate (and, optionally, adjuncts).

In contrast to German, in many languages with impersonal passive, an expletive subject must be inserted. Examples are Danish, Swedish, Norwegian (Sten Vikner, p.c.) and Dutch (Jan van Kuppevelt, p.c.), as shown in (20).

(20) a. Vielleicht wird getanzt. — German
perhaps is danced

b. Måske bliver **der** danset. — Danish
perhaps be-PRES there danced

c. Kanskje blir **det** danset. — Norwegian
perhaps be-PRES it danced

d. Kanske dansas **det**. — Swedish
perhaps danced-be-PRES it

e. Misschien wordt **er** gedanst. — Dutch
perhaps is there danced

In the following it will be argued that this difference is due to the role of verbal morphology in the different languages.

## 4.3 The Role of the Verbal Agreement Morphology

We have seen that in German the subject agrees with the finite verb in person and number. Following the analysis of subject-verb agreement in Kaplan and Bresnan (1982, p. 205) and Bresnan (2001, chap.8), the subject-verb agreement is encoded on the verbal affix.

The verbal affix contains, on the one hand, information about tense and mood, and on the other hand, it specifies that its subject must have certain number and person values. The verb is able to specify features of the subject because it is the f-structure head of the clause (i.e., this is an instance of head-marking). To illustrate, the entry of the third person singular verbal affix is given in (21):

(21) -t $V_{infl}$ (↑ TENSE) = PRESENT
(↑ MOOD) = INDICATIVE
(↑ SUBJ) = ↓
(↓ PERS) = 3
(↓ NUM) = SG

The person and number features of the subject, provided by the verbal agreement morphology, are unified with the features of the subject

DP and guarantee subject-verb agreement. For example, the agreement features of the verbal affix -*t* are compatible with the agreement features of the pronoun *er* (*he*). The lexical entry of *er* is given in (22):

(22) er N (↑ PRED) = 'pro'
(↑ NUM) = SG
(↑ PERS) = 3
(↑ GEND) = MASC
(↑ CASE) = NOM

Hence the information of the affix -*t* and the pronoun *er* can be unified, as shown in (23):[5]

(23) ... dass er lacht.
that he laughs

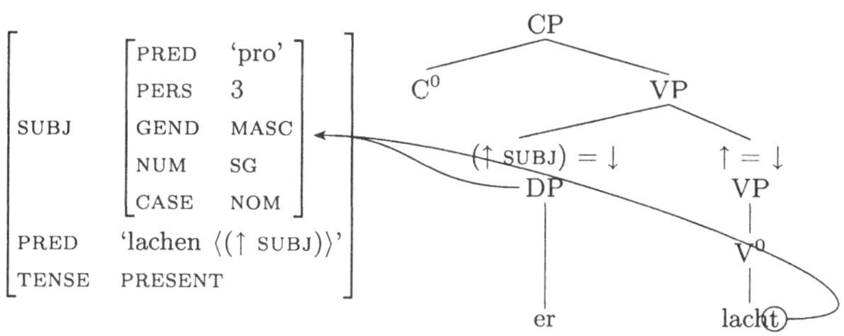


Subject-verb agreement is an instance of head-marking. The subject is specified on the head of the clause, the verb. But since the verbal affix specifies only the person and number features of the subject, a corresponding DP is usually obligatory, in order to provide the semantic features selected by the predicate. But what about sentences like (16b), (17) or (18), where no subject DP is present and thus no unification can take place?

There are languages in which arguments do not have to be represented in c-structure. For example, Bresnan and Mchombo (1987) claim that in Chicheŵa, the optional absence of the subject NP can be analyzed as an instance of pro-drop. The object in Chicheŵa, however, is specified only by the verbal morphology and is an example of pronoun incorporation. Hence, in this case, no object NP can occur. To see whether clauses without a c-structure subject in German can be analysed along these lines, I will briefly summarize the analysis of pro-drop and pronoun incorporation given in Bresnan and Mchombo (1987) and

[5]Here and subsequently I omit the mood feature from the f-structure for simplicity, since it plays no role in the present work.

Bresnan (2001).[6]

### 4.3.1 Pronoun Incorporation and Pro-Drop

Bresnan (2001, chap. 8, p. 144) suggests that "*pronoun incorporation* or *pronominal inflection* can be analyzed in this way: an incorporated pronoun or pronominal inflection is a bound morpheme that specifies a complete pronominal f-structure. The functional specification of a pronoun is incorporated with the functional specifications of the stem to which the morpheme is bound." In Chicheŵa the affix *-wá* specifies an object f-structure, containing semantic and agreement features. This is illustrated by the following example (Bresnan 2001, p.150 (13b)):

(24) Njûchi zi-ná-wá-lum-a
10.bee 10.S-PST-2.O-bite-FV
'The bees bit them'

The object marker (OM) *-wá* carries the following information:

(25) OM- $V_{infl}$ $(\uparrow \text{OBJ}) = \downarrow$
$(\downarrow \text{PRED}) = \text{'pro'}$
$(\downarrow \text{AGR}) = \alpha$

Since *-wá* specifies the PRED-feature of the object, the occurrence of an object-NP is excluded by the Uniqueness Condition. This is also the case if the PRED-features which are specified by *-wá* and the object-NP are identical, since PRED-features are treated as instantiated symbols which can't be unified, even if they are identical (Kaplan and Bresnan 1982, p. 225):

(26) a. * $\left[\text{SUBJ} \quad \left[\text{PRED} \quad \text{'pro}_i\text{' \& 'hunters}_j\text{'}\right]\right]$

b. * $\left[\text{SUBJ} \quad \left[\text{PRED} \quad \text{'pro}_i\text{' \& 'pro}_j\text{'}\right]\right]$

Suppose an additional corresponding NP occurs, as in the following example (Bresnan 2001, p.150 (13a)):

(27) Njûchi zi-ná-wá-lum-a a-lenje
10.bee 10.S-PST-2.O-bite-FV 2-hunter
'The bees bit them, the hunters.'

Bresnan and Mchombo (1987) argue, based on syntactic, phonological and discourse evidence, that the NP functions as a TOP to which the OBJ is anaphorically linked:

[6] On pronominal incorporation and pro-drop, see also Mereu (1997) and Börjars and Chapman (1998).

(28)

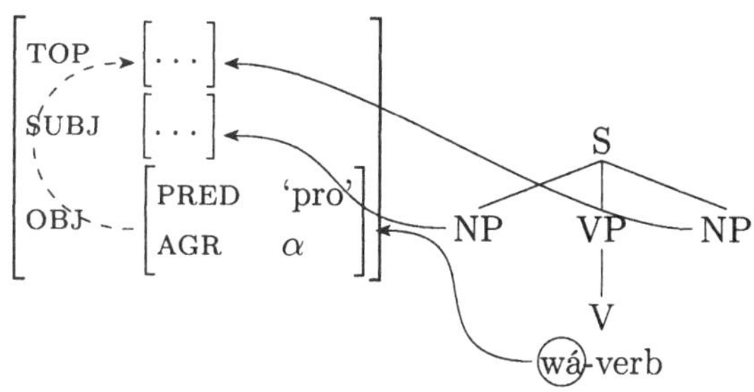


If *wá* is not present an object-NP can occur (Bresnan 2001, p.150 (10a)):

(29) Njûchi zi-ná-lúm-a a-lenje
10.bee 10.S-PST-bite-FV 2-hunter
'The bees bit the hunters.'

If both *wá* and the object-NP are absent, the clause is ungrammatical (Bresnan 2001, p.151 (13c)):

(30) *Njûchi zi-ná-lúm-a
10.bee 10.S-ST-bite-FV
'The bees bit.'

In contrast to the object marker, the subject marker (SM) *zi* is obligatory. According to the analysis of Bresnan and Mchombo (1987), the subject in Chicheŵa is also specified by the verbal morphology, with the difference that in this case the semantic feature is optional:

(31) SM- $V_{infl}$ $(\uparrow \text{SUBJ}) = \downarrow$
$((\downarrow \text{PRED}) = \text{'pro'})$
$(\downarrow \text{AGR}) = \alpha$

This gives two possibilities: (i) if the semantic feature is present, the subject is specified by the morphology, as in (32) (Bresnan 2001, p.150 (10b)); (ii) if the semantic feature is absent, it is provided by the corresponding DP and we have subject-verb agreement, as in (33) (Bresnan 2001, p.150 (10a)).

(32) Zi-ná-lúm-a a-lenje
10.S-PST-bite-FV 2-hunter
'They bit the hunters.'

(33) Njûchi zi-ná-lúm-a a-lenje
10.bee 10.S-PST-bite-FV 2-hunter
'The bees bit the hunters.'

In contrast to Chicheŵa, in German pro-drop and pronoun incorporation are not possible, since a thematic subject can never be omitted,[7] as shown in (34):

(34) … weil *(er) lacht.
because he laughs

This indicates that in German, the verbal agreement morphology does not provide a PRED-feature either optionally or obligatorily. Hence, in (34) where the verb *lachen* subcategorizes for a thematic subject, the SUBJ-DP, providing the semantic feature, has to be present and we have subject-verb agreement.

We have seen that in LFG the difference between pronominal incorporation, pro-drop and agreement is minimally captured by the obligatory or optional presence or absence of the PRED-feature[8]. This implies that with pronominal incorporation an additional NP in the same function can't occur, while with pro-drop a corresponding NP is optional and with agreement a corresponding NP is obligatory. However, it was shown that there are verbs in German which do not subcategorize for a subject, namely certain verbs with lexically case-marked arguments, and impersonal passives. In the following I will argue that in these cases the verbal agreement morphology can specify a subject—just as we have seen with pronominal incorporation or pro-drop—however, not a thematic subject but an expletive (non-thematic) subject.

### 4.3.2 Specifying Expletive Subjects

We have seen that in German the verbal morphology does not provide a semantic feature. Notice, however, that the verbal agreement morphology nevertheless specifies a subject containing only person and number information, as exemplified for the present tense in (35):

(35)
$$\left[\begin{array}{ll} \text{SUBJ} & \left[\begin{array}{ll}\text{PERS} & 3\\ \text{NUM} & \text{SG}\end{array}\right] \\ \text{TENSE} & \text{PRESENT}\end{array}\right] \quad \text{-t} \quad V_{infl} \quad \begin{array}{l} (\uparrow \text{TENSE}) = \text{PRESENT}\\ (\uparrow \text{SUBJ}) = \downarrow \\ \quad (\downarrow \text{PERS}) = 3 \\ \quad (\downarrow \text{NUM}) = \text{SG}\end{array}$$

Normally this information is unified with the features of the subject DP. But what happens if no subject DP is present? In this case too, the

[7] Except in the case of Topic Drop, where a subject or an object in sentence-initial position may be omitted under certain pragmatic conditions; cf. Huang (1984) and chapter 7, section 7.4.

[8] Cf. Nordlinger (1998, sect. 3.2) for a general discussion of head-marking non-configurationality.

verbal agreement morphology introduces a subject in the f-structure, namely a subject without a semantic feature. A subject which has no semantic feature, but only agreement features, is an expletive subject. If a verb subcategorizes for a thematic, semantically contentful subject, like the verb *lachen* ('laugh'), the subject provided by the morphology does not satisfy Completeness, since it has no semantic feature. However, if the verb does not subcategorize for a thematic subject, the specification of an expletive subject is fine and furthermore required to satisfy the Subject Condition. Notice, too, that the insertion of the expletive subject by the verbal morphology is just a consequence of subject-verb agreement and does not need to be stipulated. On the contrary, further constraints would be necessary in order to prevent the insertion of the expletive subject.

The mapping from c- to f-structure of a sentence without a subject DP is illustrated in (36). *Grauen* has a lexically case-marked argument which is mapped onto OBJ$_\theta$. The Subject Condition is satisfied by the verbal agreement morphology:

(36) ... weil mir graut.
because me-DAT dreads

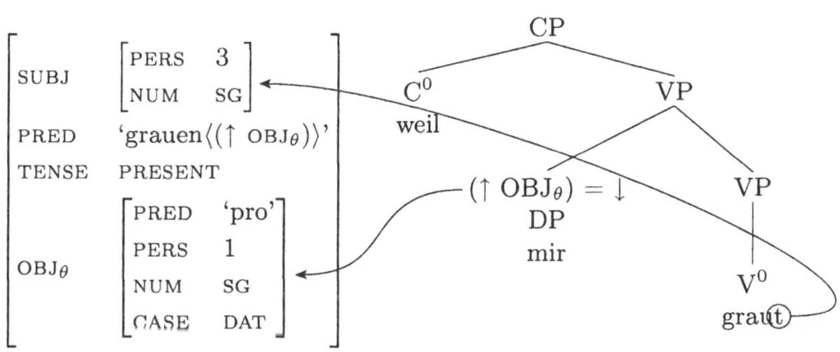


According to this analysis every finite clause satisfies the Subject Condition, since either the subject, specified by the agreement morphology, is unified with a subject DP or the agreement morphology specifies an expletive subject.

Notice that sentences like the following

(37) a. *... weil lacht.
because laughs

b. *... weil sieht den Löwen.
because sees the lion

do satisfy the Subject Condition under this analysis, but violate Completeness, since *lachen* and *sehen* subcategorize for a thematic subject.

However, there is a restriction: an expletive subject can only be introduced by the affix which is marked third person singular. All the other morphological forms lead to ungrammaticality:

(38) a. ... weil getanzt wird. (3.pers.sg)
b. *... weil getanzt wirst. (2.pers.sg)
c. *... weil getanzt werde. (1.pers.sg)
d. *... weil getanzt werden. (1./3 pers.pl)
e. *... weil getanzt werdet. (2.pers.pl)

But this is in accordance with the observation that the expletive DP in other languages is also third person singular, as for example Swedish or Norwegian *det* or Icelandic *það*. It seems that this is the only specification that allows a construal without semantic content. This observation can be captured by the following wellformedness condition on f-structures:[9]

(39) All f-structures must have a PRED-feature, unless they are specified for third person singular.
$(\forall f)\ [\neg\ (f\ \textsc{pred}) \Rightarrow [(f\ \textsc{num}) = \textsc{sg}, (f\ \textsc{pers}) = 3]]$

Another question which arises is why the subject introduced by the verbal morphology does not violate Coherence, since the verb does not subcategorize for a subject. Compare (36), where *grauen* subcategorizes only for an $\textsc{obj}_\theta$, or the passive of an intransitive verb as in (40), where *tanzen* in the passive voice does not subcategorize for any function at all.

[9]This condition does not capture adverbial expletives, like English *there* or Danish *der*, which lack inflectional features. I leave such cases to future research.

(40) ... weil getanzt wird.
because danced is
'... because people are dancing/there is dancing.'

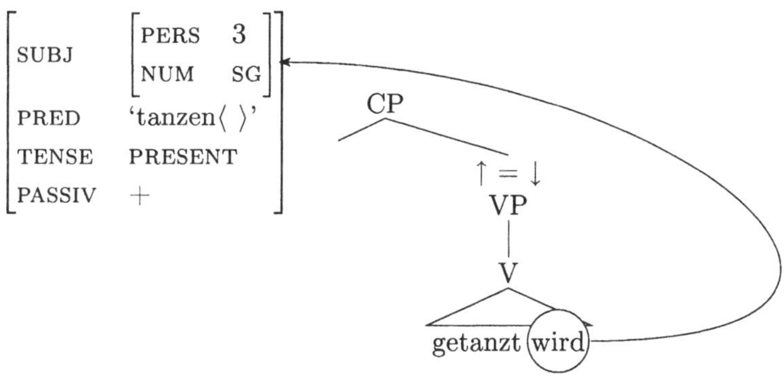


According to Alsina's formulation of Coherence, grammatical functions can be licensed in three different ways: "a direct function must be licensed either (i) by a mapping principle [...], (ii) by a general principle such as the Subject Condition [...], or (iii) by a lexical stipulation (Alsina 1996, p. 71 (59))." Following Alsina's claim that non-thematic functions are not represented in a-structure (*ibid.*, pp. 57-58), an expletive subject cannot be licensed by a mapping principle, but being a subject it is licensed by the Subject Condition itself. This is the case for expletive subjects introduced by the morphology, as in German, as well as for the expletive subject DP, as for example in Norwegian:

(41) Kanskje blir **det** danset.
perhaps be-PRES it danced

Also in the Norwegian case, the expletive subject DP *det* is not subcategorized by the verb, but it is licensed by the Subject Condition.

### 4.3.3 Predictions of the Analysis

The analysis presented here makes a prediction for other languages: a language which does not have subject-verb agreement can't introduce an expletive subject via the verbal morphology. In order for such languages to satisfy the Subject Condition, the expletive subject must be introduced in another way. This is the case for languages like Danish, Norwegian and Swedish. These languages do not have subject-verb agreement. Hence, the verbal morphology does not specify an expletive subject, rather the subject must be identified structurally.[10] The

[10] In case there is a sentence-initial locative PP or a locative adverb the expletive subject is optional (cf. Vikner 1995, p. 47 for Danish, Falk 1987, p. 2ff. and Kersti

examples are repeated for convenience:

(42) a. Måske bliver *(der) danset. — Danish
perhaps be-PRES there danced

b. Kanskje blir *(det) danset. — Norwegian
perhaps be-PRES it danced

c. Kanske dansas *(det). — Swedish
perhaps danced-be-PRES it

Yiddish and Icelandic, like German, do have subject-verb agreement. So the expletive subject can be introduced by the verbal agreement morphology. The prediction of the analysis presented here, that no expletive DP occurs, is borne out. Examples are the following (Sten Vikner p.c.):[11]

(43) a. Efsher vert (*es) getantst. — Yiddish
perhaps is it danced

b. Kannski er (*það) dansað. — Icelandic
perhaps is it danced

An apparent counterexample is English, which has both subject-verb-agreement and a structural expletive subject. In case the DP occurs in postverbal position the expletive *there* has to occupy the subject position:

(44) Perhaps *(there) arrived a man.

In Bresnan (2001) the entry of the verbal affix *-s* is specified as follows:

---

Börjars (p.c.) for Swedish; Helge Dyvik pointed out to me that it also holds in Norwegian). For example (Sten Vikner, p.c.):

(i) I huset bliver (der) danset. — Danish
in the-house be-PRES there danced

(ii) I huset blir (det) danset. — Norwegian
in the-house be-PRES it danced

(iii) I huset dansas (det). — Swedish
in the-house be-PRES-danced it

However in this case the PP functions as a subject and is an instance of locative inversion which has a specific discourse function (cf. Bresnan 1994, p. 85ff.).

[11] Yiddish *es* and Icelandic *það* can occur in front of the finite verb in a V2 clause (cf. Vikner 1995, p. 69f. (8)–(9)). However, it is plausible to assume that in this case they are functioning as placeholders and do not have the status of a subject; cf. the discussion of (56) below, which illustrates the exactly analogous behaviour of German *es*.

(45) -s $V_{infl}$ $(\uparrow \text{TENSE}) = \text{PRESENT}$
$(\uparrow \text{SUBJ}) = \downarrow$
$(\downarrow \text{PERS}) = 3$
$(\downarrow \text{NUM}) = \text{SG}$
$(\downarrow \text{CASE}) = \text{NOM}$

So if the analysis proposed for German is correct, this would seem to lead to the incorrect conclusion that also in English the verbal agreement morphology can specify an expletive subject and satisfy the Subject Condition.

Note, however, English has only partial subject-verb agreement, mainly in the present tense, third person singular. We can plausibly assume that in English the verbal morphology is too weak (cf. Rohrbacher 1999, Vikner 1997) to introduce a subject by itself. Weakness of the morphology can be expressed by constraining equations (notated as '$=_c$') on the agreement features:

(46) -s $V_{infl}$ $(\uparrow \text{TENSE}) = \text{PRESENT}$
$(\uparrow \text{SUBJ}) = \downarrow$
$(\downarrow \text{PERS}) =_c 3$
$(\downarrow \text{NUM}) =_c \text{SG}$
$(\downarrow \text{CASE}) = \text{NOM}$

Constraining equations do not assign a value to an attribute. Instead the constraining equation requires that the value be already specified in order for the f-structure to be wellformed.

Thus, in English the agreement features of the verbal morphology must be licensed by a cooccurring DP. Consequently, in sentences like the following, the verb agrees with the postverbal DP:[12]

(47) a. There is a man outside the door.
b. There are two men outside the door.

Further support for this treatment of English agreement comes from the fact that impersonal passive constructions, where no DP occurs to license the agreement feature of the verb, are ungrammatical in English:[13]

[12]On the analysis of agreement in sentences like (47) see e.g. Alsina (1996, p. 72ff.), Baker (1983, p. 6), Bresnan (1994, p. 107).

[13]Dutch is more problematic under this analysis: like English, Dutch has subject-verb-agreement and an adverbial structural subject expletive *er* (there). But in contrast to English, in Dutch impersonal passive is grammatical:

(i) Misschien wordt *(er) gedanst.
perhaps is there danced)

Constraining equations on the verbal agreement morphology wouldn't capture the Dutch data, since the expletive *er* could not license them. However, notice that there

(48) *Perhaps there was danced.

## 4.4 German as a Semi-Pro-Drop Language

The proposal that German has a phonetically unrealized expletive subject recalls the claim frequently made in the GB literature that German is a semi-pro-drop language, disallowing an argumental null subject *pro*, but licensing an expletive *pro*.[14] According to this analysis, expletive *pro* occupies the IP-Spec-position and the Extended Projection Principle[15] is fulfilled.

However, the analysis presented here and the semi-pro-drop analysis are different in several respects.

First, the proponents of the semi-pro-drop analysis claim that the expletive is represented in phrase-structure by the empty category *pro*, as shown in (49) (Vikner 1995, p. 153 (209)):

| (49) ... weil | [$_{IP}$ *pro* [$_{VP}$ getanzt | worden | ist]] |
|---|---|---|---|
| because | danced | been | is |

'... because there has been dancing'

But I have defended the claim that the functions in German are identified morphologically; hence an empty category, lacking any morphology, couldn't be identified as the subject at all. Note that even if one assumed that German has structural function specification in addition to morphological function specification (cf. Choi 1999), an empty category in the subject position would be ruled out by Economy of Expression (see below).[16] So, in contrast to the analysis proposed by Vikner and others, on the present analysis the expletive subject is not represented in c-structure by an empty element, but is introduced in f-structure by the verbal agreement morphology.

Second, the proponents of the semi-pro-drop analysis assume that in the case of an ergative or passivized verb, the argument is base-generated in the object position. Specifically, since in German NP-

is a difference between the 'weakness' of the English and the Dutch morphology. While English has neither person- nor number agreement in all tenses, Dutch has number agreement, but no person-agreement in all tenses (cf. Vikner 1997). This might suggest that the analysis of the Dutch morphology must be captured in a different way from the English morphology. However, I leave these issues for future research.

[14]See e.g. Safir (1985), Cardinaletti (1990), Grewendorf (1989), Vikner (1995). Cf. Fanselow (1991, p.80ff.), Haider (1991b) and Brandner (1993, p. 81ff.), who argue against an expletive *pro* in German.

[15]The Extended Projection Principle requires that every clause has a subject (Chomsky 1982, p. 10).

[16]This does not imply that that empty categories are incompatible with LFG; see chapter 5.

movement is not obligatory, the nominative marked DP can stay in its base position but then the subject position has to be occupied by the expletive *pro*. Grewendorf (1989, p. 147 (84)–(85)) proposes structures like (50):

(50) a. ... weil [$_S$ *pro$_i$* [$_{VP}$ dem Hans ein Fehler$_i$
because the Hans-DAT a mistake-NOM
unterlaufen ist] INFL]
happened is
'... because Hans (unknowingly) made a mistake.'

b. ... weil [$_S$ *pro$_i$* [$_{VP}$ dem Hans der Arm$_i$
because the Hans-DAT the arm-NOM
verbunden wurde] INFL]
bandaged was
'... because Hans's arm was bandaged.'

Vikner (1995, p. 243) gives the following example:

(51) ... dass [$_{IP}$ *pro* [$_{VP}$ ein Apfel gegessen wurde]]
that an apple eaten was

However, on the analysis being presented here, a nominative marked, agreeing DP is identified as the subject regardless of its thematic role and its structural position; and being identified as the subject, it will be unified with the subject specified by the verbal agreement morphology.

## 4.5 Is there an Expletive Subject DP in German?

We have seen that with impersonal passive and with certain verbs in the active voice, the Subject Condition is satisfied in German by the verbal agreement morphology. Notice that the additional insertion of the expletive DP *es* with impersonal passive is ungrammatical:

(52) ... weil (*es) getanzt wurde.
because it danced was

This follows from the present analysis straightforwardly. The subject is already specified by the verbal agreement morphology. Hence the occurrence of an additional structural expletive subject violates Economy of Expression, repeated here for convenience:

(53) **Economy of Expression** Bresnan (2001, p. 91, (1))
All syntactic phrase structure nodes are optional and are not used unless required by independent principles (completeness, coherence, semantic expressivity).

As illustrated by the following c- and f-structures, a c-structural expletive subject would give only redundant information, thus is not required:[17]

(54)

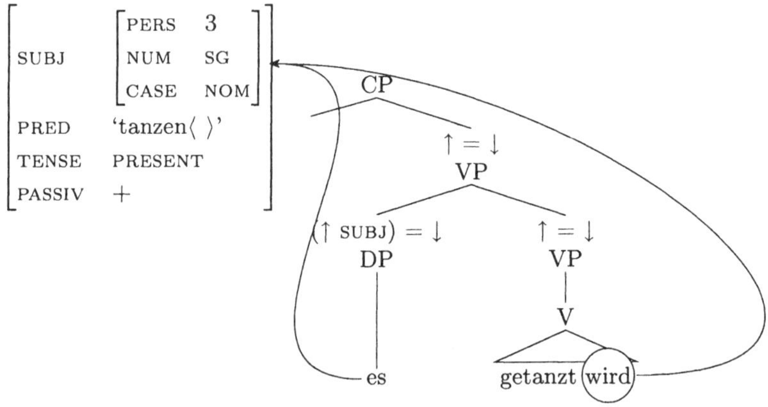


The same is true for those verbs that in the active voice lack a subject but have an obligatory $\text{OBJ}_\theta$ argument:

(55) ... weil (*es) mir an einer schnellen Lösung liegt.
because it me-DAT at a quick solution lies
'... because I am interested in a quick solution.'

Again, a structural subject expletive can't occur, since in contrast to the subject provided by the morphology, the expletive DP would require additional phrase structure nodes.

In short, according to the analysis presented here, we expect that German has no expletive subject DP at all, since every finite verb potentially specifies an expletive subject and hence the expletive *es* would always violate Economy of Expression.[18]

Examples like the following, in which expletive *es* occurs in CP-Spec, are not counterexamples to this prediction, despite initial appearances:

---

[17] Notice that in contrast to the SUBJ specified by the verbal agreement morphology, the SUBJ in (54) contains case information, provided by the lexical entry of *es*. However, the case feature does not make any difference with respect to Economy of Expression, since Completeness, Coherence and Semantic Expressivity are not affected by the case feature.

[18] Notice that an expletive object DP is not ruled out by Economy of Expression, since German does not have object-verb agreement. But since an object is not required to satisfy a principle such as the Subject Condition, an expletive object can only occur if it is lexically required by a governing element, as in the following examples:

(i) Sie hat **es** eilig.
she has it quickly
'She's in a hurry.'

(56) a. Es wird getanzt.
it is danced
'People are dancing/There is dancing.'

b. Es kamen viele Linguisten.
it came-3.PL many linguists
'There came a lot of linguists.'

In such examples, *es* is required to occupy the *Vorfeld* (i.e., CP-Spec), which, because German is a V2 language, may not remain empty in a declarative sentence. Following Grewendorf (1989), Fortmann (2001) and the analysis of traditional grammar, I assume that *es* in sentences like (56) does not function as the subject, but merely as a placeholder. Evidence for this comes from the lack of number agreement with the verb, as exemplified by (56b).

Putting aside expletive *es* in the *Vorfeld*, the prediction of the analysis is thus that *es* occurring in the *Mittelfeld* can't be an expletive. This is consistent with the position of Cardinaletti (1990), Vikner (1995) and Fortmann (2001), who claim—following Hoekstra (1983)—that *es* in the *Mittelfeld* is always a (quasi)-argument. However, this claim is not uncontested in the literature; cf. Brandner (1993, p. 84), Fanselow (1991, p. 84), who argue that German does have a structural expletive subject, for example, in middle constructions. In the following I will present some examples where the status of *es* as a quasi-argument is questionable and it will be shown how an expletive subject DP can be handled by the present analysis.

### 4.5.1 Evidence for *Es* as a (Quasi)-Argument?

*Es* can occur in the *Mittelfeld* either obligatorily (57a) and (57b) or optionally (57c) and (57d):

(57) a. ... weil es regnet.
because it rains

b. ... weil es keine Hoffnung gab.
because it no hope gave
'... because there was no hope.'

c. ... weil (es) mich friert.
because it me freezes
'... because I am cold.'

(ii) Sie hat **es** darauf angelegt.
she has it thereon on-laid
'She's determined (to do that).'

d. ... weil (es) mir graut.
   because it me is-dreadful
   '... because I dread it.'

Cardinaletti, Vikner and Fortmann support their claim that *es* here is an argument by showing that *es* can occur in control constructions (these examples are from (Fortmann 2001, p. 19 (26a-b)):

(58) a. Gestern hat es geblitzt, ohne zu donnern.
   yesterday has it flashed-lightning without to thunder
   'Yesterday there was lightning without thundering.'

b. Gestern hat es geregnet, anstatt zu schneien.
   yesterday has it rained instead to snow
   'Yesterday it rained instead of snowing.'

However, with other verbs than weather verbs, it is doubtful whether control is possible ((59a) is from Christine Czinglar, handout GGS Stuttgart 1999, example (46a), and (59b) is from Christian Fortmann (p.c.)):

(59) a. ?Es gibt in dieser Gegend viele Tümpel, ohne jemals
   it gives in this area many ponds without ever
   richtig zu regnen.
   really to rain
   'There are lots of ponds in this area without it ever really raining.'

b. ?Es friert mich, ohne mich zu schaudern.
   it freezes me without me to shiver
   'I'm cold without shivering.'

In cases where the subject can be realized by other DPs than *es*, analyzing *es* as a referential DP seems quite plausible:

(60) a. ... weil es klopft.
   because it knocks

b. ... weil die Heizung klopft.
   because the radiator knocks

c. ... weil es donnert.
   because it thunders

d. ... weil Zeus donnert.
   because Zeus thunders

However, this is not always the case:

(61) a. ... weil es mich friert.
   because it me freezes
   '... because I'm cold.'

b. *... weil die Kälte mich friert.
because the cold me freezes

(62) a. ... weil es keine Hoffnung gibt.
because it no hope gives
'... because there is no hope.'
b. *... weil das Schicksal keine Hoffnung gibt.
because the destiny no hope gives

Although the analysis presented here is consistent with the claim that there is no structural expletive in German, data like (59) and (61)-(62) provide evidence for the occurrence of a non-thematic, non-referential *es* in the *Mittelfeld.* However, in these examples an expletive subject DP does not have to be inserted to satisfy the Subject Condition, since this can be done by the verbal agreement morphology. Therefore, I assume that where an expletive subject DP occurs, the verb has to subcategorize for it and that the verb has special requirements on the realization of its subject—namely, it requires a non-thematic subject which must be realized by *es.*[19] In this regard, this use of *es* is like an idiomatic expression. Formally, this could be captured by a constraining equation in the lexical entry of the verb (cf. Kaplan and Bresnan 1982, p. 213 for the treatment of idiomatic expressions):

(63) geben V $(\uparrow \textsc{pred}) =$ 'geben $\langle(\uparrow \textsc{obj})\rangle$ $(\uparrow \textsc{subj})$'
$(\uparrow \textsc{subj form}) =_c$ es

The special requirement of the verb on its subject prevents *es* from being ruled out by Economy of Expression, since the subject that is provided by the verbal agreement morphology can't satisfy the constraining equation.

We have seen that in German the Subject Condition is always satisfied in finite clauses, since either there is a structural subject or an expletive subject is provided by the verbal agreement morphology. The question arises whether the same is true of non-finite clause. This question is addressed in the next section.

## 4.6 The Subject in Non-Finite Clauses

Non-finite clauses are another case where the subject is not represented in c-structure. Consider the following example:

(64) Er forderte sie auf, zu lachen.
he asked her PRT to laugh
'He asked her to laugh.'

[19] In fact, this requirement holds not just for subjects, but also for expletive object, cf. the examples in footnote 18.

This sentence is grammatical, although the non-finite clause *zu lachen* has no structurally realized subject, and although *lachen* is a verb which subcategorizes for a thematic subject. In order not to violate Completeness there must be a subject in the f-structure. This means that in non-finite clauses the subject must be introduced not by the mapping from a c-structure node to f-structure but in another way. In the following I will sketch how the Subject Condition is satisfied in non-finite clauses and I will show that non-finite verbs provide further evidence for the claim that the agreement morphology specifies an expletive subject.

### 4.6.1 Functional vs. Anaphoric Control

Sentences like (64) are called control structures, because the understood subject of the non-finite verb is introduced, hence controlled, by some other element. In LFG a distinction is made between functional and anaphoric control (cf. Bresnan 1982, Andrews 1982, Bresnan 2001, ch. 12–13). Example (64) and (65a) are generally taken as an instance of functional control, example (65b) and (65c) of anaphoric control (arbitrary control is an instance of anaphoric control).

(65) a. Sie versprach ihm, zu lachen.
she promised him to laugh

b. die Idee, zu lachen
the idea to laugh
'the idea of laughing'

c. Annas Idee, zu lachen
Anna's idea to laugh
'Anna's idea of laughing'

With **functional control** the subject of the non-finite verb is introduced by a control equation and functionally identified with a grammatical function of the matrix verb. The control equation is part of the lexical entry of the control verb, e.g.:[20]

(66) auffordern V $(\uparrow \text{PRED}) = \text{`auffordern} \langle (\uparrow \text{SUBJ}) (\uparrow \text{OBJ}) (\uparrow \text{XCOMP}) \rangle\text{'}$
$(\uparrow \text{OBJ}) = (\uparrow \text{XCOMP SUBJ})$

The effect of the control equation is that the f-structure of the object of the matrix clause is identified with the subject of the embedded clause and all their f-structure attributes are shared:

[20] XCOMP is the standard grammatical function in LFG for functionally controlled infinitival complements; for anaphorically controlled infinitival complements COMP is used (cf. the f-structure for (70) below).

(67) Er forderte sie auf, zu lachen.

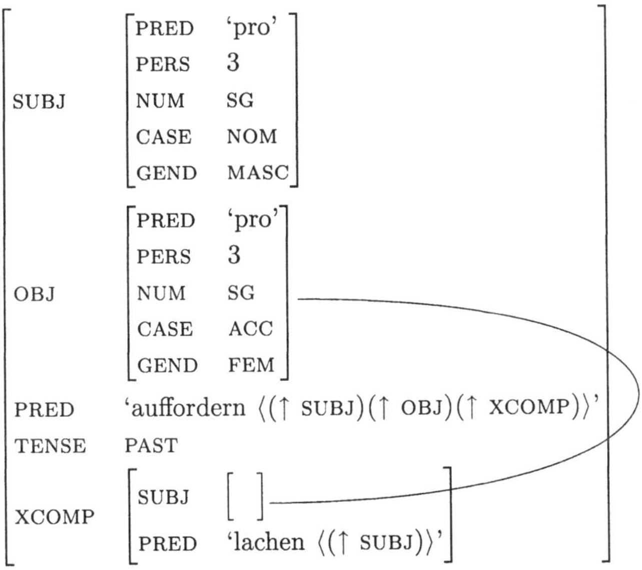


With **anaphoric control** the subject is introduced by the following lexical rule (Bresnan 2001, p. 295):

**Null subjects:** (V (nonfinite) $\Rightarrow$ (↑ SUBJ PRED) = 'pro')

Bresnan describes the property of non-finite verbs to allow a null pronominal subject as "a special case of a general crosslinguistic property by which null pronominals are provided as a lexical default to core arguments of verbal argument structure" (*ibid.*). Since in German only nonfinite verbs containing the affix *zu* ('to')[21] can be anaphorically controlled, we can assume that the equation (↑ SUBJ PRED) = 'pro' is optionally associated with *zu*, as shown in (68):

(68) zu $V_{infl}$ ((↑ SUBJ PRED) = 'pro')
...

The non-finite clause *zu lachen* therefore has the f-structure given in (69):

[21]Following Bech (1983), Haider (1990a) I assume that *zu* is a verbal affix. *Zu* occurs only as a bound morpheme, e.g., nothing can intervene between *zu* and the non-finite verb. With verbs which consist of the stem and a separable particle, *zu* has to occur after the particle: *aufzufordern* ('to ask').

(69) (die Idee,) zu lachen
the idea to laugh

$$\begin{bmatrix} \text{SUBJ} & \begin{bmatrix} \text{PRED} & \text{`pro'} \end{bmatrix} \\ \text{PRED} & \text{`lachen } \langle(\uparrow \text{SUBJ})\rangle\text{'} \end{bmatrix}$$

The optional insertion of a thematic pronominal subject (thematic since it contains a PRED-feature) in conjunction with the affix *zu* explains why the example in (69) is grammatical, although in c-structure no subject is realized. With anaphoric control the controller is anaphorically linked to the controllee. In this case it is not their f-structure values but only the referential index of the two functions that is identified, e.g. in (70):

(70) Annas Idee, zu lachen

$$\begin{bmatrix} \text{PRED} & \text{`Idee'} \\ \text{POSS} & \begin{bmatrix} \text{PRED} & \text{`Anna}_i\text{'} \end{bmatrix} \\ \text{COMP} & \begin{bmatrix} \text{SUBJ} & \begin{bmatrix} \text{PRED} & \text{`pro}_i\text{'} \end{bmatrix} \\ \text{PRED} & \text{`lachen } \langle(\uparrow \text{SUBJ})\rangle\text{'} \end{bmatrix} \end{bmatrix}$$

Anaphoric control provide further evidence for the claim that the agreement morphology specifies an expletive subject. Compare the following examples (cf. Haider 1991b, p. 61 (22a–b)):

(71) a. die Möglichkeit, dass getanzt wird
the possibility that danced is
'the possibility that there is dancing'

b. *die Möglichkeit, getanzt zu werden
the possibility danced to be

c. die Möglichkeit, verstanden zu werden
the possibility understood to be
'the possibility of being understood'

(71c) shows that anaphoric control of the passive of a transitive verb is grammatical. However, impersonal passive is only possible in finite clauses (71a), and not in non-finite clauses (71b).[22]

This follows straightforwardly from the analysis presented in section 4.3.2. Non-finite verbs in German do not have agreement inflection, i.e. morphology marking person and number. Hence, non-finite verbs can't specify an expletive subject, unlike finite verbs as in (71a). Thus,

[22] For discussion and alternative analyses see, e.g., Grewendorf (1989, p. 153ff.), Haider (1990a, p. 125ff.), Haider (1991b, p. 61f.), Fanselow (1991, p. 80), Kiss (1995, p. 140ff.).

in (71b) the non-finite clause will not have with a subject function in f-structure, in violation of the Subject Condition. In contrast, with a non-finite transitive passive, as in (71c), anaphoric control supplies the understood thematic subject.

### 4.6.2 Non-Representation of the Subject of Non-Finite Clauses on C-Structure

The structural representation of the subject of non-finite clauses is always ungrammatical:

(72) a. *Er forderte sie auf, sie zu lachen.
he asked her PRT she zu laugh

b. *Sie versprach ihm, sie zu lachen.
she promised him she zu laugh

c. *die Idee, man zu lachen
the idea one zu laugh

d. *Annas Idee, Anna/sie zu lachen
Anna's idea Anna/she to laugh

This fact can be explained by Economy of Expression, since providing the subject by a control equation or by the infinitive particle *zu* requires fewer c-structure nodes than a c-structurally represented subject. Economy of Expression also prohibits the representation of the subject of non-finite clauses by an empty category (PRO in GB):

(73) Er forderte Maria auf, (*PRO) zu lachen.
he asked Maria PRT to laugh

Notice, however, that the following example should be grammatical, according to the principles that have been introduced so far:

(74) *Gestern hat versucht, er zu lachen.
yesterday has tried he to laugh

As with the previous sentences that contain a non-finite clause, in this example the subject is also represented only once on c-structure, but in this case in the non-finite clause instead of the finite clause. Likewise, the f-structure of the subject of the embedded clause is identified with the f-structure of the subject of the matrix clause by the control equation. Further, claiming that the subject can't occur in the c-structure of non-finite clauses since non-finite clauses are of the category VP, can't capture the German data, since, as we have seen, in German the subject occurs adjoined to the VP and not in the specifier of IP or as daughter of the exocentric category S. Hence, there must be another principle which excludes the structural subject from occurring inside the non-finite clause.

A similar case we have to look at is the insertion of an expletive subject with anaphoric control. Why is it not possible to introduce a structural expletive subject in cases like the following?

(75) a. *die Möglichkeit, es getanzt zu werden

b. *die Möglichkeit, es viele Tümpel zu geben
the possibility, it a lot of ponds to give
'the possibility of there being a lot of ponds'

Since the morphology does not provide an expletive subject, the structural expletive subject shouldn't be excluded by Economy of Expression. In (75b) the lexical realization as *es* should even be required by a constraining equation in the lexical entry of the verb (cf. (63)).

King (1995, p.179) restricts nominative case-assignment to finite verbs, i.e., verbs with a TENSE attribute:[23]

(76) $(\uparrow \text{TENSE}) \Rightarrow [(\uparrow \text{SUBJ CASE}) = \text{NOM}]$

King argues that case-features must be licensed (they have constraining equation in the lexical entries). Hence a nominative DP can occur only in finite clauses. In Bresnan (2001) the nominative case is likewise assigned by the verbal affix, cf. the lexical entry of the English affix *-s* in (45).

In German, however, nominative case is not necessarily restricted to finite clauses, as the following observations due to Höhle (1983) and Oppenrieder (1991) show.

Höhle (1983, chap.6) claims that the implicit subject of non-finite clauses is also marked nominative. He observed that the adverbial phrase *ein- nach d- ander-* has to agree with its antecedent in gender and case (see also Müller 2001, p. 117f., Meurers 1999, p. 194):

(77) a. Einer nach dem anderem haben wir die Burschen
one-NOM after the other have we-NOM the boys
runtergeputzt.
polished-down
'One after the other we read the boys the riot act.'

b. Einen nach dem anderen haben wir die Burschen
one-ACC after the other have we the boys-ACC
runtergeputzt.
polished-down

*Ein- nach d- ander-* can also occur in non-finite clauses:

[23] King uses the notation TNS.

(78) a. Wir sind es leid, eine nach der anderen den Stuhl
we-NOM are it sorry one-NOM after the other the chair
vor die Tür gesetzt zu kriegen.
before the door placed to get
'We're tired of getting thrown out one after the other.'

b. Ich habe den Burschen geraten, im Abstand von
I have the boys-DAT advised in-the separation from
wenigen Tagen einer nach dem anderen zu kündigen.
few days one-NOM after the other to quit
'I advised the boys to quit one after the other within a few days.'

In a non-finite clause a subject can't be realized structurally. Hence the nominative marked phrase in (78) can't function as the subject. However *ein- nach d- ander-* refers to the implicit subject of the non-finite clause. Since we have seen that *ein- nach d- ander-* has to agree with its antecedent in gender and case, we expect the subject of the non-finite to be marked nominative too. This is unproblematic in (78a) since by functional control the subject of the non-finite clause will be identified with the subject of the matrix clause *wir* which is also marked nominative. However in (78b) the controller *den Burschen* is marked dative. Hence by functional control the controlled subject should also be marked dative. But the agreeing adverbial phrase *einer nach dem anderen* is marked nominative (on its head constituent *einer*) which shows that its antecedent has to be marked nominative too. This shows on the one hand that the restriction of nominative case-assignment to finite verbs can't be right and on the other hand it provides evidence against the assumption that (78b) is an instance of functional control, since by functional control "the controlled subject will have all of the grammatical features (CASE, PERSON, NUMBER, etc.) of the controller." (Bresnan 1982, p.326).

A nominative marked phrase can also occur in sentences which are instances of arbitrary control ((79b) is from Oppenrieder 1991, p. 216):

(79) a. die Idee, **einer nach dem anderen** zu kündigen
the idea one after the other to quit
'the idea of quitting one after the other'

b. Es muss schön sein, **ein Vogel** zu sein/ **wie ein Vogel**
it must nice be a bird to be/ like a bird
fliegen zu können.
fly to be-able
'It must be nice to be a bird/to be able to fly like a bird.'

In view of the preceding data, I assume that the occurrence of a structural subject in non-finite clauses is not excluded because of the lack of nominative case. Instead I propose that a nominative marked DP can't be identified as the subject unless it agrees with the verb. Formally this can be done by the functional equation proposed earlier (6), repeated here:

(80) $(\downarrow \text{CASE}) = \text{NOM} \wedge (\downarrow \text{NUM}) = (\uparrow \text{SUBJ NUM}) \wedge (\downarrow \text{PERS}) = (\uparrow \text{SUBJ PERS}) \Rightarrow (\uparrow \text{SUBJ}) = \downarrow$

Since non-finite verbs do not show agreement morphology in German, the identification of a structural subject is impossible in non-finite clauses. The ungrammaticality of a structural subject in non-finite clauses as in (72) and (75) is therefore prohibited not by the case filter but by the lack of verbal agreement.[24]

## 4.7 Summary

In this chapter it was argued that German is a language which, despite having clauses without a c-structural subject, does satisfy the Subject Condition and is therefore consistent with the claim that the Subject Condition is universal. In particular, I argued that the expletive subject is provided by the verbal agreement morphology, which follows from the analysis of subject-verb agreement without further assumptions. Economy of Expression prohibits the representation of the subject on c-structure in this case, since it would require unnecessary c-structure nodes. With non-finite verbs, the subject also can't be represented on c-structure but is introduced either via a control equation (functional control) or by the affix *zu* (anaphoric control).

We have also seen that neither the expletive subject inserted by the verbal agreement morphology nor the thematic subject of non-finite verbs are c-structurally represented, not even by an empty category. In the next chapter we will investigate whether empty categories are ever required in German, and if so, how their occurrence is motivated.

[24] Evidence for this claim can be found in Portuguese, which has inflected infinitives. The inflected infinitive is marked for agreement (with the subject of the clause) and it can take lexical subjects (Raposo 1987, p. 87, (6b)):

(i) Eu penso/afirmo [**ter*em*** **os deputandos** trabalhado pouco.]
I think/claim to-have-AGR the deputies worked little

This is exactly what is predicted by my analysis.

# 5

# Weak Crossover and the Status of Empty Categories

We have seen in the preceding chapter that an empty category corresponding to an expletive subject or to the subject of non-finite verbs is excluded in German by Economy of Expression. This chapter is concerned with the question whether there is any necessity and evidence for empty categories in LFG at all or whether empty categories in general violate Economy of Expression.[1]

In Bresnan (1998, p. 73f.) and Bresnan (2001, ch. 9) the effects of Economy of Expression with regard to empty categories are illustrated by topicalization in English versus Russian. In English, a configurational language, the functions are defined structurally. According to the analysis proposed in Bresnan (2001), the topicalized constituent is adjoined to IP. By the Endocentric Mapping Principles the adjoined position is annotated with a non-argument function, i.e., an adjunct or a discourse function (cf. (18e) in chapter 1). Since English, lacking almost any morphological marking, does not have morphological function specification, the argument function of the topicalized constituent can't be identified in the adjoined position. Thus, in order for its argument function to be identified, it must be linked to an empty category in its canonical position (Bresnan 2001, p. 187; Bresnan 1998, p. 74):

[1]This chapter is a modified and elaborated version of Berman (1997).

(1) The old boat, we sold.

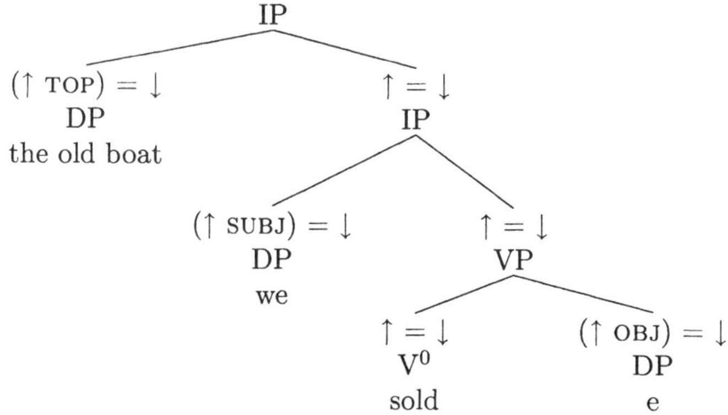


It is only by the structural position which is marked by the empty category that the argument function of the topicalized phrase can be specified, because, as sister of a lexical category, the DP dominating the empty category is annotated with a complement function. Therefore, in this situation the empty category does not violate Economy of Expression, since it provides information which is necessary to satisfy Completeness.

Russian, in contrast, has rich morphological marking. According to King (1995), in Russian the functions are identified both structurally and by the morphology. Since the topicalized constituent which is adjoined to IP is case-marked, the argument function can be identified in the topicalized position, independently of its canonical position, cf. (2). Thus, an empty category would violate Economy of Expression, since the argument function is already specified by the case morphology.

(2) Staruyu lodku my prodali.
old-ACC boat-ACC we-NOM sold-PL

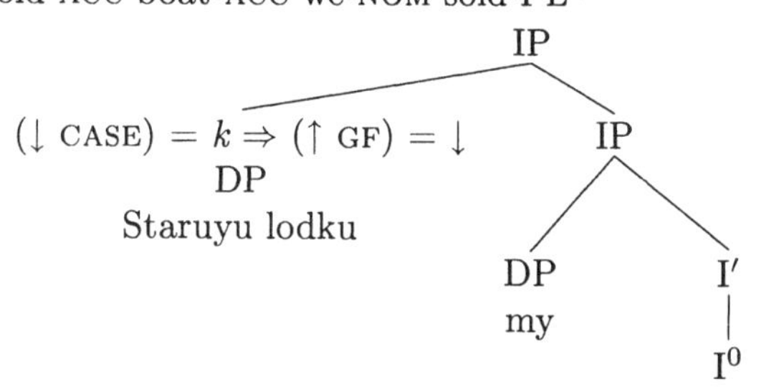


In short, in Russian morphological marking provides information which in English can only be specified by the syntactic structure. Hence, in English, an empty category is licensed if the structural position which provides information about the grammatical function is not lexically filled, as in the case of topicalization.

In German, syntactic functions are also morphologically marked, and identified by the morphology. Hence, as in Russian, we expect that with topicalization of an object-DP an empty category inside the VP is not needed. This is illustrated by the topicalization structure in (3).

(3) Den alten Kahn haben wir verkauft.
the old boat-ACC have (pl) we-NOM sold

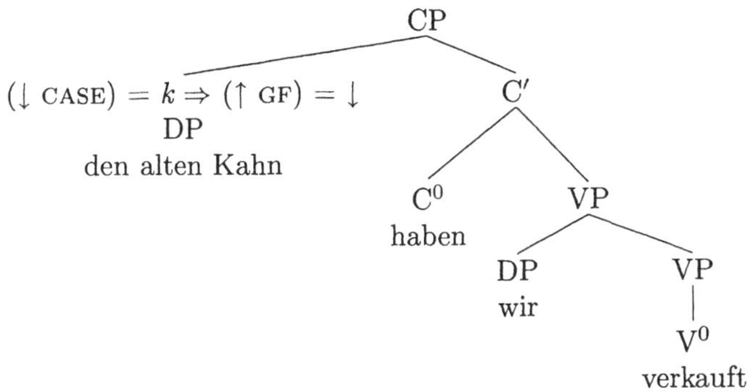


Consequently, in such a structure an empty category is, by Economy of Expression, not permitted.

Bresnan (1998) shows that weak crossover effects might detect the presence or absence of empty categories. In the following we will see how the weak crossover data in German can be captured and what predictions they make for empty categories in German. We begin by presenting the theory of operator binding in Bresnan (1998).

## 5.1 The Analysis of Weak Crossover — Bresnan (1998)

In order for a pronoun to have a bound interpretation, it has to be in the domain of the binder. The domain of a binder is defined as follows (Bresnan 1998, p. 75):

(4) The **domain** of a binder is the minimal clause or predication structure containing it (formally modelled as the minimal f-structure).

Operator binding is restricted by the so-called Prominence Principle (*ibid.*):

(5) **Prominence Principle**: A binder excludes from its domain any element more prominent than it.

At each level of representation the relation of prominence is determined by properties specific to that level: syntactic rank for f-structure, linear order for c-structure, and thematic prominence for a-structure. These relation are defined as follows (cf. Bresnan (1998, p. 76 (31)))[2]:

(6) a. $\alpha$ **outranks** $\beta$ if $\alpha$ and $\beta$ belong to the same f-structure and $\alpha$ is more prominent than $\beta$ on the functional hierarchy or $\alpha$ outranks some $\gamma$ that contains $\beta$.

b. **Syntactic rank**: a relation of prominence among (expressed or unexpressed) syntactic arguments, based on the **functional hierarchy** SUBJ > OBJ > $\text{OBJ}_\theta$ > $\text{OBL}_\theta$ > COMPL > ADJ.

(7) a. The **linear order** of $\alpha$ and $\beta$ is determined by the right edges of their lexical expressions; reduces to simple linear order in the string whenever the correspondence between arguments and the XPs that express them is one-to-one.

b. The **lexical expression** of an argument consists of any c-structure word or bound form that lexically carries the semantic features of the argument, together with all nonterminal phrase structure nodes that also correspond to the f-structure of the argument.

(8) **Thematic prominence**: a relation of prominence among arguments associated with the same argument structure; inherited from the underlying semantic or role structure (e.g. Dowty 1991, Jackendoff 1990, Bresnan and Zaenen 1990, Alsina 1996.)

What results from these distinct notions of prominence are the following level-specific instantiations of the Prominence Principle:

(9) **Resulting domain constraints on pronominal binding:**

(i) The domain of $\alpha$ excludes any $\beta$ that outranks $\alpha$ (in f-structure).

(ii) The domain of $\alpha$ excludes any $\beta$ that precedes $\alpha$ (in c-structure).[3,4]

---

[2]The definitions in (7) slightly revise Bresnan's definitions, referring to XPs rather than any nodes in (7a), and in (7b) requiring that the correspondence be to the f-structure of the argument rather than the argument itself. I owe these corrections to the comments of an anonymous reviewer.

[3]Notice that according to (7a), in the configuration [... $A_1$ ... C ... $A_2$ ...], where $A_1$ and $A_2$ are mapped onto the same f-structure, C precedes the complex $\{A_1, A_2\}$.

[4]In Bresnan (1995b) and Bresnan (2001) linear order is captured by the notion of f-precedence, which is defined as follows: Given a correspondence mapping $\phi$ between a c-structure and its f-structure, and given two subsidiary f-structures $\alpha$ and $\beta$, $\alpha$ **f-precedes** $\beta$ if the rightmost node in $\phi^{-1}(\alpha)$ precedes the rightmost node

(iii) The domain of $\alpha$ excludes any $\beta$ that is thematically more prominent than $\alpha$ (in a-structure).

Since the notion of prominence differs according to syntactic level, the effect of the Prominence Principle may differ at each level of representation. Moreover, cross-linguistic differences in the distribution of operator binding may be accounted for by assuming that languages observe different combinations of the level-specific constraints. Bresnan (1998) proposes the following illustrative weak crossover typology, based on the domain constraints at f-structure (i) and c-structure (ii):[5,6]

| languages | domain constraints |
|---|---|
| Palauan | (i) & (ii) |
| German, Korean, English | (i) $\vee$ (ii) |
| Chicheŵa, Kiswahili | (i) |
| Malayalam, Hindi | (ii) |

TABLE 5 Weak Crossover Typology (Bresnan 1998)

## 5.2 Weak Crossover in German

### 5.2.1 Scrambling — Choi (1995)

The idea that operator binding in languages like Korean and German is constrained by the disjunction of the f-structure and c-structure constraints is due to Choi (1995). She showed that this directly accounts for the possibilities of scrambling in Korean and German; her German examples are given in (10).

in $\phi^{-1}(\beta)$. Hence the relation of f-precedence has the same effect as the definition of linear order given in (7).

[5]In Bresnan (1998) English was classified like Palauan; however, in Bresnan (2001) it was shown that English can be explained under the assumption that it behaves like Korean or German. In the following I will assume with Bresnan (2001) that English observes the same constraints as German and Korean.

[6]In Bresnan (2001, p. 200) the binding condition for German and English is formulated as follows:

**Precedence-rank condition on pronominal binding:**
A pronominal that both f-precedes a binder and is contained in a constituent that outranks the binder is excluded from the domain of the binder.

This formulation has the same effect as the formulation in Bresnan (1998). I will follow the formulation in Bresnan (1998), since I will shortly discuss the role of argument structure with operator binding in German, which is not taken into account in the formulation of Bresnan (2001).

(10) a. . . . dass jeder$_i$ seine$_i$ Mutter mag.
that everyone-NOM his mother-ACC likes
'. . . that everyone likes his mother.'

b. . . . dass jeden$_i$ seine$_i$ Mutter mag.
that everyone-ACC his mother-NOM likes.
'. . . that his mother likes everyone.'

c. . . . dass seine$_i$ Mutter jeder$_i$ mag.
that his mother-ACC everyone-NOM likes
'. . . that everyone likes his mother.'

d. *. . . dass seine$_i$ Mutter jeden$_i$ mag.
that his mother-NOM everyone-ACC likes
'. . . that his mother likes everyone.'

In (10a) the pronoun *seine* neither precedes nor outranks the operator *jeder*, so binding is excluded neither on c-structure nor on f-structure and the bound reading is available. In (10b) the pronoun does not precede the pronoun, but it outranks the operator.[7] Thus, though in (10b) binding is excluded in f-structure, it is not excluded in c-structure, so again the bound reading is correctly permitted. In (10c) the pronoun does not outrank the operator but it does precede the operator, so again binding is possible. Only in (10d) does the pronoun both outrank and precede the operator, i.e., the pronoun is excluded from the operator's binding domain in both c-structure and f-structure. Thus, here the bound reading of the pronoun is not available.

### 5.2.2 Topicalization

As a comparison of the sentences in (10) above with those in (11) below makes clear, the pattern of operator binding is the same in both scrambling and clause-internal topicalization (cf. Haider 1987, Haider 1993a, Frey 1993). Thus, Choi's account will also apply directly to the latter.[8]

[7]That the pronoun outranks the operator in (10b) follow only on the assumption that $\beta$ in (9i) stands for not just the outer f-structure (corresponding to the DP node of the phrase 'seine Mutter' in (10)) but also all f-structures it may contain—in particular the one corresponding to the possessive pronoun *seine*. The earlier formulation of the f-structure condition on operator binding given in Bresnan (1995b, p. 252 (20)) is less ambiguous in this respect; it reads: "The pronominal binding domain of an operator O is restricted to the set of f-structure elements that O outranks." Note that there is no ambiguity in the formulation of the c-structure constraint (9ii), due to the nature of linear orders.

[8]Notice that, as specifier of a functional category, CP-Spec is annotated with a discourse-function. The discourse functions TOP and FOC are not contained in the functional hierarchy as given in Bresnan (1998) or Bresnan (2001, p. 198). It can be shown that the assumption that TOP and FOC are integrated in the functional hierarchy and are more prominent than the subject would give the wrong result;

(11) a. Jeder$_i$/ Wer$_i$ mag seine$_i$ Mutter
everyone-NOM/ who-NOM likes his mother-ACC
'Everyone likes his mother.'/'Who likes his mother?'

b. Jeden$_i$/ Wen$_i$ mag seine$_i$ Mutter
everyone-ACC/ who-ACC likes his mother-NOM
'Everyone, his mother likes.'/'Who does his mother like?'

c. Seine$_i$ Mutter mag jeder$_i$.
his mother-ACC likes everyone-NOM
'His mother, everyone likes.'

d. *Seine$_i$ Mutter mag jeden$_i$.
his mother-NOM likes everyone-ACC
'His mother likes everyone.'

This analysis succeeds only because no trace of the scrambled or topicalized constituent is assumed. If there were an empty category in the canonical position of the antecedent in (10b) and (11b), the sentences would have the following structures:

(12) a. Jeden$_i$/Wen$_i$ mag seine$_i$ Mutter e$_i$
b. ... weil jeden$_i$ seine$_i$ Mutter e$_i$ mag.

In both of these structures, the pronoun precedes the right edge of the operator, so by (7) it precedes the operator, and is therefore excluded from its domain in c-structure. Thus, with an empty category the bound reading would be wrongly ruled out. In short, the weak crossover data in (10) and (11) confirm that neither scrambling nor topicalization structures involve empty categories.

Notice that with topicalization in German the annotation of an argument function does not conform to the Endocentric Mapping Principles. As we saw in chapter 1, only adjoined positions were considered to admit optional annotation which allows for exocentric specification of an argument function. However, in German the topicalized constituent occupies the specifier of CP, which is annotated with a discourse function. Hence, lexocentric function specification has to be possible in this position, too.

Let us now compare the pattern of operator binding in German with that found in English, illustrated by the following examples:

(13) a. Everyone$_i$ likes his$_i$ mother.
b. *His$_i$ mother likes everyone$_i$.
c. *Everyone$_i$, his$_i$ mother likes.
d. His$_i$ mother, everyone$_i$ likes.

---

see also footnote 9.

If we assume, following Bresnan (2001), that English has to fulfill the same constraints on operator binding as German, then this pattern is directly predicted. In (13a) the pronoun neither precedes nor outranks the operator, so binding is possible. In (13b) the pronoun both outranks and precedes the operator, hence binding is ungrammatical. In (13c) and (13d) the object-DP is topicalized. Since the function of the topicalized object can only be identified in its canonical position in English, there must be a corresponding empty category inside the VP:

(14) a. *Everyone$_i$, his$_i$ mother likes e$_i$
 b. His$_i$ mother, everyone$_i$ likes e$_i$

(14a) is ungrammatical, in contrast to the corresponding German construction (11b). While in both the English and German constructions the pronoun outranks the operator, in German the pronoun does not precede the operator, hence binding is possible. But in English, due to the empty category, the pronoun does precede the operator, since it precedes its right edge, so it is excluded from the operators binding domain and binding is impossible.[9] Finally, in (14b) the pronoun precedes the operator in spite of the empty category (notice, however, that the topicalized DP does not precede the operator; see section 5.2.6) but since the pronoun does not outrank the operator, binding is possible.

The analysis of weak crossover confirms the structures proposed in (1) and (3), for English and German, respectively. While in German topicalization and scrambling involve no empty category, topicalization in English requires an empty category in its canonical position.

In the remainder of this section we apply the analysis to further constructions of German involving weak crossover: adjuncts (sec. 5.2.3), two objects (sec. 5.2.4), complex sentences (sec. 5.2.5), long distance dependencies (sec. 5.2.6), and infinitives (sec. 5.2.7).

### 5.2.3 Weak Crossover Involving Adjuncts

According to the functional hierarchy given in (6b), the adjunct is the lowest function. We therefore expect that an operator inside an adjunct can bind a pronoun only if it is more prominent on c-structure than the pronoun. That this is the case is shown by the following examples:

(15) a. Hinter [jedem Präsidenten]$_i$ wartete sein$_i$ Leibwächter.
 Behind every president waited his bodyguard-NOM
 b. *Sein$_i$ Leibwächter wartete hinter [jedem Präsidenten]$_i$

[9] Notice that if discouse functions were integrated into the functional hierarchy we would get the wrong result for (14a). The topicalized operator is a TOP, so the pronoun would not outrank the operator and binding should be available, although due to the empty category the pronoun does not precede the operator.

In contrast, a pronoun which is contained in an adjunct-PP can be bound regardless of the position of the adjunct, since a pronoun in an adjunct is always outranked by a non-adjunct operator, e.g.:[10]

(16) a. In seiner$_i$ Freizeit sollte sich jeder$_i$ entspannen.
in his free-time should REFL everyone-NOM relax
'Everyone should relax on his free time.'

b. Jeder$_i$ sollte sich in seiner$_i$ Freizeit entspannen.

(17) a. An seinem$_i$ Geburtstag bekommt jeder$_i$ eine Torte.
on his birthday gets everyone-NOM a cake
'Everyone gets a cake on his birthday.'

b. Jeder$_i$ bekommt an seinem$_i$ Geburtstag eine Torte.

### 5.2.4 Weak Crossover between Objects

Binding between objects is more problematic. According to Frank, Lee, and Rambow (1992) and Frey (1993), backwards binding is possible only for subjects; this is illustrated by the following sentences (from Frank/Lee/Rambow 1992: (17b), (21a)):

(18) *Ich glaube, dass der Jörg seinem$_i$ Vater jeden$_i$
I think that the J.-NOM his$_i$ father-DAT everyone$_i$-ACC
gezeigt hat.
shown has
'I think that Jörg has shown his$_i$ father everyone$_i$.'

(19) *Ich glaube, dass der Jörg seinen$_i$ Vater jedem$_i$
I think that the J.-NOM his$_i$ father-ACC everyone$_i$-DAT
gezeigt hat.
shown has
'I think that Jörg has shown everyone$_i$ his$_i$ father.'

To account for this Bresnan (1998) suggested that in any sentence in German the domain constraints must be satisfied in at least two of the three levels of representation. Here are the preceding examples with functions and thematic roles spelled out:

(20) a. *Ich glaube, dass der Jörg seinem$_i$ Vater (OBJ$_\theta$, goal) jeden$_i$ (OBJ, theme) gezeigt hat.

b. *Ich glaube, dass der Jörg seinen$_i$ Vater (OBJ, theme) jedem$_i$ (OBJ$_\theta$, goal) gezeigt hat.

In (20a) the constraint is satisfied only at f-structure and in (20b) only at a-structure (assuming the thematic hierarchy in Bresnan and

[10] The examples in (17) are due to Hubert Haider (p.c.).

Zaenen 1990: agent > beneficiary > experiencer/goal > instrument > patient/theme > locative). Hence binding is ungrammatical.

However, Choi (1995, p. 4 (7b)) reports an acceptable example of backwards binding from the dative object to the accusative object, and I share this judgment:

(21) ... dass man seine$_i$ Tanzpartnerin jedem$_i$ vorstellte.
that one his dance partner-ACC everyone-DAT introduced
'... that they introduced to everyone his dance partner'

And in Büring (1997, p. 17 (9)) the following example is given:

(22) Sein$_i$ erstes Buch würde ich keinem$_i$ Autor abkaufen.
his first book would I no author buy-from
'His first book I would buy from no author.'

In both of these examples the pronoun precedes and outranks the operator. Nevertheless the bound reading is possible. The bound reading is also available if this configuration of pronoun and operator occurs in the *Mittelfeld*:

(23) ... weil ich sein$_i$ erstes Buch keinem$_i$ Autor abkaufen würde.

Contrary to the predictions of Bresnan's analysis, in (21), (22), and (23) the domain constraints are satisfied only at one level of representation, namely on a-structure. To account for the grammaticality of these data, it might be proposed that operator binding in German is constrained by the disjunction of the a-structure and c-structure constraints, instead of the disjunction of f-structure and c-structure constraints—at least in the dialects of those speakers who accept these data.

Examples with psych-verbs, like the following, can also be explained on this proposal:

(24) ... weil seine$_i$ Mutter jeden$_i$ interessiert.
because his mother everyone interests
'... because everyone's mother interests him.'

Binding is possible although the pronoun precedes the operator and although the operator, which is an OBJ, is lower-ranked than the pronoun, which is contained in the SUBJ-DP. Only on a-structure does the operator (experiencer) outrank the pronoun (theme). Notwithstanding data like (21)–(24), since the role of a-structure does not directly bear on the question of empty categories, I will continue to classify German as proposed by Choi (1995) and Bresnan (1998).

### 5.2.5 Weak Crossover and Complex Sentences

With complex sentences we have to look carefully at the definition of the binding domain. Consider the following examples:

(25) a. *Seine$_i$ Kinder wissen, dass jeder$_i$ nun heimgeht.
his children know that everyone now goes-home

b. *Dass jeder$_i$ nun heimgeht, wissen seine$_i$ Kinder.

At first sight both constraints appear to be violated in (25a). The pronoun precedes and outranks the operator, so the sentence is predicted to be ungrammatical. By this reasoning, however, (25b) should be grammatical, since the operator precedes the pronoun. However, recall that according to (4) the domain of the binder is restricted to "the minimal clause or predication structure containing it". The minimal predication structure containing the operator in (25) is the embedded *dass*-clause, as can be clearly seen from its f-structure:[11]

(26)
$$\left[\begin{array}{ll} \text{DF} & [\;] \\ \text{SUBJ} & \left[\begin{array}{ll} \text{PRED} & \text{'Kinder'} \\ \text{POSS} & \left[\text{PRED} \;\; \text{'seine'}\right] \end{array}\right] \\ \text{PRED} & \text{'wissen } \langle(\uparrow \text{SUBJ})\ (\uparrow \text{COMP})\rangle\text{'} \\ \text{COMP} & \left[\begin{array}{ll} \text{PRED} & \text{'heimgehen } \langle(\uparrow \text{SUBJ})\rangle\text{'} \\ \text{SUBJ} & \left[\text{PRED} \;\; \text{'jeder'}\right] \end{array}\right] \end{array}\right]$$

The pronoun is outside the domain of the binder and therefore not accessible to the binder. And (25a) is ungrammatical for the same reason.

We have seen that the German weak crossover data can be captured if we assume that there is no empty category in either scrambling or topicalization constructions.[12] However, when we look at data involving long distance dependencies, the situation is different. We turn to this next.

[11] COMP is the traditional LFG grammatical function for sentential arguments. In chapter 7 I will argue that sentential arguments in German bear the same grammatical function as their nominal or prepositional alternatives. In the present chapter and the following one I will continue to use the traditional notation for simplicity, since the function of sentential arguments does not bear on the analysis of weak crossover or long distance depedencies.

[12] One unresolved problem for this account is VP-topicalization containing the operator:

(i) *Jeden$_i$ geliebt hat seine$_i$ Mutter.
everyone loved has his mother

Although in this case the operator precedes the pronoun, nevertheless binding is ungrammatical.

### 5.2.6 Weak Crossover Involving Long Distance Dependencies

The following example involves a long distance dependency: the topicalized operator is the direct object of the embedded verb. Unlike topicalization within a single clause, in this case the pronoun cannot be understood as bound by the operator:

(27) *Jeden$_i$/*Wen$_i$ meinte seine$_i$ Mutter, habe sie
everyone/who-ACC said his mother-NOM has she
getröstet
consoled
'*Everyone$_i$, his$_i$ mother said she consoled.'
'*Who$_i$ did his$_i$ mother say she consoled?'

The analysis presented above fails to account for this. The operator is extracted from the embedded clause and occupies the CP-Spec-position, i.e., it functions as a discourse-function in the matrix clause. This means that the domain of the binder is extended to the matrix clause, as seen in the following f-structure:

(28)
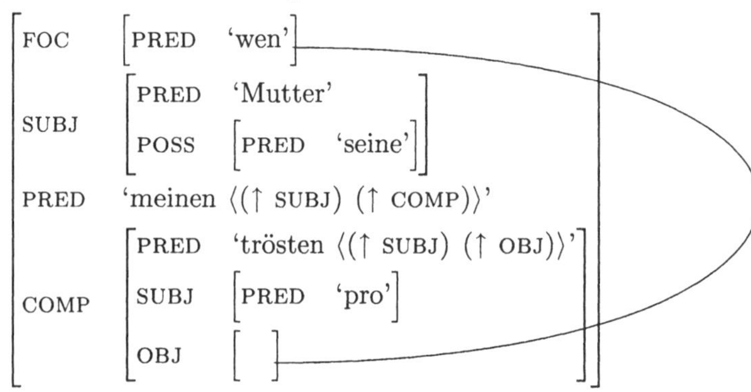


Although the binding condition is not satisfied in f-structure, since the pronoun is contained in an element that outranks the operator, still the operator precedes the pronoun, which should be sufficient to sanction binding.

Bresnan (1998) discusses an analogous example in Hindi (from Mahajan 1990). According to the weak crossover typology in Hindi, operator binding is possible if the Prominence Principle is satisfied on c-structure. Hindi is a scrambling language and uses morphological function specification. Bresnan observes that on the assumption that function specification by morphology is only locally accessible, there must be an empty category inside the local clause in order to assign the correct argument-predicate relation between the operator and the embedded verb. Note that, since in this case the empty category is required in order to satisfy Completeness, it does not violate Economy of Expression. Under this assumption the ungrammaticality of (29) is correctly predicted:[13]

(29) *kis-ko$_i$/kab-ko$_i$ uskii$_i$ bahin-ne socaa [ki
who-EDO/everyone-EDO his sister-SUBJ thought that
raam-ne [e]$_i$ dekhaa thaa]
Ram-ESUB see be.PST
'Who$_i$ was it that his$_i$ sister thought that Ram had seen him$_i$?'
'Everyone was such that his sister thought that Ram had seen him.'

The empty category, which is the right edge of the operator, follows the pronoun, so by the definition of linear order the pronoun precedes the operator and is excluded from its binding domain. Thus, the presence of the empty category correctly predicts the absence of the bound reading in (29).

Applying this proposal to German, (27) must be analyzed as having a structure like the following:

(30) *Jeden$_i$/*Wen$_i$ meinte seine$_i$ Mutter, habe sie e$_i$ getröstet

Again, the right edge of the operator does not precede the pronoun and the absence of the bound reading is correctely predicted.

One piece of evidence for the claim that morphology identifies syntactic functions only locally is that in German free word order is restricted to the local clause. Within the local clause almost every order is grammatical, but outside the clause there is only one position for long distance dependencies available, namely CP-Spec. In other words, in German, long distance scrambling is ungrammatical.

Now consider the long distance dependency in (31) below. Here, in contrast to (29), the bound reading is possible. This shows that the position of the empty category cannot be in the canonical position of the antecedent (indicated in (31) by (*e$_i$)), since then by (7) the pronoun would precede the operator.

(31) Jeden$_i$/ Wen$_i$ sagte sie, habe seine$_i$ Mutter
everyone-ACC/ who-ACC said she have his mother-NOM
(*e$_i$ ) getröstet
consoled
*'(Of) everyone$_i$, she said his$_i$ mother consoled (him$_i$).'
*'Who$_i$ did she say his$_i$ mother consoled?'

[13]In the glosses, EDO stands for 'embedded direct object' and ESUB for 'embedded subject'.

Again the analogous fact obtains in Hindi (cf. Mahajan 1990):

(32) kis-ko$_i$/sab-ko$_i$ raam-ne socaa [ki uskii$_i$
who-EDO/everyone-EDO Ram-SUBJ thought that his
bahin-ne (*[e]$_i$) dekhaa thaa]?
sister-SUBJ seen be.PST
'Who$_i$ did Ram think was seen by his$_i$ sister?'
'Everyone$_i$ Ram thought was seen by his$_i$ sister'

To account for this Bresnan (1998) proposed (based on Mahajan 1990) that the trace of the extractee may be freely ordered (this was also proposed by Haider 1987 for German).[14] Then the trace may occur before the subject, as shown in (33), and the possibility of binding is correctly predicted:

(33) Kis-ko$_i$ raamne socaa [ki [e]$_i$ uskii$_i$ bahin-ne dekhaa thaa]?

Since German is a scrambling language we can assume that also in German the trace may be freely ordered. If we assume that the object trace may precede the subject, we get the right result:

(34) Jeden$_i$/Wen$_i$ sagte sie, habe e$_i$ seine$_i$ Mutter getröstet.

Finally, let us consider the case where the DP which contains the pronoun is topicalized:

(35) a. *Sein$_i$ Hund glaubt Maria, dass jeden$_i$ Mann schon
his dog believes Maria that every man-ACC already
mal gebissen hat.
once bit hat
'*His dog, Maria believes has already bitten every man sometime.'

b. Sein$_i$ Hund glaubt jeder$_i$, sei der Beste.
his dog believes everyone is the best-one
'His (own) dog, everyone believes is the best.'

We would obtain the right result already without the presence of an empty category. But since we assumed that the morphology can identify grammatical functions only locally, we predict that also in this case there is an empty category in the embedded clause. On the assumption

[14]The desired effect, namely that the gap may precede its base position, is also achieved with the proposal made by Frey (1993), who claims that an extracted binder or bindee has to be reconstructed into the structurally highest position of its chain within its local domain. For example, in a configuration like (i) (Frey 1993, p. 87), the binder or the bindee has to be reconstructed into the lowest IP-Spec-position, namely $t'_1$.

(i) [XP$_1$ ... [$_{\text{Vmax}}$ ... [$_{\text{IP}}$ $t''_1$ [$_{\text{Vmax}}$ ... [$_{\text{IP}}$ ($t'_1$) [$_{\text{Vmax}}$ $t_1$ ... V] ...]]]]]

that the empty category is freely ordered, the following configuration is interesting:

(36) *[Sein$_i$ Hund]$_j$ glaubt Maria, dass jeden$_i$ Mann e$_j$ schon mal gebissen hat.

Here the operator precedes the empty category. But notice that the empty category is not the right edge of the pronoun *sein*. Although by the definition of linear order the operator precedes the DP that contains the pronoun, due to the empty category, yet it does not precede the pronoun itself. Hence (36) is correctly predicted to be ungrammatical, since the pronoun precedes and outranks the operator regardless of the position of the empty category.

### 5.2.7 Weak Crossover and Infinitives

Finally, we consider the interaction of weak crossover and infinitives. As the following examples show, operator binding is possible only with so-called coherent infinitives, as in (37a), but not with incoherent infinitives, as in (37b).

(37) a. Wen$_i$ versucht seine$_i$ Mutter zu trösten.
who-ACC tries his mother-NOM to console
*'Who$_i$ is his$_i$ mother trying to console.'

b. *Wen$_i$ zwingt seine$_i$ Mutter Maria, e$_i$ zu heiraten.
who-ACC forces his mother-NOM Maria-ACC to marry
*'Who$_i$ is his$_i$ mother forcing Mary to marry.'

Sentences with coherent infinitives have properties of monoclausal sentences (cf. Bech 1983, Haider 1991a, Haider 1993a and others). This means that (37a) is an instance of local topicalization, i.e., the operator is inside its local domain. In contrast, sentences with incoherent infinitives are biclausal, so the operator in (37b) is extracted from the embedded non finite clause and occupies the specifier position of the the matrix clause. Hence it is outside its local domain. So lexocentric function specification is not possible. Assuming, as we have been, that morphological function specification is local, it follows that an empty category must be present with incoherent infinitives but not with coherent ones and this gives us the right results. In both examples in (37) the pronoun outranks the operator (so the pronoun is excluded from the operator binding domain in f-structure). However in (37a) it is not excluded from the operator binding domain in c-structure, since no empty category is required, while in (37b) it is, because the empty category is necessary for function specification.

Binding by a lower-ranked operator is also possible in the so-called 'third construction', illustrated by the following example:

(38) ... weil jeden$_1$ seine$_1$ Mutter versucht hat zu
because everyone-ACC his mother-NOM tried has to
trösten.
console
'... because his mother has tried to console everyone.'

In the third construction the non-finite VP is extraposed, but one argument of the extraposed VP (here *jeden*) is in the *Mittelfeld*. Since binding is possible, it follows on the present analysis that there is no empty category of the operator in the extraposed phrase.[15] This entails that the third construction is not biclausal, but monoclausal.

## 5.3 A Traceless Account of Weak Crossover

Although Bresnan's account of weak crossover in terms of empty categories is empirically adequate, and extends straightforwardly to German, Dalrymple, Kaplan, and King (2001) reject the use of traces on conceptual grounds. They claim that a traceless theory is preferable, since it is less redundant, more restrictive and more tractable mathematically. In the following I will sketch their account and point out some conceptual questions that it raises. After that I will discuss the status of traces in the theory of Bresnan (2001).

### 5.3.1 Dalrymple *et al.* (2001)

Dalrymple, Kaplan, and King (2001) accept the basic insight of Bresnan's analysis of weak crossover that operator binding relations are constrained by prominence relations between an operator and a pronoun that it binds. However, in order to eliminate traces they reformulate the prominence relations. First they introduce the following definitions:

**Coarguments** The arguments and adjuncts of a single predicate

**CoargPro** The f-structure of the coargument in which the pronoun is contained

**CoargOp** The f-structure of the coargument in which the operator is contained

The prominence relation on f-structure is now formulated between the f-structure which contains the operator (CoargOp) and f-structure which contains the pronoun (CoargPro):

**Syntactic Prominence** An operator O is more prominent than a pronoun P if and only if CoargOp is at least as high as CoargPro on the functional hierarchy.

[15] This was also proposed by Bayer and Kornfilt (1994) in the framework of GB.

Linear prominence is formulated between the pronoun itself and CoargOp:

**Linear Prominence** An operator O is more prominent than a pronoun P if and only if CoargOp f-precedes[16] P.

Although Dalrymple *et al.* do not explicitly formulate a Prominence Principle analogous to (5), it is clear that they assume such a principle with reference to the above prominence relations. In other words, binding is possible (in German) only if at least one of the prominence relations is satisfied.

Dalrymple *et al.*'s analysis of German is essentially the same as Bresnan's for single-clause sentences. Let us therefore examine the case of long distance dependencies, which involve traces on Bresnan's analysis. Consider again example (27), repeated here:

(39) *Jeden$_i$ meinte seine$_i$ Mutter, habe sie getröstet.
everyone-ACC said his mother-NOM has she consoled
*'Everyone$_i$, his$_i$ mother said she consoled.'

In Dalrymple *et al.*'s analysis the coarguments of *meinen* are the SUBJ f-structure which contains the pronoun and the f-structure of the complement clause (COMP) which contains the operator (the operator is the object of the embedded verb *trösten*). Since SUBJ (i.e., CoargPro) is higher on the functional hierarchy than COMP (i.e, CoargOp), the operator is syntactically not more prominent than the pronoun. Moreover, the pronoun precedes (and hence f-precedes) CoargOp, thus the operator is also linearly not more prominent than the pronoun. Since neither prominence relation is satisfied, binding is correctly ruled out.

Since the configuration in (39) is the only one in German where an empty category is needed, Dalrymple *et al.*'s modification appears to make traces superfluous.[17]

### 5.3.2 Discussion

In short, the analysis of Dalrymple, Kaplan, and King (2001) has the same coverage as Bresnan's, and in particular accounts for the failure of binding in long distance weak crossover configurations, without appealing to empty categories. This would seem to make it conceptually preferable. However, there are some conceptual questions raised by Dalrymple *et al.*'s analysis that I would like to briefly address.

[16]Dalrymple *et al.* use a different definition of f-precedence than the one given above in footnote 4, but there is no empirical difference for the cases discussed here.

[17]I have only presented Dalrymple *et al.*'s analysis of the German weak crossover data. However, they also examine data from other language and conclude that traces are generally not necessary to account for weak crossover.

First, while Dalrymple *et al.*'s analysis avoids traces, it relies on three other notions: coargument, CoargPro and CoargOp. Thus the question arises whether these notions play a role elsewhere in the grammar; if not, then this weakens their claim that their analysis is theoretically more parsimonious than an account with traces. Second, there is an asymmetry between the two types of prominence relations between an operator and a pronoun: while prominence on f-structure is defined in terms of CoargPro and CoargOp, prominence on c-structure is defined in terms of the pronoun and CoargOp. (Note, however, that Bresnan's account has a similar asymmetry, cf. the reference to the containing element in the definition of the outranking relation (6a) above.)

A more significant conceptual issue is raised by Dalrymple *et al.*'s notion of linear prominence. Looking at the coargument in which the operator is embedded and not at the operator itself suggests that it should be irrelevant for the binding relation whether the operator is extracted from the embedded clause or not. But in fact there is an important difference. If the operator is not extracted, binding is still ungrammatical, not because of the Prominence Principle but because the pronoun is not in the binding domain of the operator, as we have seen (cf. section 5.2.5). In fact, although they do not mention it explicitly, Dalrymple, Kaplan, and King (2001) have to take the definition of the binding domain into account in any case, as the following example shows:

(40) Dass sie jeden$_i$ tröstet, meint seine$_i$ Mutter.
that she everyone-ACC consoles thinks his mother
'Everyone$_i$'s mother thinks she consoles him$_i$.'

Here CoargOp (f-)precedes the pronoun, which should be enough to allow binding. Only by appealing to the binding domain—i.e., the embedded *dass*-clause—can binding in this sentence correctly be ruled out on the account of Dalrymple, Kaplan, and King (2001) (as on Bresnan's account). Analogously, the following sentence is excluded by reference to the binding domain, rather than the Prominence Principle (cf. (25a) in section 5.2.5):

(41) *Seine$_i$ Mutter meint, dass sie jeden$_i$ tröstet.

However, this contrasts with the case of extraction of the binder from an embedded clause, as in (39), repeated here:

(42) *Jeden$_i$ meinte seine$_i$ Mutter, habe sie getröstet.

Both Bresnan's and Dalrymple *et al.*'s accounts implicitly assume that the extraction of the binder extends the binding domain. Hence, the ungrammaticality of binding can't be captured by the binding domain here but has to be accounted for by the Prominence Principle. Yet it is curious that precisely in the case of extraction of the binder, the binder itself plays no role in the analysis of Dalrymple, Kaplan, and King (2001). Instead Dalrymple *et al.*'s linear prominence relation refers to the complement clause which contains the operator (CoargOp), without any reference to the extracted operator. But if the binding domain is simply taken to be the embedded clause, then the ungrammaticality would follow from the fact that the pronoun is outside the binding domain. These considerations raise the question of whether the binding domain is in fact extended in the case of extraction of the binder or remains confined to the embedded clause. If the binding domain is extended, then it seems to me that the extraction of the binder should be taken in consideration by the Prominence Principle, as it is in Bresnan's analysis but not in Dalrymple *et al.*'s. But whether there is independent evidence for extending the binding domain must be left for future research.

Even if the preceding considerations indicate some conceptual reservations about of the account of weak crossover by Dalrymple, Kaplan, and King (2001), we still have to acknowledge that they do capture all the data without reference to traces. However, there is independent reason for adopting traces in LFG.

Recall from section 5.2.2 Bresnan's argument that in English, we need the empty category with both local and non-local topicalization. Since the grammatical functions are specified structurally, with long distance dependencies, an empty category is needed in the structural subject or object position to get the right annotations. In the topicalized position the function of the phrase can't be identified in English. In contrast, in German I have argued that the grammatical functions are identified by the morphology and moreover, based on the absence of long distance scrambling I have claimed that morphological function specification in German is possible only locally, namely with scrambling and local topicalization (cf. section 5.2.6). Hence in the case of long distance topicalization, in order to determine the grammatical function of the extracted phrase there must be an empty category in the local domain on which the annotations for morphological function specification appear. Although the empty category lacks morphology itself, it corresponds to the same f-structure as the extracted phrase through which the case and agreement features appear (see chapter 6, section 6.2.2 for discussion and examples).

While Dalrymple, Kaplan, and King (2001) do not explicitly discuss grammatical function specification, it seems clear that, since long distance dependencies involve no traces in their account, the grammatical function of the extracted phrase must be introduced by its uncertainty path (how this is done is shown in chapter 6). In this case the grammatical function will be specified independently of the Endocentric Mapping Principles and morphological function specification.[18] However, the mapping principles and morphological function specification are among the underlying assumptions of my analysis of German syntax, and Bresnan (1998), which is based on these assumptions, provides a consistent theory of weak crossover. Hence, I accept Bresnan's conclusion that empty categories are sometimes necessary for function identification, depending on the structural and morphological properties of the language. In German, they are needed only in the case of long-distance topicalization.

## 5.4 Summary

In this chapter it was shown that the analysis of weak crossover proposed in Bresnan (1998) and Choi (1995) not only captures the German weak crossover data in scrambling (Choi 1995), but also in other constructions, including (local and non-local) topicalization, adjuncts, double objects, complex sentences, long distance dependencies, and infinitives. Assuming the Endocentric Mapping Principles and morphological function specification in German, weak crossover provides evidence for the existence of an empty category in long distance dependencies, i.e., in non-local topicalization but not in scrambling and local topicalization. With long distance dependencies the extracted constituent has to be linked with an empty category in its local domain (its minimal clause). In this situation the empty category is independently motivated by a locality requirement on function specification (empirically supported by the fact that free word order in German is restricted to the local clause). Since it is needed to satisfy Completeness, the empty category does not violate Economy of Expression.

In the next chapter we will look in more detail at how the empty category is related to its antecedent and how restrictions on extraction can be captured.

[18]In this connection it is interesting that Dalrymple (2001, p.71ff.) appeals to Bresnan's Endocentric Mapping Principles. However, she notes that in case the arguments of a predicate appear in the specifier position of a functional projection which is annotated with a DF-function, they are linked to their within-clause function "by means of purely functional specifications (p. 76)" (i.e. by the uncertainty path).

# 6

# Long Distance Dependencies

We have seen that on the assumption that morphological function specification is only locally accessible, constructions involving non-local extraction must have an empty category inside the local clause in order to guarantee the correct predicate-argument relation. We turn now to the question of how the empty category is related to its antecedent. For example, the following f-structure is not wellformed, because the OBJ of *marry* has no PRED-feature and the TOP is not appropriately integrated:

(1) Mary$_i$, he said that John married e$_i$

$$
\left[\begin{array}{ll}
\text{TOP} & \left[\text{PRED} \quad \text{`Mary'}\right] \\
\text{SUBJ} & \left[\text{PRED} \quad \text{`he'}\right] \\
\text{PRED} & \text{`say } \langle(\uparrow \text{SUBJ})\ (\uparrow \text{COMP})\rangle\text{'} \\
\text{COMP} & \left[\begin{array}{ll}
\text{PRED} & \text{`marry } \langle(\uparrow \text{SUBJ}),\ (\uparrow \text{OBJ})\rangle\text{'} \\
\text{SUBJ} & \left[\text{PRED} \quad \text{`John'}\right] \\
\text{OBJ} & \left[\ \right]
\end{array}\right]
\end{array}\right]
$$

According to the analysis of topicalization in Bresnan (2001, ch. 9), the relation between the TOP and the OBJ is captured by the **Principle for Identifying Gaps**, which Bresnan (2001, p. 181, (2)) formulates as follows:

(2) Associate XP $\rightarrow$ *e* with $((x \uparrow)\ \text{DF}) = \uparrow$

In applying this principle Bresnan makes use of functional uncertainty. Functional uncertainty was introduced to model long distance dependencies in LFG without appealing to movement operations (see Kaplan and Maxwell 1988, Kaplan and Zaenen 1989) and has become the standard means of analysing these constructions in LFG. In the next section I review the mechanism of functional uncertainty and show that there are two ways of applying it, so-called outside-in and inside-out functional uncertainty. It turns out that the latter is more consistent with the analysis developed in the preceding chapter. Therefore, in section 6.2 I apply inside-out functional uncertainty to the analysis of long distance dependencies in German. In section 6.3 I present an alternative to functional uncertainty for analysing long distance dependencies, namely, as locally bounded cyclic dependencies and apply this approach to the German data. In section 6.4 I then compare the two approaches and examine how they deal with additional aspects of long distance dependencies.

## 6.1 Modeling Extraction with Functional Uncertainty

In a long distance dependency the f-structure of the extracted element in the higher clause, which functions as the TOP or FOC, is identified with the f-structure of the clause internal grammatical function by means of a functional equation which is annotated to the corresponding c-structure. Since a long distance dependency may in principle involve indefinitely many intermediate clauses, the path (the sequence of f-structure attributes) between the discourse function and the clause internal function (the so-called *within clause function*) may be indefinitely long. Hence, in describing the path variable strings of attributes have to be allowed. Functional uncertainty accomplishes this by extending the domain of functional descriptions from attribute strings to sets of attribute strings.

The idea of functional uncertainty can be viewed from two perspectives. On one, the functional equation is annotated to the higher c-structure node of the dependency relation (e.g., the node of the TOP). This has the effect that the uncertainty path is traversed from top to bottom, i.e., from the least to the most embedded f-structure in the dependency relation. Hence, this is called outside-in functional uncertainty. On the other perspective, the functional equation is annotated to the lower c-structure node of the dependency relation (i.e., the node of the canonical argument position of the extracted element). This has the effect that the uncertainty path is traversed from bottom to top. Hence, this is called inside-out functional uncertainty.

In the next two sections I will show in more detail how each type of functional uncertainty models long distance dependencies.[1] We begin

[1]See also Falk (2001, p. 153–156) for a comparison of the two types of functional uncertainty.

with outside-in functional uncertainty, since it was introduced first and is conceptually perhaps easier to grasp.

### 6.1.1 Outside-in Functional Uncertainty

Since functional uncertainty is based on the idea of traversing a path of f-structure attributes, it is first necessary to extend the domain of function application from single attributes to strings of attributes, as originally pointed out by Kaplan and Zaenen (1989); this is what the following definition (from Bresnan 2001, p. 64) does:

(3) $(f\epsilon) = f$, where $\epsilon$ is the empty string, and $(fax) = ((fa)x)$, where $a$ is an attribute and $x$ a possibly empty string of attributes.

Using this, outside-in functional uncertainty is then defined as follows (Bresnan 2001, p. 64):

(4) **Outside-in Functional Uncertainty:**
For $\alpha$ any set of strings of attributes, $(f\alpha) = v$ holds if and only if for some $x$ in the set of strings $\alpha$, $(fx) = v$.

To see how this works, consider again sentence (1), repeated below, as example of extraction out of a single embedded clause (this and the following example are based on the analysis of English topicalization in Kaplan and Zaenen 1989):

(5) Mary, he said that John married.

In this sentence *Mary* is not only the TOP of the clause, but is also understood as the OBJ of the embedded clause. The problem is that it does not occur in the canonical OBJ position. However, we can capture the relation between the TOP and the OBJ by identifying their f-structures, in the following way. The DP which is adjoined to the IP is annotated with the equation $(\uparrow \text{TOP}) = \downarrow$ (by the Endocentric Mapping Principles). The TOP and the embedded OBJ are functionally identified by the equation $(\uparrow \text{TOP}) = (\uparrow \text{COMP OBJ})$, which is also annotated to the DP. Here is the relevant phrase-structure rule:

(6)
$$\text{IP} \rightarrow \underset{\substack{(\uparrow \text{TOP}) = \downarrow \\ (\uparrow \text{TOP}) = (\uparrow \text{COMP OBJ})}}{\text{DP}} \quad \underset{\uparrow = \downarrow}{\text{IP}}$$

The resulting f-structure for (5) is given in (7):

(7)
$$\left[\begin{array}{ll}
\text{TOP} & \left[\text{PRED} \quad \text{`Mary'}\right] \\
\text{SUBJ} & \left[\text{PRED} \quad \text{`he'}\right] \\
\text{PRED} & \text{`say} \langle(\uparrow \text{SUBJ})\ (\uparrow \text{COMP})\rangle\text{'} \\
\text{TENSE} & \text{PAST} \\
\text{COMP} & \left[\begin{array}{ll}
\text{PRED} & \text{`marry} \langle(\uparrow \text{SUBJ}),\ (\uparrow \text{OBJ})\rangle\text{'} \\
\text{TENSE} & \text{PAST} \\
\text{SUBJ} & \left[\text{PRED} \quad \text{`John'}\right] \\
\text{OBJ} & \left[\ \right]
\end{array}\right]
\end{array}\right]$$

Of course, the TOP may be separated from the canonical OBJ position by multiple intermediate clauses, as in the following example:

(8) Mary, he claimed that Bill said that John married.

In principle, there is no specific limit to the number of intermediate clauses, and this is the reason for introducing functional uncertainty, so that the string of attributes may, for instance, contain multiple COMPs, reflecting multiple embeddings. The effect of functional uncertainty is encoded in the notation of functional equations by extending this to regular expressions over functional attributes—in particular, the use of the Kleene iteration operator *. For example, the following equation relates the TOP to an arbitrarily deeply embedded OBJ function:

(9) $(\uparrow \text{TOP}) = (\uparrow \text{COMP}^* \text{ OBJ})$

There are two points to be noted about this equation. First, it does not follow from the Endocentric Mapping Principles ((18) in chapter 2), since these associate the specifier of functional projections or adjoined positions only with $(\uparrow \text{DF}) = \downarrow$ or $(\uparrow \overline{\text{AF}}) = \downarrow$, respectively. (e.g., $(\uparrow \text{TOP}) = \downarrow$ in (6) above). Second, not only does it identify the f-structures of the TOP and the arbitrarily deeply embedded OBJ, but it also introduces the OBJ-function into the embedded f-structure. Hence, by appealing to (9), the OBJ does not have to have a representation on c-structure—in fact an empty category would be ruled out by Economy of Expression, since the OBJ-function is already specified by the functional uncertainty equation. In other words, the analysis of long-distance extraction by means of outside-in functional uncertainty is inconsistent with the position that this construction involves empty categories.

However, we have argued in chapter 5 that in configurational languages such as English the grammatical functions are identified structurally and can't be specified in non-canonical position. Hence, the empty category is necessary for function identification. This contrasts with Kaplan and Zaenen (1989), who assume that topicalization in English does not involve any c-structure gaps. They note that "[t]his formulation is possible only because subcategorization in LFG is defined on f-structure via the Completeness and Coherence conditions... and is independent of phrase-structure configurations" (Kaplan and Zaenen 1989, p. 27). However, as we have seen, the Endocentric Mapping Principles formulated in Bresnan (2001) do associate functions with specific phrase structure positions in configurational languages. Hence, on Bresnan's account subcategorization is not independent of phrase-structure. In the next section we will see how long distance dependencies can be captured on the assumption that we do have an empty category inside the local clause, by means of inside-out functional uncertainty.

### 6.1.2 Inside-out Functional Uncertainty

Inside-out functional uncertainty was introduced by Halvorsen and Kaplan (1988) and has been used to model anaphoric binding (Dalrymple 1993) and extraction (Bresnan 2001, Berman 1997). This section recapitulates the extraction analysis.

Since the intuition behind inside-out functional uncertainty involves traversing the attribute path from bottom to top, it is first necessary to invert the notion of function application and then extend it analogously to the definition in (3) above. The following definition is a slight revised of the one in (Bresnan 2001, p. 65):[2]

(10) **Inside-out function application:**

a. For any f-structure $f'$ and attribute $a$, $(af')$ designates an f-structure $f$ such that $(fa) = f'$.

b. For any f-structure $f'$, attribute $a$ and string of attributes $x$, $(\epsilon f') = f'$ ($\epsilon$ the empty string), and $(xaf') = (x(af'))$.

Using this, inside-out functional uncertainty is then defined as follows (Bresnan 2001, p. 66):

(11) **Inside-out functional uncertainty:**
For $\alpha$ any set of strings of attributes, $(\alpha f) = v$ holds if and only if for some $x$ in the set of strings $\alpha$, $(xf) = v$.

To see how this works, consider again the sentence in (5). As before, by the Endocentric Mapping Principles the DP *Mary*, which is adjoined to IP, will be annotated with $(\uparrow \text{TOP}) = \downarrow$. In the embedded clause the

[2] I replaced "designates the f-structure" by "designates an f-structure", since it is not necessarily unique. I owe this observation to an anonymous reviewer.

canonical OBJ position is occupied by a DP which dominates the empty string. This allows the function specification of the dislocated DP inside the embedded clause. As sister to the verb, the DP will be annotated with (↑ OBJ) = ↓. As required by the Principle for Identifying Gaps (2), the empty category dominated by the OBJ-DP will be annotated with the inside-out functional uncertainty equation. Here are the c-structure, with the relevant annotations, and the corresponding f-structure:

(12)

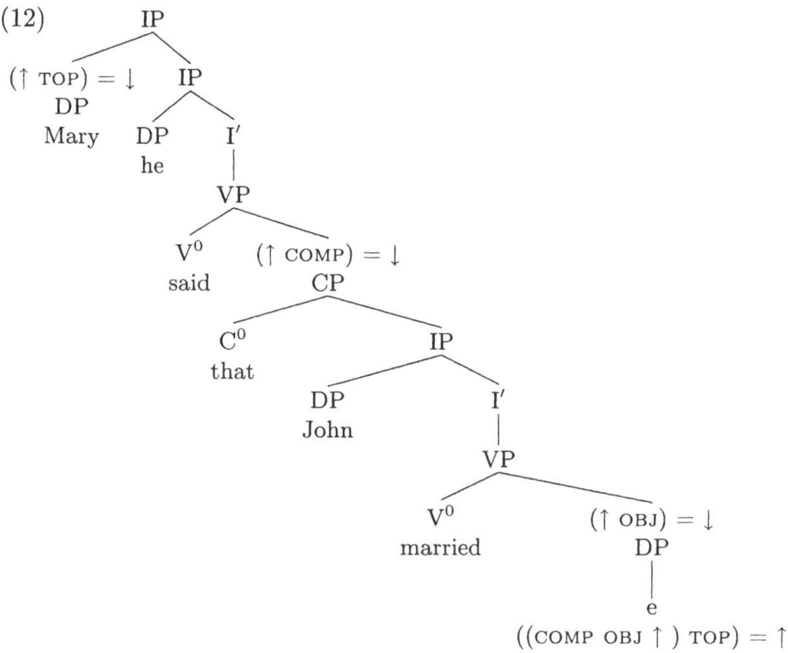


(13)

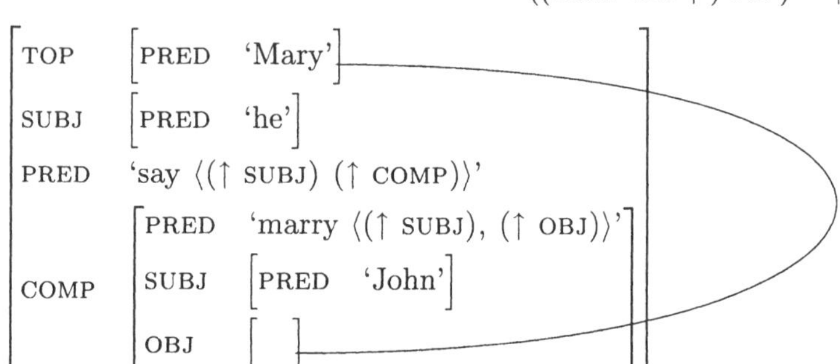


To clarify this analysis it may be helpful to decompose the inside-out functional annotation ((COMP OBJ ↑) TOP) = ↑. By inside-out function application, the expression (OBJ ↑) denotes the f-structure whose OBJ attribute has the f-structure of the OBJ-DP as its value; i.e., the f-structure of the embedded CP. Correspondingly, the expression (COMP OBJ ↑) denotes the f-structure whose COMP attribute has the f-structure of the CP as its value; i.e., the f-structure of the matrix IP. Finally, this f-structure has the attribute TOP, whose f-structure is identified with the f-structure which the inside-out equation is annotated to, i.e., the f-structure of the OBJ-DP.

Again, we can also think of this in terms of the notion of traversing an attribute path from bottom to top. The f-structure identifier ↑ refers to the f-structure of the OBJ-DP. From there one can follow a path outwards through the attributes OBJ and COMP to the higher f-structure (the f-structure of the matrix clause), which has the TOP attribute. The f-structure of the TOP is identified with the f-structure of the embedded OBJ. This establishes the long-distance dependency.

As with outside-in functional uncertainty, we can use the Kleene star operator to construct the inside-out functional annotation ((COMP* OBJ ↑) TOP) = ↑, which allows the identification of a multiply embedded OBJ with the TOP of the matrix clause. In short, by means of inside-out functional uncertainty long-distance dependencies can be modelled under the assumption that there is an empty category in the c-structure.

## 6.2 An Analysis of Long Distance Dependencies in German Based on Inside-Out Functional Uncertainty

As we have seen, German requires an empty category in the case of long distance dependencies, i.e., a c-structure gap is necessary in German to identify the grammatical function of the extracted phrase in the embedded clause. In this section we will see how we can account for the German data involving long distance dependencies in terms of inside-out functional uncertainty. But before presenting this analysis, let us first look at some German data involving extraction.

### 6.2.1 German Data Involving Extraction

Consider the following representative examples of extraction:[3]

[3]These data show only basic properties of extraction in German. The goal of the following analysis is to illustrate how extraction in German can be captured by using inside-out functional uncertainty. No deep investigation of extraction in German is intended. For more detailed discussion of the data and more fine-grained analyses see (in the GB framework) e.g. Bayer (1994), Fanselow (1987), d'Avis, Beck, Lutz, Pafel, and Trissler (1993), Müller (1995a) and (in the HPSG framework) Müller

(14) a. Wer glaubst du, kommt morgen?
who-NOM believe you-NOM comes tomorrow
'Who do you think is coming tomorrow?'

b. Wer glaubst du, dass morgen kommt?
who-NOM believe you-NOM that tomorrow comes
'Who do you think is coming tomorrow?'

c. Wen glaubst du, hat sie eingeladen?
who-ACC believe you has she invited
'Who do you think she's invited?'

d. Wen glaubst du, dass sie eingeladen hat?
who-ACC believe you that she invited has
'Who do you think she's invited?'

e. Wie lange hat er behauptet, geschlafen zu haben?
how long has he claimed slept to have
'How long did he claim to have slept?'

f. *Wen bedeutet nichts, dass Maria gelobt hat?
who-ACC means nothing that Maria praised has
'Whom does (it) mean nothing that Maria praised?'

g. *Welchen Zug hat sie sich beeilt, damit sie noch erreicht?
which train-ACC has she REFL hurry so that she still reaches
'Which train did she hurry so that she would make?'

h. *Was hat Peter das Buch geschrieben, ohne vorher zu lesen?
what has Peter the book written without before to read
'What did Peter write the book without reading before?'

These examples illustrate two generalizations about extraction in German: (i) Extraction is possible out of a finite or non-finite object clause, but impossible out of a subject or an adjunct clause.[4,5] (ii) The extractable constituents themselves include all types of functions: ad-

(1999).

[4]Extraction out of a *dass*-clause is only possible in some dialects of German. In Standard German extraction out of a *dass*-clause is ungrammatical. In section 6.3 we will see one possibility for how this difference can be captured.

[5]Reis (1995) argues that extraction out of a verb-second-clause is not possible at all in German. In her view all these cases are 'Verb-first Integrated Parentheticals'. However as Hubert Haider pointed out to me, there are some distinctions between parentheticals and the extraction-configuration. For example, true parentheticals (as determined by their position in the string) do not permit certain particles such as *denn*, as in (i), or wh-in-situ, as in (ii):

juncts, subjects and objects. These generalizations imply that extraction in German can be analyzed in functional terms and that restrictions on extraction can be captured by formulating conditions on the uncertainty path, as proposed by Kaplan and Zaenen (1989). We show how this is done in the next section.

### 6.2.2 Conditions on the Path — Kaplan and Zaenen (1989)

As noted above, Kaplan and Zaenen (1989) account for long distance dependencies in terms of outside-in functional uncertainty. Kaplan and Zaenen (p. 32 (40)) subdivide the uncertainty path into the BOTTOM, which contains the potential functions at the end of the path, and the BODY, which contains the functions in the middle of the path:

(15) $(\uparrow \text{DF}) = (\uparrow \text{BODY BOTTOM})$

The BODY therefore contains all the functions out of which extraction is possible, while the BOTTOM contains all extractable functions. This allows functional constraints on extraction to be expressed directly in the uncertainty equation. For example, for English topicalization Kaplan and Zaenen formulate the following equation (p. 31 (39)):

(16) $(\uparrow \text{TOP}) = (\uparrow \{\text{COMP}|\text{XCOMP}\}^{*}\ (\text{GF}-\text{COMP}))$

where GF−COMP denotes the set of grammatical functions other than COMP. This equation states that (in English) extraction is possible out of indefinitely many finite and non-finite complement clauses and that all GFs except sentential complements are extractable.

The distinction made by Kaplan and Zaenen between BODY and BOTTOM can, of course, also be applied to the above analysis of extraction in terms of inside-out functional uncertainty; the empty category is then associated with the following annotation:

---

(i) *Wo habe Karl, sagte sie denn, es versteckt?
where has Karl said she PRT it hidden
'Where did Karl, so she said, hide it?"

(ii) *Womit soll Karl, hat wer behauptet, den Tresor geknackt haben?
with-what is-supposed Karl has who claimed the safe cracked has
'*What is Karl supposed, who claimed, to have cracked the safe with?"

In constrast, the following sentences are fine, which implies they do not involve parentheticals:

(iii) Wo sagte sie denn, habe Karl es versteckt?
where said she PRT has Karl it hidden
'So where did she say Karl hid it?'

(iv) Womit hat wer behauptet, soll Karl den Tresor geknackt haben?
with-what has who claimed is-supposed Karl the safe cracked has
'Who claimed that Karl is supposed to have cracked the safe with what?'

So I assume that German has both extraction from verb-second clauses as well as verb-first-parenthetical expressions.

(17) ((BODY BOTTOM $\uparrow$) DF)= $\uparrow$

As we have seen, in German it is grammatical to extract out of finite and non-finite object clauses, but ungrammatical to extract out of a subject or an adjunct clause; and further, all GFs, arguments as well as adjuncts, are extractable. The BODY can therefore be specified as {COMP|XCOMP}* and the BOTTOM as GF.[6] The annotation on the empty category therefore reads:

(18) (({COMP|XCOMP}* GF $\uparrow$) DF) = $\uparrow$

For sentences like (14a), repeated here:

(19) Wer glaubst du, kommt morgen?
who-NOM believe you-NOM comes tomorrow
'Who do you think is coming tomorrow?'

we get the c-structure in (20) and the f-structure in (21):

[6] As discussed above, in Kaplan and Zaenen's analysis of English COMP is excluded from the BOTTOM functions. Analogous restrictions in German were observed by Webelhuth (1992). I put these aside for the moment, but discuss them in chapter 7.

(20)

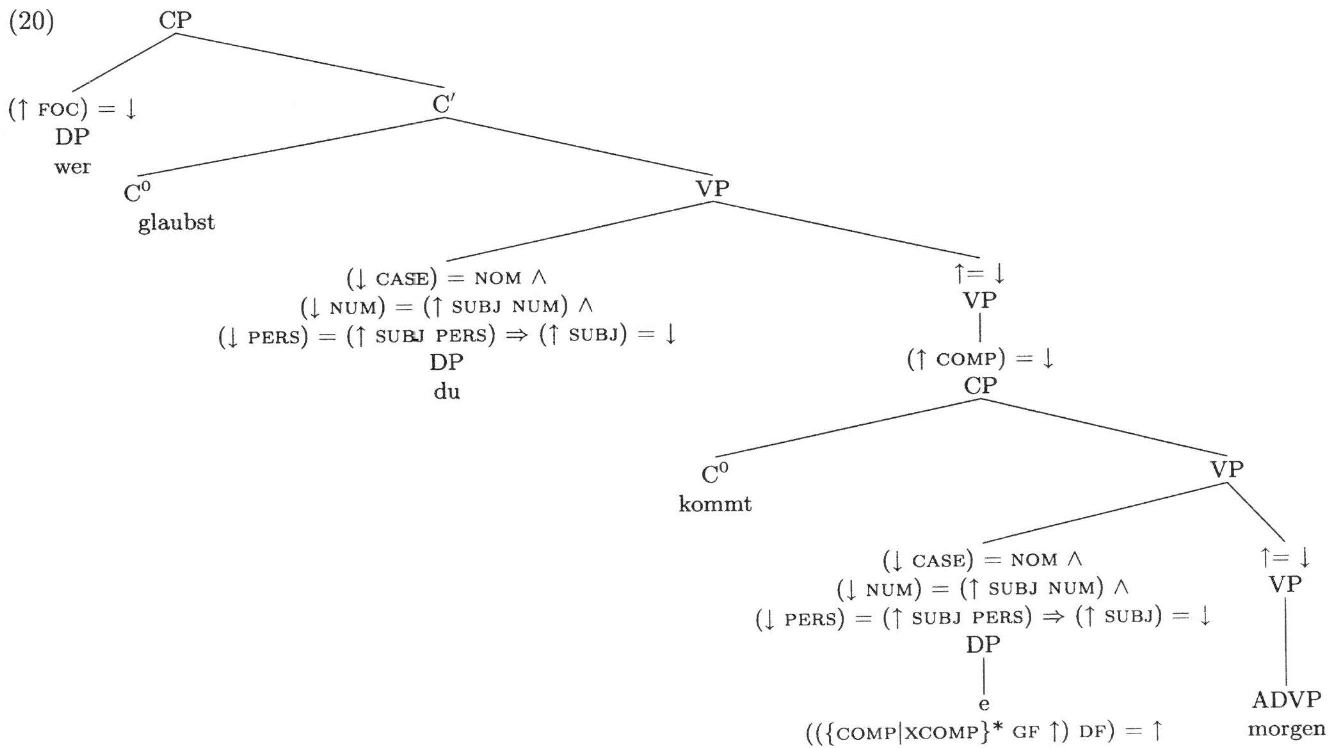
CP
(↑ FOC) = ↓
DP
wer
C′
C0
glaubst
VP
(↓ CASE) = NOM ∧
(↓ NUM) = (↑ SUBJ NUM) ∧
(↓ PERS) = (↑ SUBJ PERS) ⇒ (↑ SUBJ) = ↓
DP
du
↑= ↓
VP
(↑ COMP) = ↓
CP
C0
kommt
VP
(↓ CASE) = NOM ∧
(↓ NUM) = (↑ SUBJ NUM) ∧
(↓ PERS) = (↑ SUBJ PERS) ⇒ (↑ SUBJ) = ↓
DP
e
(({COMP|XCOMP}* GF ↑) DF) = ↑
↑= ↓
VP
ADVP
morgen

(21)

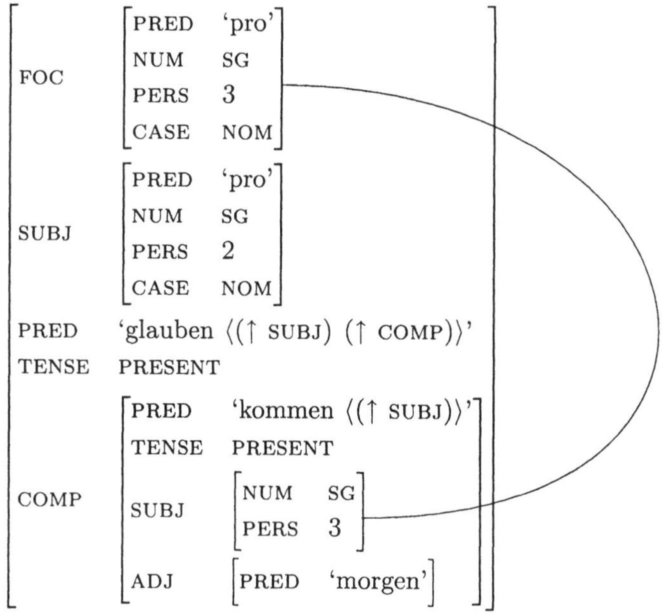


By inside-out functional uncertainty the f-structure of the empty category is identified with the discourse function of the matrix clause. This implies that the within clause function has the same information as the DF of the matrix clause, although the empty category lacks any morphological or lexical information. The person and number information of the embedded subject is specified in the lexical entry of the finite verb *kommt*, as was shown in chapter 4. The DP dominating the empty string is annotated with the conditionals for morphological function specification. Since *wer* carries nominative case marking and agrees with the finite verb of the embedded clause in person and number, the within clause function, which has the same information, can be identified as SUBJ and hence satisfies Completeness.

### 6.2.3 A Further Restriction on Long Distance Dependencies

But restricting the uncertainty path in the way proposed in (18) cannot account for certain word order restrictions in the clause that is extracted out of. In particular, the finite verb must be the first word in the extraction clause (in Standard German; in some dialects, *dass* is also possible, cf. footnote 4), as shown by the examples in (22):[7]

[7] Cf., e.g., Staudacher (1990), Haider (1993b), among many others.

(22) a. Diesen Teilnehmer glaube ich, [$_{CP}$ kennt niemand].
this participant-ACC think I knows nobody-NOM
'This participant, I think nobody knows.'

b. *Diesen Teilnehmer glaube ich, [$_{CP}$ niemand
this participant-ACC think I nobody-NOM
kennt].
knows
'This participant, I think nobody knows.'

c. *Diesen Teilnehmer sagte man mir, [$_{CP}$ warum
this participant-ACC said one me why
niemand kennt].
nobody-NOM knows
'This participant, they told me why nobody knows.'

The clause which is extracted out of is a complement clause. The extracted function is an OBJ. Hence, according to the conditions on the BOTTOM and the BODY, the sentences in (22) should all be grammatical. Since they are not, we need another way to account for this additional restriction.

### 6.2.4 Off-Path Constraints

If the finite verb is the first word in the extraction clause, then according to German sentence structure the verb must be in $C^0$ and the specifier position must be empty. Since the specifier of a functional category is associated by the Endocentric Mapping Principles with a discourse function, we can conclude that clauses out of which extraction is possible can't have a syntactized discourse function. The same can be observed with embedded complement clauses introduced by a wh-word. Extraction is ungrammatical, since the wh-word occupies the specifier position, where it functions as FOC.

Extraction is also possible out of multiply embedded clauses. However, the same condition holds for all intermediate clauses. Extraction is only grammatical if all intermediate clauses lack a discourse function, e.g.:

(23) [Den Peter]$_i$ glaube ich, sagte der Hans gestern, hat
the Peter-ACC think I said the Hans-NOM yesterday has
die Maria $e_i$ eingeladen.
the Maria-ACC invited
'Peter (is who) I think Hans said yesterday Maria invited.'

If the specifier of an intermediate clause is occupied by another constituent, as in (24), the sentence is ungrammatical:

(24) *[Den Peter]$_i$ glaube ich, gestern sagte der Hans, hat
the Peter-ACC think I yesterday said the Hans-NOM has
die Maria e$_i$ eingeladen.
the Maria-ACC invited

To account for this, I propose that the empty category must be linked with the nearest potential antecedent, that is, the next higher filled CP-Spec. This can be thought of as a kind of economy requirement.

In (23), the nearest potential antecedent is *den Peter* in the matrix CP-Spec, since the intermediate CP-Spec position is not filled, and this is an appropriate object of *einladen*. In (24), on the other hand, the nearest potential antecedent is *gestern*. But identifying the f-structure of *gestern* and the empty category would violate Completeness, since the adverb *gestern* lacks case features and can't be identified as an OBJ. Moreover it would violate Extended Coherence, since as TOP, *den Peter* is not identified with an integrated function.

This condition can be formalized by applying **off-path constraints** (cf. Dalrymple 2001, p. 151). These are constraints on the f-structures through which the path (in our case the BODY) can pass and refer to attributes of the f-structure of the path. Consequently, we can formulate the necessary condition by restricting the BODY-path so that the BODY does not pass an f-structure containing a discourse function. The resulting equation is given in (25):[8]

(25) $((\{\text{XCOMP, COMP}\}^* \quad \text{GF} \uparrow) \quad \text{DF}) = \uparrow$
$\neg\ (\rightarrow \text{DF})$

By the Principle for Identifying Gaps (2) this equation is annotated to the empty category. The right arrow ($\rightarrow$) points to the f-structure which is the value of the attribute it is associated with and requires that the f-structure of XCOMP or COMP not have a DF.

Let us see how the off-path constraint captures the examples in (22).

[8] In Berman (1997) it was argued—based on work by Frey (1993)—that the specifier position of the functional category is the only position in which the empty category is licensed. Restricting the empty category to the local CP-Spec position captures the fact that the specifier of the clause which is extracted out of can't be lexically filled. However, since the empty category is required for function specification only inside the local domain of the extractee, Economy of Expression prevents intermediate traces in the case of extraction out of a multiply embedded clause. Hence the fact that the specifiers of the intermediate clauses also have to be unfilled was not captured by the position of the empty category. Therefore it was suggested that off-path constraints capture the restrictions with intermediate clauses. However, since the off-path constraint $\neg\ (\rightarrow \text{DF})$ also captures the fact that the specifier of the clause which was extracted out of must be unfilled, the localization of the empty category in the local CP-Spec is not necessary to capture the restrictions on extraction and therefore no longer pursued.

In (26) the f-structure of the BODY, i.e. COMP, does not contain a discourse function. Hence, the OBJ can be identified with the TOP.

(26) Diesen Teilnehmer glaube ich, kennt niemand.
this participant believe I knows nobody
'This participant I believe nobody knows.'

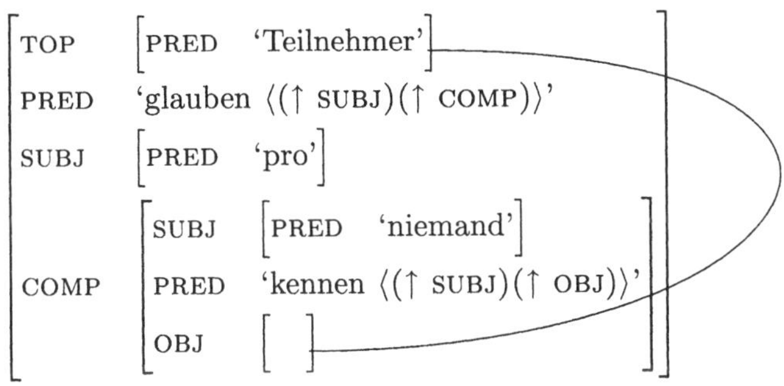


However in (27), the f-structure of COMP does contain a discourse function. This is excluded by the off-path constraint. Hence, the identification of the embedded object and the discourse function of the matrix clause is not possible:

(27) *Diesen Teilnehmer glaube ich, niemand kennt.

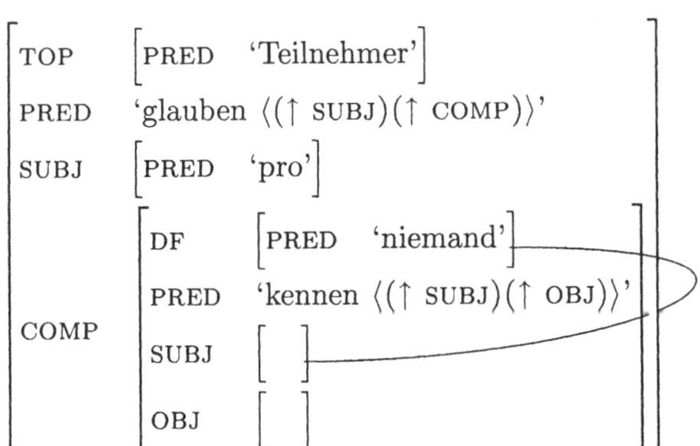


This analysis also yields the right results for examples like (28), where the extracted element is not sentence initial, but occupies an intermediate specifier position:

(28) a. Ich frage mich, wen er glaubt, dass Maria eingeladen
I ask myself whom he believes that Maria invited
hat.
has
'I wonder who he thinks Mary invited.'

b. Ich glaube, den Hans hat er gesagt, dass Maria eingeladen
I believe the Hans has he said that Maria invited
hat.
has
'I think it was Hans that he said Mary invited.'

Since the path can't pass an f-structure containing a DF, the empty category is linked to *wen* in (28a) and *den Hans* in (28b), which are the nearest potential antecedents and appropriate objects of the verb *einladen*.

While we have followed Kaplan and Zaenen (1989) in using the functions COMP and XCOMP in the BODY of the uncertainty path for extraction, in chapter 7 it will be claimed that clauses may have the same functions as DPs, e.g., SUBJ or OBJ. If this is so, we can simplify the conditions on the BODY to the single function OBJ. However, in the present work only extraction out of CPs is taken into consideration. Whether extraction out of DPs is possible in German is controversial (cf. Fanselow 1991, p. 174ff., Müller 1995a, p. 46) and I will not try to enter into this controversy here. If it turned out that extraction out of DPs is not possible, the BODY would have to be restricted to those OBJ functions which correspond to a CP in c-structure. This can be done by using the CAT-operator (Ron Kaplan (p.c.)), which relates f-structures and category labels; CAT is defined as follows:[9]

(29) CAT$(f, c)$ is true iff $f$ is an f-structure, $c$ is a category, and there exists a node $n$ in $\phi^{-1}(f)$ such that $\lambda(n) = c$ (where $\lambda$ is a function that assigns labels to nodes).

The categorial restriction can be added to the path by the following off-path constraint:

(30) ((OBJ* GF ↑) DF) = ↑.
CAT (→, CP)
¬ (→ DF)

[9]The definition is taken from Sells (1999, p. 10), who himself refers to Kaplan (p.c.).

## 6.3 Long Distance Dependencies as Locally Bounded Dependencies

An alternative to the analysis of long distance dependencies with functional uncertainty is to analyze them as cyclic, locally bounded dependencies.[10] On this account, the annotation which is associated with the empty category contains no uncertainty path, but is related to the local DF by inside-out function application: $((\text{GF}\ \uparrow)\ \text{DF}) = \uparrow$. For convenience, the definition of inside-out function application is repeated here:

(31) **Inside-out function application:**
For any f-structure $f'$ and attribute $a$, $(a\ f')$ designates an f-structure $f$ such that $(f\ a) = f'$.

The equation $((\text{GF}\ \uparrow)\ \text{DF}) = \uparrow$ states that attributes DF and GF are in the same f-structure and that the f-structure of DF is identical to the f-structure of GF.

Let us apply this account to the same example (19), repeated here for convenience, that we analyzed above in terms of functional uncertainty.

(32) Wer glaubst du, kommt morgen?
who-NOM believe you-NOM comes tomorrow
'Who do you think is coming tomorrow?'

The c-structure differs only in the annotation associated with the empty category:[11]

---

[10] This account was suggested to me by Peter Sells in the discussion after my talk during the LFG97-conference in San Diego. See also Sells (2000) for an analysis of dependency constructions in the Phillippine languages, according to which dependencies are local links through nominative adjuncts.

[11] For the sake of simplicity and compactness, I omit the annotations for morphological function specifications from this representation, since they are already reproduced in (20).

(33)

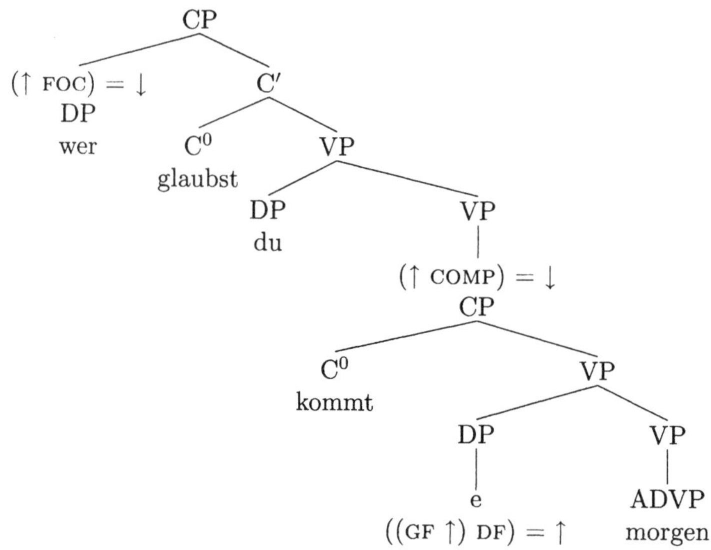


And the f-structure differs from that in (21) in the presence of the DF attribute in the f-structure of COMP:[12]

(34)

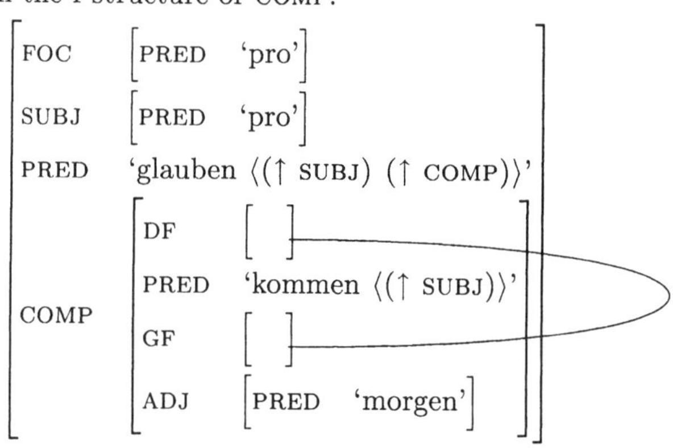


Since the empty category is annotated with the inside-out equation ((GF ↑) DF) = ↑, where GF denotes all extractable functions, this results in the GF being linked to the DF of the local f-structure. However, the extracted phrase occupies the specifier position of the matrix clause. Hence the relation between the empty category and its antecedent is still missing. The f-structure in (34) therefore violates Extended Coherence (the FOC is not linked to an argument or an adjunct) as well as Completeness (the grammatical function can't be specified, since the

[12]For simplicity the agreement features are omitted.

GF lacks sufficient morphological marking and the grammatical function has no semantic feature).

But suppose this relation is established by the lexical properties of certain verbs, i.e., that it is encoded in the lexical entry of these verbs. A distinction is commonly made between verbs which allow extraction out of their complement clause—so-called bridge verbs—and non-bridge verbs, which do not allow extraction, even if their complement clause lacks a discourse function. (35a-b) are examples of bridge verbs, (35c-d) of non-bridge verbs:

(35) a. Was glaubst du, hat der Hans gesehen?
what believe you has the Hans seen
'What do you think Hans saw?'

b. Was meinst du, hat der Hans gesehen?
what mean you has the Hans seen
'What do you think Hans saw?'

c. *Was bezweifelst du, hat der Hans gesehen?
what doubt you has the Hans seen

d. *Was flüsterst du, hat der Hans gesehen?
what whisper you has the Hans seen

We can obtain the right result if we assume that a lexical property of bridge verbs is that they identify the matrix discourse function with the discourse function of their complement clause. This property can be encoded in the lexical entry of these verbs by the optional equation (($\uparrow$ DF) = ($\uparrow$ COMP DF)). The effect is that long distance dependencies are modeled as locally bounded cyclic dependencies. By the Principle for Identifying Gaps (2), the within clause function is linked to the local DF. The local DF is identified with the next higher DF by the lexical entry of the bridge verbs, and so on.

Thus, via the lexical entry of the bridge verb *glauben*, we get the following f-structure for (32), which is wellformed, unlike (34):

(36)

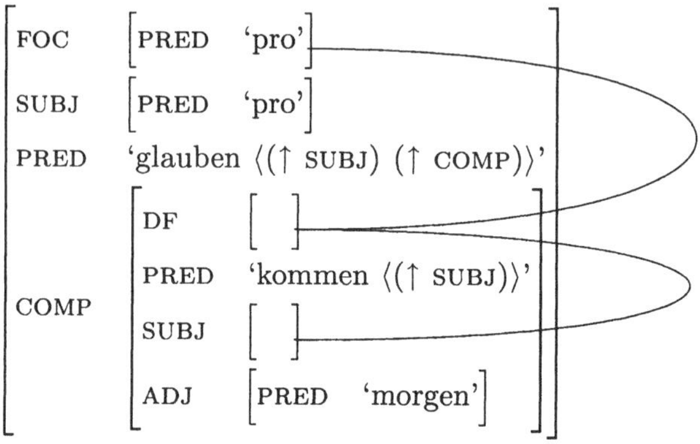


Since non-bridge verbs do not identify the DF with the DF of the complement clause, the relation between the empty category and its antecedent can't be established and extraction is ungrammatical.

(37) *Wer flüsterst du, kommt morgen?

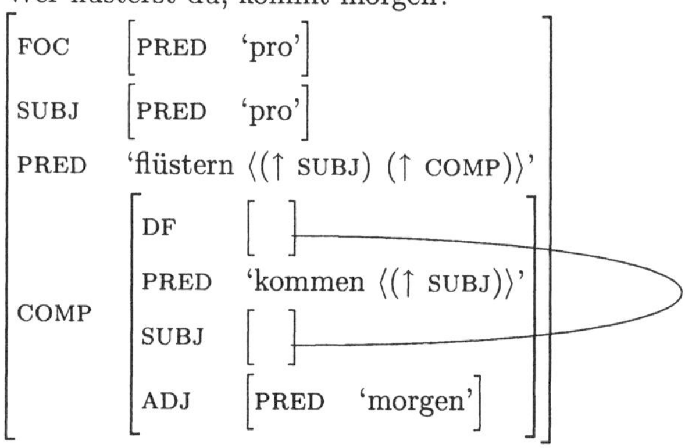


If there are intermediate clauses, extraction is only possible if all the intermediate clauses contain bridge verbs, i.e., only verbs which introduce the equation (↑ DF) = (↑ COMP DF). The result is that in every intermediate f-structure a DF occurs which is identified with the DF of the embedded clause (which results in cyclic identification of the DFs) although in c-structure no specifiers occur. For example:

(38) Wer glaubst du, meint der Peter, wird kommen?
who believe you means the Peter will come
'Who do you believe Peter thinks will come?'

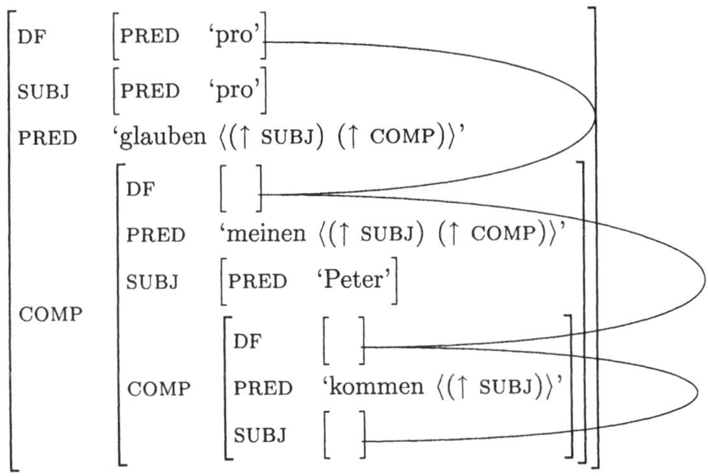


If there are intermediate clauses which do not contain bridge verbs, the cyclic identification of the within clause function with the extracted phrase is blocked. Hence examples like (39) are correctely ruled out:

(39) *Wen glaubst du, hat er geflüstert, hat der Hans gesehen?
whom believe you has he whispered has the H.-NOM seen

If the specifier of the embedded clause is lexically filled, then by functional uniqueness, the identification can't take place (see f-structure (27)).

The ungrammaticality of extraction out of an adjunct or subject clause is also accounted for, since the bridge verbs identify the DF only with the DF of their complement clause.

## 6.4 A Comparison of the Two Accounts

I have presented two approaches to modelling long distance dependencies in German. One uses inside-out functional uncertainty, reflecting the long distance dependency by means of indefinitely long attribute paths at f-structure. On the other approach, long distance dependencies are analyzed as lexically conditioned locally bounded dependencies which propagate cyclically.

On both accounts it is assumed that we need an empty category in the local clause (and only there) to guarantee the right predicate-argument relation. In both accounts the f-structure of the empty category and the f-structure of the antecedent are identified. Where the accounts differ is in the question of whether the empty category is linked to its antecedent directly (via functional uncertainty), or indirectly (via cyclic identification of intermediate DFs).

Now let us see whether there is any empirical evidence in favour of the one or the other account. I will investigate how the following phenomena can be handled within the two approaches: the distinction between bridge verbs and non-bridge verbs, Split NP constructions and extraction out of *dass*-clauses.

Since the cyclic account is lexically conditioned, it captures the distinction between bridge verbs and non-bridge verbs without further assumptions. Only bridge verbs contain the equation $(\uparrow\text{DF}) = (\uparrow\text{COMP DF})$ in their lexical entry. In contrast, the functional uncertainty approach as presented does not distinguish between bridge verbs. However, as Dalrymple (2001, p. 392) points out, with functional uncertainty this property can be captured by an off-path constraint. She assumes that non-bridge verbs specify the attribute LDD (for long distance dependencies) with the value '$-$' in their COMP. Hence, non-bridge verbs have the following equation in their lexical entry: $(\uparrow\text{COMP LDD}) = -$. By adding the off-path constraint $(\rightarrow \text{LDD} \neq -)$ to the BODY we can restrict the path so that it does not pass an f-structure containing the feature LDD $= -$:

(40)
$$\begin{array}{l} ((\{\text{XCOMP}, \text{COMP}\}^* \quad \text{GF}\uparrow) \quad \text{DF}) = \uparrow \\ \quad\quad \neg\,(\rightarrow \text{DF}) \\ \quad (\rightarrow \text{LDD}) \neq - \end{array}$$

The off-path constraint prevents extraction in examples like (35d), repeated below in (41) with its f-structure in (42), since the f-structure of the complement clause contains the feature LDD $= -$:

(41) *Was flüsterst du, hat der Hans gesehen?
what whisper you has the Hans seen

(42)
$$\left[\begin{array}{ll} \text{FOC} & [\text{PRED} \ \text{`pro'}] \\ \text{PRED} & \text{`flüstern} \langle(\uparrow \text{SUBJ})(\uparrow \text{COMP})\rangle\text{'} \\ \text{SUBJ} & [\text{PRED} \ \text{`pro'}] \\ \text{COMP} & \left[\begin{array}{ll} \text{SUBJ} & [\text{PRED} \ \text{`Hans'}] \\ \text{PRED} & \text{`sehen} \langle(\uparrow \text{SUBJ})(\uparrow \text{OBJ})\rangle\text{'} \\ \text{LDD} & - \\ \text{OBJ} & [\ ] \end{array}\right] \end{array}\right]$$

So both accounts are able to capture the distinction between bridge verbs and non-bridge verbs. However, the functional uncertainty approach seems more ad hoc, because the feature LDD has to be introduced especially to prevent extraction, while on the cyclic approach the syntactic function DF is a function which appears in embedded clauses independently of extraction.

A possible problem for the cyclic analysis is the so-called Split NP construction. According to the analysis by Kuhn (2001), the different parts of the split NP are mapped onto the same function. For example, in

(43) Bücher sieht Anna drei.
books sees Anna three
'(Speaking of) books, Anna sees three.'

(Kuhn 2001, p.177 (1)) both parts of the split NP behave syntactically like autonomous NPs, yet both NPs are mapped onto the OBJ-function of *sehen*. Hence, this construction shows that a single grammatical function can be realized in more than one c-structural position by independent phrases, as long as they are compatible in terms of instantiation. Given this, the cyclic analysis predicts that, with long-distance extraction, it should be possible for the lower part of the split NP to occupy intermediate DF-positions which are functionally identified. But in fact, this is not the case:

(44) a. *Bücher glaube ich, hat er gesagt, drei hat er gesehen.
books believe I has he said three has he seen.
b. *Bücher glaube ich, drei hat er gesagt, hat er gesehen.

The only grammatical configuration is where the nounless NP remains in the *Mittelfeld*:

(45) Bücher glaube ich, hat er gesagt, hat er drei gesehen.
books believe I has he said has he three seen.
'(Speaking of) books, I think he said he saw three.'

This problem does not arise on the functional uncertainty approach, since the occurrence of a DF in the intermediate clauses is prohibited by the off-path constraint.

However, it appears that there is an independent reason for the ungrammaticality of (44a) and (44b). As Kuhn (2001, p. 191, (18)) observes, the two NPs in (43) cannot be exchanged:

(46) *Drei sieht Anna Bücher.

Since this example involves only local topicalization, the fact that it is ungrammatical suggests that there is a general constraint on split NPs against the nounless NP (i.e. *drei*) occupying the specifier position. This may have an independent syntactic or semantic explanation; see Kuhn (2001) for a semantic account in terms of linear logic.[13]

Recapitulating, while the Split-NP construction is compatible with the functional uncertainty approach, at first glance it seems to be problematics for the cyclic account. But closer inspection suggests that the apparent wrong predictions may well have an independent explanation. In short, this construction, too, does not decide between the two analyses.

Let us turn to the third phenomenon, extraction out of *dass*-clauses. It is well-known that German dialects differ with respect to the grammaticality of this construction. On the cyclic account it is easy to capture this difference, as we will now see.

In dialects such as Bavarian extraction out of a *dass*-clause is possible, while in Standard German extraction out of a *dass*-clause is ungrammatical. Hence in Bavarian but not in Standard German, clauses like (47) are grammatical:

(47) #Wen$_i$ sagst du, dass e$_i$ der Hans liebt?
who-ACC say you that the Hans-NOM loves
'Who are you saying that Hans loves?'

This correlates with the fact that in Bavarian CP-Spec and $C^0$ can be occupied simultaneously, while this is ungrammatical in Standard German:

(48) #Ich sage nicht, wen dass der Hans liebt.
I say not, who-ACC that the Hans-NOM loves
'I'm not saying who Hans loves.'

This shows that in Bavarian the complementizer *dass* is compatible with a DF in the same clause. The cyclic analysis therefore predicts that in such dialects it is possible to extract out of a *dass*-clause, since on this analysis a DF is introduced by the lexical entry of the bridge verbs (cf. the optional equation on page 113) which is compatible with the occurrence of *dass*.[14] In the literature it is often assumed that the lexical entry of the declarative complementizer (i.e., *dass*, *that*, etc.) contains the feature ($\uparrow$ TYPE) = DECL or ($\uparrow$ MOOD) = DECL[15]. So we

[13]The conclusion that the nounless NP my not occupy the specifier position is my interpretation of the data; Kuhn merely observes that the two NPs cannot be "swapped".

[14]While this correlation is predicted by the cyclic analysis, it is not clear whether all German dialects which allow extraction out of a *dass*-clause also allow CP-Spec and $C^0$ to be filled simultaneously.

[15]See e.g. Bresnan (2001, p. 406), Falk (2001, p. 217); Bresnan uses the attribute

get the following f-structure for (47):

(49)

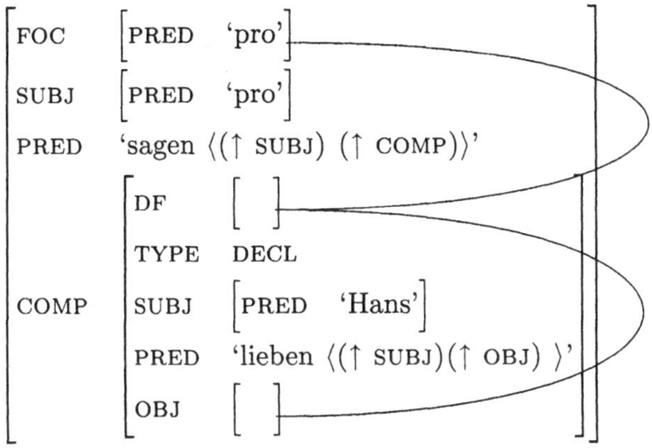


The cyclic account also correctly predicts that in such dialects extraction is ungrammatical if the specifier position is lexically filled, since then the f-structures of the DFs can't be identified:

(50) *Den Hans sage ich nicht, wer dass liebt.
the Hans-ACC say I not who-NOM that knows
*'Hans, I'm not saying who loves.'

Since Standard German does not allow CP-Spec and $C^0$ to be simultaneously occupied, this implies that the complementizer *dass* is incompatible with a DF in the same clause. Hence the cyclic analysis correctly predicts that in Standard German both a lexically filled DF as well as extraction out a of *dass*-clause are ungrammatical. This can be captured by the following lexical entry for *dass* in Standard German:

(51) dass C (↑ TYPE) = DECL
¬ (↑ DF)

In Bavarian, in contrast, the lexical entry of *dass* lacks the negative constraint ¬ (↑ DF).

On the inside-out functional uncertainty approach, since the long-distance dependency is established directly, the prediction is that extraction out of *dass*-clauses should also be possible. Thus, dialects like Bavarian are straightforwardly accounted for; however, additional constraints are required to prevent the extraction out of *dass*-clauses in Standard German. But again, this is possible with an off-path constraint. If in Standard German the complementizer *dass* introduces the feature (↑ TYPE) = DECL in the f-structure of the complement clause,

---

MOOD and Falk TYPE.

then extraction out of a *dass*-clause can be prevented by adding the off-path constraint ($\rightarrow$ TYPE) $\neq$ DECL to the extraction path.

(52) (({ XCOMP, COMP}* GF $\uparrow$) DF) = $\uparrow$
$\neg$ ($\rightarrow$ DF)
($\rightarrow$ LDD)= $\neq$ –
($\rightarrow$ TYPE) $\neq$ DECL

Summarizing, with respect to extraction out of a *dass*-clause it appears once again that the two approaches are equally capable of capturing the data: on the cyclic approach the lexical entry of *dass* prevents the occurrence of DF, hence blocking extraction (in Standard German); and with functional uncertainty extraction is prevented by requiring the path not to contain the feature ($\uparrow$ TYPE) = DECL. Notice, however, that embedded V2-clauses are also declarative, but do allow for extraction. This implies, on the functional uncertainty approach, that V2-clauses can't carry the feature ($\uparrow$ TYPE) = DECL, but have to be distinguished from interrogative clauses by means of a different feature. In other words, it is incumbent on the functional uncertainty approach to motivate such a distinction. On the cyclic analysis, in contrast, reference is made directly to *dass*, not to clausal features, so this issue does not arise.

## 6.5 Summary

In this chapter two analyses of long distance dependencies in German were presented. Both analyses assume an empty category in the local clause. According to one analysis, long distance dependencies are captured by means of iterating local dependencies, which is conditioned by a lexical property of bridge-verbs, by which the DF of a higher clause is identified with DF of the immediate embedded clause. Further restrictions can be encoded in the lexical entry of the complementizer by making reference to the grammatical function DF. According to the other analysis, the dependency is established directly in terms of unbounded attribute paths, by inside-out functional uncertainty. Restrictions are captured by off-path constraints by making reference to the grammatical function DF and features introduced in the lexical entries of the complementizer and the non-bridge-verbs. A question raised by the functional uncertainty approach is whether these features are independently motivated. The absence of independent evidence for these features favours the cyclic approach; nevertheless, it does not seem warranted at this time to definitively reject or accept either approach.

On both accounts the extractable functions are not limited, i.e., all GFs are allowed as extractable functions, as BOTTOM-functions. But as we have seen, on Kaplan and Zaenen (1989)'s analysis of English topicalization, sentential complements were excluded from the extractable functions. Webelhuth (1992) observed similar facts in German. In the following chapter these and related facts will be discussed and analyzed.

# 7

# Distribution of Sentential Arguments

This chapter is concerned with the distribution of sentential arguments, in particular, how their occurrence in sentence-initial position can be captured. As we will see, the distribution of sentential arguments is closely related to their grammatical function.

In Kaplan and Zaenen (1989) an analysis is proposed for the fact that in English some verbs allow the topicalization of their sentential arguments, while with other verbs this is ungrammatical. Similar facts were observed in German by Webelhuth (1992). To see if we can apply the analysis of Kaplan and Zaenen to the German data as well, I will briefly discuss their analysis in the following section.[1] After presenting the relevant German data, in section 7.3 I examine several previous analyses of these data. In sections 7.4–7.6 I then develop my analyses of the phenomena.

## 7.1 Topicalization of Sentential Arguments in English

As we have seen in the previous chapter, Kaplan and Zaenen formulate the following equation for English topicalization:

(1) $(\uparrow \textsc{top}) = (\uparrow \{\textsc{comp}, \textsc{xcomp}\}^*(\textsc{gf}-\textsc{comp}))$

They assume that all grammatical functions are extractable except COMP (i.e. except sentential complements). Kaplan and Zaenen (p. 34 (47)) provide the following VP rule for English:

(2) VP $\rightarrow$

| V | (NP) | (NP) | PP* | ... | (S′) |
|---|---|---|---|---|---|
| | $(\uparrow \textsc{obj}) = \downarrow$ | $(\uparrow \textsc{obj2}) = \downarrow$ | $(\uparrow (\downarrow \textsc{pcase})) = \downarrow$ | | $(\uparrow \textsc{comp}) = \downarrow$ |

This rule is formulated in accordance with the constraints on the possible associations between syntactic categories and grammatical functions proposed by Bresnan (1982); in Bresnan (1994) these constraints

[1] Cf. also Kaplan and Bresnan (1982), Bresnan (1995a) for related analyses.

are captured by the following principle:

(3) If C is a c-structure position restricted to subjects or objects, then C is nominal. (Bresnan 1994, p. 104 (88))

Grimshaw (1982) also argues that there is a correlation between category and function. She proposes that only nominals can be assigned the OBJ function; for sentential complements she introduces the function CLAUSE. She bases this on an asymmetry she notes in the distribution of nominal and sentential arguments in English: there are transitive verbs whose complement must be realized by a clausal constituent and not by a noun phrase, but there are no verbs whose subject can only be realized by a clause. That is, all verbs that semantically select a proposition as the subject argument can realize this argument either as an NP or as a clause. Grimshaw cites as examples *pray*, for the complement, and *surprise* for the subject (the following examples are from Grimshaw 1982, p. 47–48 (35)–(36)):

(4) John prayed that Reagan would resign (*and I prayed that too).

(5) a. That Reagan resigned surprised everyone.
  b. Reagan resigned. That surprises me.

To account for this asymmetry, Grimshaw proposes that both nominal and sentential phrases can be assigned the function SUBJ, but only noun phrases can be assigned the function OBJ; sentential complements have the function CLAUSE (or COMP in the terminology of Kaplan and Zaenen).

Kaplan and Zaenen claim that with these two assumptions, namely that there are general constraints on the possible association between categories and grammatical functions and that COMP is excluded from the BOTTOM-functions, contrasts such as the following can be explained (p. 34–35 (49)–(52)):[2]

(6) a. Kevin persuaded Roger that these hamburgers were worth buying.
  b. *That these hamburgers were worth buying, Kevin persuaded Roger.

(7) a. Louise told me that Denny was mean to her.
  b. That Denny was mean to her, Louise told me (already).

With both verbs the sentence-final position of the *that*-clause is grammatical, but only *tell* allows the topicalization of the *that*-clause.

[2]The examples are from Stowell (1981).

According to Kaplan and Zaenen this is related to the fact that only *tell* can take a nominal complement, while a nominal complement with *persuade* is ungrammatical (p. 35 (53)–(54)):

(8) a. *Kevin persuaded Roger the news.
 b. Louise told me the story.

That is, they assume the following subcategorization frames in the lexical entries of these verbs (p. 35 (55)):

(9) tell: a. (↑ PRED) = 'tell ⟨(↑ SUBJ) (↑ OBJ) (↑ OBJ2)⟩'
 or
 b. (↑ PRED) = 'tell ⟨(↑ SUBJ) (↑ OBJ) (↑ COMP)⟩'

(10) persuade: (↑ PRED) = 'persuade ⟨(↑ SUBJ) (↑ OBJ) (↑ COMP)⟩'

Topicalization of the *that*-clause is possible with *tell*, since according to (9a) the function OBJ2 ($\text{OBJ}_\theta$ following more recent terminology) can be chosen as BOTTOM. On f-structure nothing prevents the *that*-clause, which is annotated with a DF in the matrix clause, from being functionally identified (via functional uncertainty) with the OBJ2-function:[3]

(11)
$$\left[\begin{array}{ll} \text{DF} & \left[\text{“that Denny was mean to her”}\right] \\ \text{PRED} & \text{‘tell}\ \langle(\uparrow \text{SUBJ})\ (\uparrow \text{OBJ})\ (\uparrow \text{OBJ2})\rangle\text{’} \\ \text{SUBJ} & \left[\text{PRED}\ \ \text{‘Louise’}\right] \\ \text{OBJ} & \left[\text{PRED}\ \ \text{‘me’}\right] \\ \text{OBJ2} & \left[\ \ \right] \end{array}\right]$$

When the clause occurs in sentence-final position, as in (7a), the alternative subcategorization frame of *tell* (9b) has to be chosen, since the c-structure position of the CP in sentence-final position is annotated with COMP.

Topicalization of the *that*-clause of *persuade* is ungrammatical, since *persuade* does not subcategorize alternatively for an OBJ2. And according to (1), COMP is excluded from the extractable functions. In sentence final position, however, the *that*-clause is fine with *persuade*, given its subcategorization frame (10).

Similar facts were observed in German by Webelhuth (1992). Topicalization of the sentential complement is only possible with verbs

[3]With outside-in functional uncertainty OBJ2 is not represented on c-structure at all. With inside-out functional uncertainty the OBJ2 would be annotated to an NP which dominates the empty category.

which allow their complement to be realized either by a CP or a DP. According to Webelhuth this is the reason for the following contrast:

(12) a. Dass Hans krank ist, glaube ich.
that Hans ill is believe I
'That Hans is ill, I (do) believe.'

b. *Dass Hans krank ist, ärgere ich mich.
that Hans ill is, annoy I REFL
'That Hans is ill, I'm annoyed.'

In the following sections I will look at the German data more carefully. I will show that excluding sentential arguments from the BOTTOM functions in German—that is, claiming that only those verbs allow topicalization of the sentential complement which subcategorize for either an OBJ (hence a DP) or a COMP (hence a CP)—not only misses an important generalization but also does not account for all the facts and I will propose an alternative analysis.[4]

## 7.2 German Data

Sentential arguments (SA) in German can appear as an alternative realization of a DP in the function of a SUBJ, an OBJ or an $OBJ_\theta$ or to a PP (or pronominal adverb) in the function $OBL_\theta$.[5] The following examples illustrate these generalizations.

(13) a. Ihn hat gewundert, dass die Erde rund ist.
him has surprised that the earth round is
'It surprised him that the earth is round.'

b. Ihn hat das/es gewundert.
him has that/it-SUBJ surprised
'That surprised him.'

(14) a. Er hat nicht gewusst, dass die Erde rund ist.
he has not known that the earth round is
'He didn't know that the earth is round."

[4]This proposal is based on Berman (1996).

[5]The functions $OBL_\theta$ and $OBJ_\theta$ correspond to what traditional German grammar calls *prepositional object* and either *dative*, *genitive*, or *accusative object* (depending on which case is lexically selected), respectively. I will use both the LFG and the traditional grammatical terminology.

Sentential arguments as an alternative to a dative object-DP, as in (i) (Hans Altmann, lecture notes; NB: *sich widersetzen* takes a dative object-DP), are extremely rare, for reasons that remain to be elucidated.

(i) Sie widersetzte sich, ins Freie gebracht zu werden.
she resisted REFL into-the open brought to be
'She resisted being brought into the open.'

Clauses as an alternative realization to a genitive DP are more frequent.

b. Er hat das/es nicht gewusst.
he has that/it-OBJ not known
'He didn't know that.'

(15) a. Sie war sich bewusst, dass die Erde rund ist.
she was REFL aware that the earth round is
'She was aware that the earth is round.'
b. Sie war sich dessen bewusst.
she was REFL of-it-$OBJ_\theta$ aware
'She was aware of it.'

(16) a. Sie hat sich gewundert, dass die Erde rund ist.
she has REFL surprised that the earth round is
'She was surprised that the earth is round.'
b. Sie hat sich über das/darüber gewundert.
she has REFL about that/about-it$OBL_\theta$ surprised
'She was surprised about that/it.'

SA can occur both sentence-finally and sentence-initially.[6] However, while sentence-initial SA that stand for a subject or accusative object can be topicalized or left-dislocated, SA which stand for a genitive or prepositional object are obligatorily left-dislocated (cf. Altmann 1981, p. 172):

(17) Dass die Erde rund ist, (das) hat ihn gewundert.
that the earth round is that-SUBJ has him surprised
'That the earth is round surprised him.'

(18) Dass die Erde rund ist, (das) hat er nicht gewusst.
that the earth round is that-OBJ has he not known
'That the earth is round, he didn't know.'

(19) Dass die Erde rund ist, *(dessen) war sie sich bewusst.
that the earth round is, that-GEN was she herself aware
'That the earth is round, of that she wasn't aware.'

(20) Dass die Erde rund ist, *(darüber) hat sie sich gewundert.
That the earth round is it-about has she herself surprised
'That the earth is round she was surprised about that.'

Hence we can state generally that all SA can be both extraposed and left-dislocated. But only some SA can be topicalized.

[6]Their occurrence in medial positions within the sentence (the *Mittelfeld*) is, if possible at all, extremely marked (see section 7.5 for further discussion).

## 7.3 Previous Analyses

### 7.3.1 Webelhuth (1992)

Webelhuth (1992) assumes that sentential arguments are base-generated in the *Nachfeld* (postfield). The verb theta-marks CPs to the right. If a SA is topicalized or occurs in the *Mittelfeld*, then it must form a chain with an empty DP that is licensed by a lexical element. Webelhuth calls this *The Sentence Trace Universal* (Webelhuth 1992, p. 94):

(21) **The Sentence Trace Universal**
Sentences can only bind DP-traces, i.e., traces with the categorial specification [+N, −V].

According to Webelhuth it follows from this principle that verbs such as *sich wundern* and *sich ärgern*, which do not subcategorize for DP in addition to CP, do not permit their sentential complements to topicalize (cf. the examples (118–120G) from Webelhuth (1992, p. 104f.):

(22) Ich wundere mich [$_{\text{CP}}$ dass Hans krank ist]
I am-surprised REFL that Hans sick is

(23) * Ich wundere mich [$_{\text{DP}}$ das]
I am-surprised REFL that

(24) * [$_{\text{CP}}$ Dass Hans krank ist]$_i$ wundere ich mich [$_{\text{DP}}$ $e$]$_i$
that Hans sick is am-surprised I REFL

This stands in contrast to verbs such as *glauben* and *wissen*, which can take either CP or DP:

(25) Er glaubt nicht, [$_{\text{CP}}$ dass sie kommt]
he believes not that she comes
'He doesn't believe that she's coming.'

(26) Er glaubt [$_{\text{DP}}$ das] nicht
He believes that not
'He doesn't believe that.'

(27) [$_{\text{CP}}$ Dass sie kommt]$_i$, glaubt er nicht [$_{\text{DP}}$ $e$]$_i$

Webelhuth's account, however, provides no explanation for why sentential arguments related to a subcategorized genitive object position also cannot undergo topicalization (cf. (19)), since the trace is evidently a DP:[7]

[7]Similarly, in the analysis of Kaplan and Zaenen (1989) it would be unexplained why a topicalized clause annotated with a DF can't be identified with an OBJ$_\theta$ (in their terminology with an OBJ2).

(28) *[Dass die Erde rund ist] vergewisserte er sich [$_{DP}$ *e*]
that the earth round is made-sure he REFL

Moreover, Webelhuth doesn't discuss the fact that the verbs he cites as taking CP but not DP also take PP:

(29) Ich wundere mich über das/darüber.
I am-surprised REFL about that/about-it.

Hence, all the *dass*-clauses that Webelhuth cites as not undergoing topicalization do have an alternative non-sentential realization, not as DP, but as a PP or a pronominal adverb.

In light of these facts about German, let us look again at the English data and Kaplan and Zaenen's analysis. Recall that Kaplan and Zaenen claim that verbs like *persuade* subcategorize only for a COMP (hence only for a sentential complement). Note, however, that the complement can also be realized as a PP:

(30) a. Kevin persuaded Roger that these hamburgers were worth buying.
b. Kevin persuaded Roger of it/that.

The subcategorization frame of *persuade* should therefore be the following, instead of (10):

(31) persuade:
(↑ PRED) = 'persuade ⟨(↑ SUBJ) (↑ OBJ) (↑ COMP)⟩'
or
(↑ PRED) = 'persuade ⟨(↑ SUBJ) (↑ OBJ) (↑ $OBL_\theta$)⟩'

According to this lexical entry it should be possible to topicalize the *that*-clause and identify it with the within clause function $OBL_\theta$. But in fact, this results in ungrammaticality:

(32) *That these hamburgers were worth buying, Kevin persuaded Roger of.

Interestingly, exactly this analysis is proposed by Kaplan and Zaenen for the verb *think*. That is, they assign *think* the following two alternative lexical entries:

(33) a. think: (↑ PRED) = 'think ⟨(↑ SUBJ) (↑ COMP)⟩'
b. think: (↑ PRED) = 'think ⟨(↑ SUBJ) (↑ $OBL_{of}$)⟩'

As evidence for this they cite the following contrast:

(34) a. That he might be wrong he didn't think of.
b. *That he might bc wrong hc didn't think.

Example (34a) corresponds to the lexical entry (33b); the BOTTOM is (↑ $\text{OBL}_{of}$) and topicalization is permitted. Example (34b) corresponds to the lexical entry (33a); COMP is excluded form the BOTTOM functions, hence (34b) is ungrammatical.

It is not clear why *persuade* and *think* differ with respect to topicalization of their clausal complement. Note, however, that even with *think* the *persuade*-pattern appears to be possible, as in the following contrast (Steve Berman, p.c.):

(35) a. *That he might be wrong he didn't think of for a moment.
b. That he might be wrong he didn't think for a moment.

Thus, the status of the data is not clear and this makes it inappropriate to draw conclusions about the analysis of Kaplan and Zaenen. What we can conclude, however, is that even verbs which do not allow the topicalization of their sentential complement may also subcategorize for an alternative function to COMP.

The preceding observations may cast new light on the data discussed by Grimshaw. Recall that she cited *pray* as a verb that takes only a clausal and not a nominal object; her example is repeated here:

(36) John prayed that Reagan would resign (*and I prayed that too).

Notice, however, that the object of *pray* can also be realized by a PP:

(37) John prayed that Reagan would resign (and I prayed for that too).

If it is assumed that the sentence embedded by *pray* has the function of a prepositional object (i.e. $\text{OBL}_{\theta}$), then the contrast observed by Grimshaw between the syntactic realizations of the subject and the object functions would not require appealing to a CLAUSE function. In German prepositional object sentences, the proform is an adverb incorporating the preposition (cf. archaic English *The man whereof I spoke*).[8] The correct generalization would instead be that all sentential arguments, not just sentential subjects, can be instantiated by a proform. As a consequence, all sentential arguments would have the same function as their corresponding nominal or prepositional counterparts,

[8]Bresnan (2001, p. 22) claims that the English verb *care* does not allow for a nominal OBJ but only for a sentential complement, citing the following contrast:

(i) I don't care *that languages are learnable.*

(ii) *I don't care *that.*

However, *care* can also take a PP as a complement:

(iii) I don't care *about it.*

On the other hand, there is arguably a semantic difference between *care* and *care about*, which might mean that (i) and (iii) involve distinct lexical items.

namely SUBJ, OBJ, $\text{OBJ}_\theta$ and $\text{OBL}_\theta$.

What the function of sentential complements is remains a very complex and controversial issue.[9] Notwithstanding this, for German I will tentatively assume that sentential arguments and their corresponding nominal or prepositional arguments do have the same function (this view was also taken in Berman and Frank 1996). The advantage of this analysis is that we can differentiate between different sentential arguments, just as in the case of nominal arguments.

Starting in section 7.4 I will therefore present an alternative analysis of the distribution of sentential arguments in German, which is independent of the assumption that verbs in German may have different subcategorization frames depending on the categorial realization and the structural position of their arguments. But first we conclude the discussion of previous analyses.

### 7.3.2 Büring (1995b)

Büring (1995, p. 373) also argues that the verbs which according to Webelhuth take only a CP and not a DP complement, are actually verbs which subcategorize for a PP. Büring assumes that sentential arguments are base-generated to the left of the verb and can move into the *Nachfeld*. He proposes that "verbs that select for a PP may in turn contain a clause." In this case the CP is always embedded within an NP and a PP, even when the heads of both of these are phonetically empty (Büring 1995, p. 375):

(38) ... $[_{\text{VP}}\ [_{\text{PP}}\ e\ [_{\text{NP}}\ [_{\text{N}}\ e]\ t_1]]$ gefreut$]$ $[_{\text{CP}}$ dass ...$]_1$

Büring thus derives the restriction on topicalization of sentential arguments in structures like (38) from the fact that topicalization is subject to the same locality conditions as, for example, relativization and movement out of noun complements.

However, this analysis raises several questions and problems:

- Why can't the PP be empty when the SA is not extraposed, i.e., when it remains in the *Mittelfeld*?[10] With a phonetically realized PP, in contrast, the SA can remain in the *Mittelfeld*:

---

[9] See for example the discussion on the LFG mailing list following the 1996 LFG conference, starting with the posting at <`http://listserv.linguistlist.org/cgi-bin/wa?A2=ind96&L=lfg&P=11516`>.

[10] Büring himself notes this unresolved problem of his analysis, cf. his footnote 5.

(39) a. Ich habe mich [$_{PP}$ darüber, [dass sie gekommen ist]],
I have myself about-that that she come is
gefreut.
pleased
'I was happy that she came (about her having come).'

b. *Ich habe mich [$_{PP}$ *e* [$_{NP}$ [$_{N}$ *e*] dass sie gekommen ist]] gefreut.

- Why can't an empty PP containing the nonextraposed SA be topicalized?[11] This would generate precisely the kind of sentences that Büring's analysis is intended to rule out, namely, topicalization of a prepositional object SA:

(40) * [$_{PP}$ *e* [$_{NP}$ [$_{N}$ *e*] Dass sie gekommen ist]] habe ich mich gefreut.

- On the other hand, why is it possible in just this case to topicalize a nonfinite SA (in contrast to a finite SA), since according to Büring's analysis infinitive SA should, like finite SA, be embedded under a PP and an NP and be subject to the same locality conditions?[12] In the following examples, the verbs take both a clausal argument and a PP:[13]

(41) Unser Versteck zu verraten werde ich mich hüten.
our hideaway to reveal will I myself guard
'I will be careful not to reveal our hideaway.'

---

[11]Hubert Haider (p.c) drew this problem to my attention.

[12]With verbs that take a prepositional object there are numerous properties that influence the occurrence of correlative pronouns, which also may depend on whether the SA is realized as a finite or a nonfinite sentence; for discussion see Breindl (1989).

[13]It should be noted that these constructions involve so-called incoherent, i.e. fully clausal, infinitives. According to Haider (1993a, p. 251), building on Bech (1983), a coherent construction is only possible if the infinitive is an internal, structural argument. Control verbs that take infinitive clauses in the function of a prepositional object, such as *verpflichten* ('to commit') and *verzichten* ('to renounce'), do not exhibit the properties of optionally coherent infinitives (monosentential *Mittelfeld*, verb complex). For example, preposing a pronoun to the so-called Wackernagel position of the matrix sentence is not possible, unlike with a coherent construction ((ii) is from Haider 1993a, p. 250 (55-c)):

(i) *... weil ihr der Hans sich zu helfen verpflichtet.
because her the Hans himself to help committed.
'... because Hans committed himself to helping her.'

(ii) *... dass sie Max nicht wiederzusehen verzichtete.
that she Max not meet renounced
'... that she refrained from meeting Hans.'

(42) Dass ich unser Versteck verrate *(davor) werde ich mich
that I our hideaway reveal against-it will I myself
hüten.
guard
'I will be careful not to reveal our hideaway.'

(43) Zu kommen hat er sich verpflichtet.
to come has he himself committed
'He committed himself to coming.'

(44) Dass er kommt *(dazu) hat er sich verpflichtet
that he comes to-it has he himself committed
'He committed himself to coming.'

Moreover, Büring's contention that structures like (38) (i.e., prepositional object SA, to use the traditional grammatical term) always constitute extraction islands is not correct, as the following examples show:[14]

(45) Wen bittet er uns, dass wir besuchen sollen?
who-ACC requests he us that we visit should
'Who is he asking us to visit?'

(46) Wen hat man ihn gezwungen zu heiraten?
who-ACC has one him forced to marry
'Who was he forced to marry?'

They are islands precisely when a correlative prepositional proform occurs in the *Mittelfeld*:[15]

(47) *Wen bittet er uns darum, dass wir besuchen sollen?
who-ACC asks he us about-it that we visit should

(48) *Wen hat man ihn dazu gezwungen zu heiraten?
who-ACC has one him to-it forced to marry

This contrast and the differential behavior of finite and nonfinite SA show that Büring's proposal of obligatory embedding in a PP cannot be right.

### 7.3.3 Dalrymple and Lodrup (2000)

Dalrymple and Lodrup (2000) propose an LFG analysis of complement clauses in several languages, including German. They claim that restricting the function of complement clauses to COMP is inadequate, and that finer distinctions among different grammatical functions are

[14]This implies that $\text{OBJ}_\theta$ is also an admissible BODY function.

[15]Concerning the internal structure of these proforms, see e.g. Bayer (1994, p. 27ff.).

necessary to describe the syntax of complement clauses. They propose that there are two grammatical functions a clausal complement can bear to a predicate, namely COMP or OBJ. While in some languages all clausal complements have the same grammatical function, in so-called mixed languages clausal complements can vary between OBJ and COMP, depending on the requirements of the matrix predicate.[16] Dalrymple and Lodrup claim that German (like English and Swedish) is a so-called mixed language.

According to Dalrymple and Lodrup *glauben* (*believe*) is a verb which subcategorizes for an OBJ, while *sich freuen* (*be happy*) subcategorizes for a COMP (Dalrymple and Lodrup 2000, p.4 (3), (4)):

(49) a. Ich glaube, dass die Erde rund ist. (OBJ)
I believe that the earth round is
'I believe that the earth is round.'

b. Ich freue mich, dass Hans krank ist. (COMP)
I am-glad REFL that Hans ill is
'I'm happy that Hans is ill.'

Let us look at some evidence they give in favour of their claim:

- **Alternation with NP object**
  Dalrymple and Lodrup claim that verbs that take a clausal OBJ also take a nominal OBJ as an alternative. In contrast, verbs which take COMP clausal complements do not allow nominal proforms (Dalrymple and Lodrup 2000, *ibid.*):

(50) a. Ich glaube, dass die Erde rund ist.
I believe that the earth round is

b. Ich glaube es.
I believe it

(51) a. Ich freue mich, dass Hans krank ist.
I am-glad REFL that Hans ill is

b. *Ich freue mich es/das.
I am-glad REFL it/that

- **Coordination**
  If an embedded clause can be coordinated with an NP OBJ, the clause also bears the OBJ function, as in (52a).[17] They claim that a

[16]Recall that Kaplan and Zaenen (1989) also assumed that some clauses can be identified with the OBJ-function, but only if the clause was topicalized. In contrast, Dalrymple and Lodrup assume that a complement clause can be an OBJ also in extraposed position.

[17]This is an instance of the widely accepted generalization that conjoined constituents must have the same grammatical function. See also Berman and Frank

PP $\text{OBL}_\theta$ can't be coordinated with a clause (Dalrymple and Lodrup 2000, p.5 (6), p.14 (45)), citing example ( 52b):

(52) a. Er vergaß [die Verabredung] (NP OBJ) und [dass es
he forgot the appointment and that it
wichtig war, pünktlich zu sein] (clausal OBJ)
important is punctual to be
'He forgot the appointment and that it importantant to be on time.'

b. *Ich informierte ihn [dass Hans krank ist] (COMP) und
I informed him that Hans ill is and
[über die Situation] (PP $\text{OBJ}_\theta$)
about the situation.

- **Passive**
Assuming that COMP is a restricted function and OBJ is an unrestricted function, Dalrymple and Lodrup predict that the OBJ can be realized as a SUBJ in passive clause, while COMP can't alternate with SUBJ (Dalrymple and Lodrup 2000, p.6 (9), (10)):

(53) a. Dass die Erde rund ist, wurde nicht geglaubt.
that the earth round is was not believed
'(The claim) that the earth is round was not believed.'

b. *Dass Hans krank ist, wurde ihn nicht informiert.
that Hans ill is was him not informed

- **Unbounded Dependencies**
Dalrymple and Lodrup claim that an OBJ arguments can enter in an unbounded dependency, while a COMP argument can't enter in a unbounded dependency in German (Dalrymple and Lodrup 2000, p.6 (13), (14)):

(54) a. Dass Hans krank ist, glaube ich.
that Hans ill is believe I
'That Hans is ill, I do believe.'

b. *Dass Hans krank ist, freue ich mich.
that Hans ill ist, am-glad I REFL

Above I defended the claim that sentential arguments and their corresponding nominal or prepositional arguments do have the same function, either SUBJ, OBJ, $\text{OBJ}_\theta$ or $\text{OBL}_\theta$. Let us re-examine the data cited by Dalrymple and Lodrup on the basis of this assumption.

(1996) for further German examples.

- **Alternation with NP object**
  As we saw in section 7.2, verbs take different proforms depending on their subcategorization frame. In particular, verbs that take prepositional objects (i.e., which bear the function OBL$_\theta$) take a PP (or the corresponding pronominal adverb); *sich freuen* is such a verb:

(55) Ich freue mich über das/darüber.
I am-glad REFL about that/about-it

My claim is therefore that in Dalrymple and Lodrup's example (49b) the clausal complement has the same function as the PP or proform in (55), namely OBL$_\theta$ and not COMP.

- **Coordination**
  Dalrymple and Lodrup cite the ungrammaticality of (52b) as evidence against the clause being an OBL$_\theta$. Notice, however, that if we reverse the order of the conjuncts the example becomes grammatical:

(56) Ich informierte ihn [über die Situation] und [dass Hans krank ist].
I informed him about the situation and that Hans ill is

Moreover, Dalrymple and Lodrup take the grammaticality of (52a) as evidence that the clause can bear an OBJ. But again, reversing order of the NP and clausal complement results in ungrammaticality:

(57) *Er vergaß [dass es wichtig war, pünktlich zu sein] und [die Verabredung].
he forgot that it important was punctual to be and the appointment

It is plausible that this is due to the independent fact that finite argument clauses are generally unacceptable in the *Mittelfeld.* Note that if the clause occurs sentence-finally, as in (52a) and (56), it can be analyzed as extraposed. In addition, note that by the coordination test, (56) represents an argument that clauses may have the function OBL$_\theta$.

- **Passive**
  Dalrymple and Lodrup's predication with respect to passive carry over to the assumption that the clause with verbs like *sich freuen* bears the function OBL$_\theta$, since OBL$_\theta$ is also restricted [+r]. So the fact that the clause can't be the SUBJ of a passive does not provide evidence for COMP.

- **Unbounded Dependencies**
  My account of the data in (54) requires a more extended development, which is undertaken in the following section. We will see that

there is an explanation based on the assumption that clauses bear the same grammatical function as there nominal counterparts, thus answering Dalrymple and Lodrup's argument. This together with the preceding points means we can account for the behaviour of clausal complements without appealing to the additional function COMP.

## 7.4 Topicalization vs. Left Dislocation of Sentential Arguments

This section develops an LFG analysis of topicalization as left dislocation based on Oppenrieder (1991, p. 290-295), and Koster (1978). In section 7.2 it was shown that all types of SA can be left-dislocated, that is, occur sentence-initially with a resumptive pronoun in the corresponding function occupying the *Vorfeld* position. The examples (17)-(20) are repeated here for convenience:

(58) Dass die Erde rund ist, (das) hat ihn gewundert.
that the earth round is that has him surprised
'That the earth is round surprised him.'

(59) Dass die Erde rund ist, (das) hat er nicht gewusst.
that the earth round is that has he not known
'That the earth is round, he didn't know.'

(60) Dass die Erde rund ist, *(dessen) war sie sich bewusst.
that the earth round is, it-GEN was she herself aware
'That the earth is round, of that she wasn't aware.'

(61) Dass die Erde rund ist, *(darüber) hat sie sich gewundert.
that the earth round is it-about has she herself be surprised
'That the earth is round she was surprised about that.'

Again, notice that with genitive and prepositional object SA, as in (60) and (61), the resumptive pronoun is obligatory, while with nominative and accusative SA it is optional.

In this connection it is significant that German is a Topic Drop language; that is, a constituent in the *Vorfeld*—and only in the *Vorfeld*—that bears the discourse function of topic may be phonetically unrealized (see Huang 1984 and Oppenrieder 1991). The following examples are from Huang (1984, p.547 (49)-(50)) (*e* represents the phonetically unrealized topic):

(62) *e* hab ihn schon gesehen.
have him already seen

(63) *e* hab ich schon gesehen.
have I already seen

(64) *Ihn hab *e* schon gesehen.

Crucially, Topic Drop is permitted only with subjects or accusative objects; prepositional, genitive, and dative topics cannot be dropped:

(65) *(Darüber) hab' ich mich gewundert.
about-it have I myself surprised
'About that I was surprised.'

(66) *(Dessen) rühmt er sich immer.
it-GEN is proud of he himself always
'Of that he is always proud.'

(67) *(Mir) hilft keiner.
me-DAT helps nobody

The conclusion for the analysis of clauses in sentence-initial position is obvious: all sentence-initial SA are obligatorily left-dislocated. With SA related to the subject or object, the resumptive pronoun need not be present, in accordance with the conditions on Topic Drop (Oppenrieder 1991, p. 292).

This analysis represents a restricted version of the hypothesis of Koster (1978), according to which all root sentences have to be analyzed as left dislocation structures, with deletion of the resumptive pronoun being obligatory or optional, depending on the language. One argument against Koster's analysis—namely, that not every type of constituent that can occur in the *Vorfeld* has a corresponding proform, which would be subject to deletion—is irrelevant on Oppenrieder's more restricted proposal. This is because all SA in German, including subject and (accusative) object SA, can be left-dislocated when the resumptive pronoun is present: its omission is essentially optional and in any case independently motivated by the phenomenon of Topic Drop, as (58) and (59) show.

Implementing this analysis in LFG, we get c- and f-structures for sentences with left-dislocated clauses like the following for (58):

(68) a.

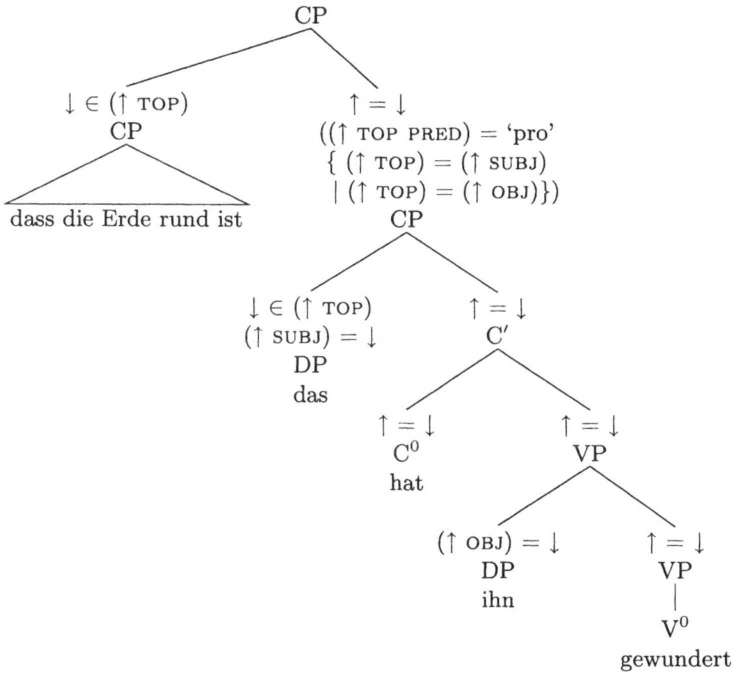
CP
↓ ∈ (↑ TOP)
CP
dass die Erde rund ist
↑ = ↓
((↑ TOP PRED) = 'pro'
{ (↑ TOP) = (↑ SUBJ)
| (↑ TOP) = (↑ OBJ)})
CP
↓ ∈ (↑ TOP)
(↑ SUBJ) = ↓
DP
das
↑ = ↓
C′
↑ = ↓
C0
hat
↑ = ↓
VP
(↑ OBJ) = ↓
DP
ihn
↑ = ↓
VP
V0
gewundert

b.

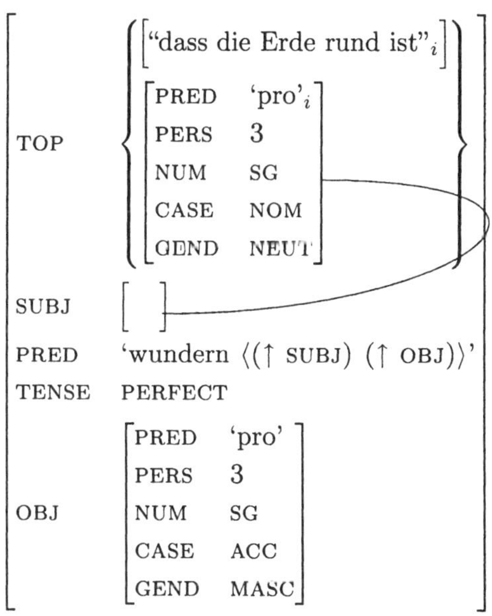
TOP
"dass die Erde rund ist"i
PRED 'pro'i
PERS 3
NUM SG
CASE NOM
GEND NEUT
SUBJ
PRED 'wundern ⟨(↑ SUBJ) (↑ OBJ)⟩'
TENSE PERFECT
OBJ
PRED 'pro'
PERS 3
NUM SG
CASE ACC
GEND MASC

The left-dislocated clause is adjoined to CP. Adjoined positions are annotated with a non-argument function, in this case with TOP. The resumptive pronoun is located in CP-Spec. As the specifier of a functional category, it is also annotated with a discourse function.[18] The TOP in CP-Spec is anaphorically linked to the DF of the left-dislocated phrase. In the local CP-Spec an argument function can be identified by the morphology. Since the resumptive pronoun is marked nominative and agrees with the finite verb, it will be identified with the SUBJ. The annotation at the matrix CP optionally introduces a PRED-feature of the TOP into the f-structure: $(\uparrow$ TOP PRED$)$ = 'PRO'. As we have seen, the identification of the 'dropped' TOP has to be restricted to SUBJ and OBJ. Further evidence for this analysis comes from the distribution of correlative pronouns, which will be discussed in chapter 8. In the next section it will be shown why it is quite plausible to assume that the *Vorfeld* is not an accessible position for SA.

## 7.5 Distribution of Nominal vs. Sentential Arguments

Let us contrast the distribution of nominal and sentential arguments in the field structure of the German sentence. Nominal arguments can occur in both the *Vorfeld* and the *Mittelfeld*. In the *Nachfeld*, however, they are, if possible at all, extremely marked:

(69) *Er hat gesehen einen Hund.
he has seen a dog

Sentential arguments, by contrast, occur readily in the *Nachfeld* but are generally impossible in the *Mittelfeld*:

(70) *Außerdem hat sie, dass sie sehr reich ist, gemeint.
furthermore has she that she very rich is thought

The prohibition on SA in the *Mittelfeld* does not, however, apply to free relatives or infinitival SA:

(71) Sie hat ihm, was er ihr erzählt hat, sofort geglaubt.
She has him what he her told has immediately believed
'She immediately believed what he told her.'

(72) Sie hat ihn, nach Hause zu gehen, mehrmals aufgefordert.
She has him to home to go several-times asked
'She asked him several times to go home.'

Free relatives have the essential properties of nominal arguments. They are the only case-marked clausal constituents; in particular, the wh-

[18]The nonargument functions TOP, FOC, ADJ allow multiple instances without violating Uniqueness.

word introducing the free relative must satisfy the case requirements not only of the embedding verb of the relative clause but also those of the main verb.[19] The grammatical function they have in the matrix clause can thus be determined from the case borne by the wh-word.

Infinitival SA, on the other hand, are like finite clauses in bearing no case information.[20] However, infinitives lack typical properties of finite clauses, such as a complementizer and agreement features. Hence, according to the nominalization scale proposed by Lehmann (1982, p. 76), they are "more nominal" than finite clauses. Oppenrieder (1991, p. 308), moreover, notes that infinitives are readily convertible into ordinary declinable nouns, and sees in this relative similarity to DPs an indication of why nonfinite SA are not strictly prohibited in the *Mittelfeld*. Notice now that there is no restriction on the occurrence of free relatives or nonfinite SA in the *Vorfeld* either; the optionality of left dislocation with infinitives even in the function of prepositional object was already observed in section 7.3.2, example (41), repeated below in (73a) (cf. also Breindl 1989, p. 248). The optionality of left dislocation with a free relative in the function of a $\text{OBL}_\theta$ is shown in (73b) (from Eisenberg 1999).

(73) a. Unser Versteck zu verraten werde ich mich hüten.
Our hideaway to reveal will I myself guard
'I will be careful not to reveal our hideaway.'

b. Wem er vertraut, hilft er auch.
who(dat) he trusts helps he also
'Whoever he trusts, he also helps.'

In short, the conditions on the licensing of arguments seem to be the same for both the *Vorfeld* and the *Mittelfeld*, with the difference that the *Vorfeld* requires certain discourse properties. Non-sentential phrases can occur in the *Mittelfeld* and in the *Vorfeld*. SA can't occur in the *Mittelfeld*, hence their occurrence in the *Vorfeld* is also prohibited. Instead, SA are only licensed at the periphery of the clause, either when extraposed or when left-dislocated.

## 7.6 Extraposition of Sentential Arguments

As we have seen in the last section all sentential arguments can occur in the *Nachfeld*. In this section we address the question of how their functions are identified.

[19]For exceptions to the case requirements, and a general treatment of free relatives in German, see e.g. Pittner (1995). For an LFG analysis of free relatives see Dalrymple and Kaplan (1997).

[20]Stowell (1981) proposes an account of the differential distribution of finite and nonfinite SA in English within the GB framework, in terms of their case properties. He hypothesizes that nonfinite SA, but not finite SA, are inherently case-marked.

In the case of left dislocation the sentential phrase is annotated with a discourse function, and is related by anaphoric linking to the resumptive pronoun in the *Vorfeld* position, whose function can be identified by the morphology. In the case of extraposition we have seen that the extraposed clause can occur without any reference to a case-marked argument. Since the clause lacks any morphological marking itself,[21] its function can't be identified in the same way as the functions of nominal arguments in German. The alternative is for the function of clauses to be identified by structural position. Let us examine what evidence there is for this. We begin by noting some conditions on the linear order of sentential phrases in the *Nachfeld*.

Argument and adjunct clauses may appear in the *Nachfeld* in any order as already noted in chapter 3. The unmarked order may depend on the adjunct-type:

(74) a. Er behauptete, als er vier Jahre alt war, dass Schweine
he asserted when he four years old was that pigs
fliegen können.
fly can
'He asserted, when he was four years old, that pigs can fly.'

b. Er behauptete, dass Schweine fliegen können, als er vier Jahre alt war.

The same can be observed for the linear order of the SUBJ- and OBJ-clauses in the *Nachfeld*: they can occur in any order. The order subject-before-object is unmarked, but both orders are grammatical:

(75) a. Vielleicht könnte beweisen, dass er hier war (SUBJ), dass er
perhaps could prove that he here was that he
unschuldig ist (OBJ).
innocent ist
'Perhaps (the fact) that he was here could prove that he is innocent.'

b. Vielleicht könnte beweisen, dass er unschuldig ist (OBJ), dass er hier war (SUBJ).

[21] Clauses are neither case-marked nor do they show agreement with the finite verb. For example, if two or more SUBJ-clauses are coordinated, the verb still has to be marked third person singular, not plural:

(i) Dass er den Hans nicht eingeladen hat und dass er nicht auf das Fest
that he the Hans not invited has and that he not to the party
gekommen ist beweist/*beweisen deine Vorhersagen.
come ist prove/prove your predictions
'That he did not invite Hans and that he did not come to the party proves/*prove your predictions.'

This can be captured with the assumption that CPs, like DPs in German, can be freely adjoined to VP. However, while DPs are adjoined to the left, CPs are adjoined to the right (cf. chapter 3, section 3.2.5):

(76)

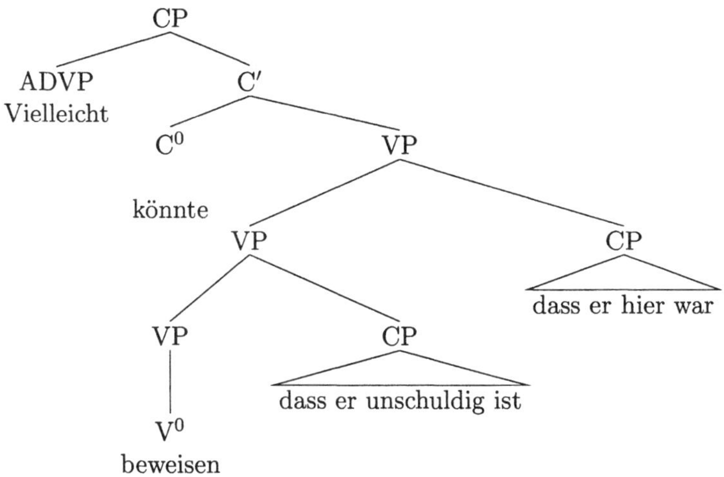


(77)

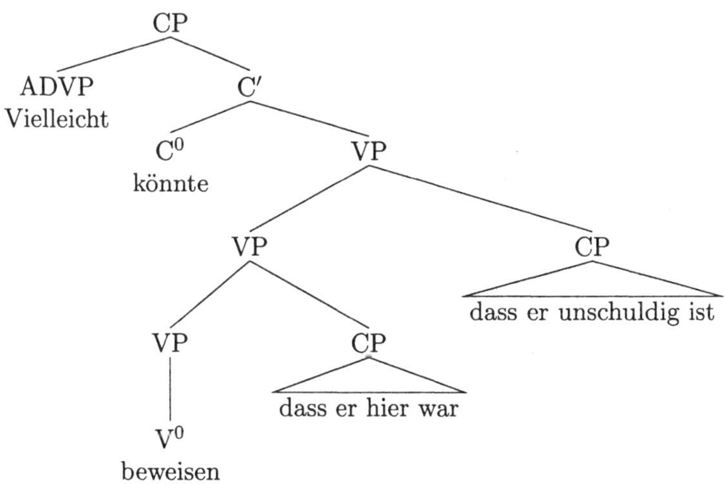


Notice, however, that VP-internal topicalization is only possible with the OBJ-clause (78a), VP-internal topicalization of the SUBJ-clause is ungrammatical (78b):

(78) a. Beweisen, dass er unschuldig ist (OBJ), könnte, dass er hier war.
prove that he innocent is could that he here was
'(The fact) that he was here could prove that he is innocent.'

b. *Beweisen, dass er hier war (SUBJ), könnte, dass er unschuldig ist.

This asymmetry might provide evidence for the claim that there are structural conditions for identifying the function of clauses: descriptively, with VP-topicalization the clause next to the verb cannot function as SUBJ (see also chapter 8).

However, the VP-internal topicalization of a subject can't be excluded in general: as we saw in chapter 3, examples (27) and (28), repeated here for convenience, VP-internal topicalization of a subject-DP is grammatical:

(79) a. Ein Fehler unterlaufen ist dabei schon manchem.
a mistake-NOM happened is thereby already many-DAT
'Many people have made a mistake with this.'

b. Ein Zug entgleist ist hier erst kürzlich.
a train-NOM derailed is here only recently
'A train derailed here only recently.'

(80) a. Kinder gespielt haben hier noch nie.
children-NOM played have hier still never
'Children have never played here.'

b. Ein Außenseiter gewonnen hat da noch nie.
An outsider-NOM won has there still never
'An outsider has never won there.'

The difference between VP-topicalization with a DP and with a CP may lie in the different ways of function specification. Since the function of CPs, unlike that of DPs, is not determined by case and agreement, configurationality may play a role in determining the functions of clauses and constraints on their occurrence. While a DP which is marked nominative and shows agreement with the verb is mapped to the SUBJ regardless of its structural position, the function of a clause, which lacks this information, will be identified by phrase-structure configuration. Thus a VP-internal topicalized argument clause, as in (78b), will be identified as an OBJ.

There is thus some evidence from VP-internal topicalization for the structural function specification of sentential arguments; still, it is too little to settle the question of the function identification of sentential arguments, which therefore remains an open question.

## 7.7 Summary

This chapter defended the thesis that all sentential arguments in German bear the same grammatical function as their nominal or prepositional alternatives. The inability of some sentential arguments to undergo topicalization can be captured by the claim that in German all sentential arguments occurring in sentence-initial position have undergone obligatory left dislocation. The resumptive pronoun that immediately follows the left-dislocated phrase may be deleted in accordance with the conditions on Topic Drop that hold for German (cf. Oppenrieder 1991). This implies that the *Vorfeld*, like the *Mittelfeld*, is unable to be occupied by sentential arguments. Hence sentential arguments always have to appear at the periphery of the clause. Either they are left-dislocated or they are extraposed. In extraposed position SA are right-adjoined to VP. VP-internal topicalization provides some evidence that the functions of extraposed sentential arguments are identified by structural position.

The next chapter examines the occurrence of nominal and sentential arguments in more detail, specifically the conditions under which they cooccur with the correlative pronoun *es*.

# 8

# Cooccurrence of *Es* with a Finite Clause

In the last chapter the distribution of sentential arguments was discussed and it was argued that SA bear the same functions as nominal arguments. Now, in German SA can cooccur with a pronominal constituent that intuitively has the same grammatical function, as the following examples illustrate:

(1) a. Ihn hat **es** gewundert, **dass die Erde rund ist**.
him has it surprised that the earth round is
'It surprised him that the earth is round.'

b. Er hat **es** nicht gewusst, **dass die Erde rund ist**
he has it not known that the earth round is
'He didn't know that the earth is round.'

c. Sie war sich **dessen** nicht bewusst,
she was REFL of-it not aware
**dass die Erde rund ist**.
that the earth round is
'She was not aware that the earth is round.'

d. Sie hat sich **darüber** gewundert,
she has REFL about-it surprised
**dass die Erde rund ist**.
that the earth round is
'She was surprised that the earth is round.'

In this chapter the interaction of these pronouns—which, borrowing from traditional German grammatical terminology will be called correlative pronouns (or simply correlatives)—and the clause they are related to will be examined in detail. In order to focus the discussion, the examination will be restricted to the neuter pronoun *es*, which is used as a correlative in conjunction with clausal constituents (CP) in the functions SUBJ or OBJ.[1]

The coocurrence of correlative *es* and CP is particulary interesting since the acceptability of this coocurrence differs according to both the syntactic construction as well as the type of the embedding verb.[2] Therefore the possibility of correlative *es* (henceforth simply *es*) and finite CP cooccurring is examined in four constructions and three verb classes for each construction. The constructions considered are (i) the CP occurring as an extraposed clause (in the *Nachfeld*); (ii) extraction out of the extraposed CP; (iii) topicalization (occurrence in the *Vorfeld*) of the matrix VP together with the embedded CP; (iv) topicalization of the CP alone.[3] The verb-types will be illustrated by *sagen* ('say')—in both the active and the passive constructions—as an example of a transitive verb which allows sentential realization of the OBJ; *beweisen* ('prove') as an example of a transitive verb which allows sentential realization of the SUBJ; and *stören* ('bother') as an example of the class of psych-verbs.

After presenting the cooccurrence patterns, the basic idea of the analysis of Hoekstra (1983) will be sketched. In section 8.3.2 this analysis—with some additional assumptions—will be implemented in LFG terms and it will be shown to account for the patterns with the *sagen* class and the *beweisen* class. It turns out, however, that this analysis fails to capture the pattern with psych-verbs. We will see that the assumption we made in chapter 4 about the thematic status of *es* together with independently motivated LFG-principles will explain the entire range of data (section 8.3.3). Finally, some consequences of this analysis for the treatment of passive constructions are briefly discussed (section 8.3.4).

## 8.1 Data

For all three verb classes, the occurrence of *es* together with an extraposed SUBJ- or OBJ-clause is optional:[4]

---

[1] This chapter is a slightly modified version of Berman (2001).

[2] In this analysis the influence of semantic, pragmatic and discourse factors on the occurrence of *es* is not considered. For discussion see e.g. Kiparsky and Kiparsky (1970), Köhler (1976), Reis (1977) and in the framework of LFG, Berman, Dipper, Fortmann, and Kuhn (1998).

[3] To be consistent with the analysis of chapter 7, we should speak here of left dislocation together with Topic Drop. But for the sake of brevity, the descriptive term 'topicalization' will be retained.

[4] For discussion of the data see e.g. Bayer (1994), Cardinaletti (1990), Haider (1995a), Müller (1995b), Oppenrieder (1991), Reis (1995), Vikner (1995), Webelhuth (1992). Cardinaletti, however, assumes that in sentences like (2c), *es* is obligatory,

(2) a. ... weil er (es) gesagt hat, dass Hans krank ist.
because he it said has that Hans sick is
'... because he said that Hans is sick.'

b. ... weil (es) gesagt wurde, dass Hans krank ist.
because it said was that Hans sick is
'... because it was said that Hans is sick.'

c. ... weil (es) deine Vorhersagen beweist, dass er den
because it your predictions proves that he the
Hans eingeladen hat.
Hans invited has
'... because (the fact) that he invited Hans proves your predictions.'

d. ... weil (es) mich stört, dass sie den Hans liebt.
because it me bothers that she the Hans loves
'... because it bothers me that she loves Hans.'

With extraction out of the extraposed clause or VP-topicalization together with the extraposed clause, however, the cooccurrence patterns vary according to the class of the embedding verb. With the *sagen* class, the presence of *es* with both extraction (3a/b) and VP-topicalization (4a/b) is ungrammatical. With the *beweisen* class, extraction (3c) and VP-topicalization (4c) are ungrammatical regardless of the presence or absence of *es*. The pattern with psych-verbs is just the opposite of the *sagen*-class: extraction (3d) and VP-topicalization (4d) are grammatical only if *es* is present.[5]

(3) a. Was hat er (*es) gesagt, dass er gelesen hat?
what has he it said that he read has
'What did he say that he read?'

---

contrary to my judgment; additional counterexamples to Cardinaletti's judgment are given in Vikner (1995, p. 237). None of these authors presents a completely worked out analysis of sentences like (2d)-(5d); Haider (1995a) remarks that "the role of the pronominal subject is not completely clear in constructions with psych predicates" (p.263), though he also states that "*überraschen* ['surprise', i.e. also a psych-verb] is a bridge verb for the subject clause and extraction is possible, but only with an expletive subject" (p.256). Cardinaletti (1990, p. 94) observes that "the theme argument of psych verbs has in some sense an intermediate status between internal and external argument, for which we have no explanation to offer." Oppenrieder (1991, p. 65) assumes that a sentential (deep) subject which is topicalized VP-internally cannot fill an argument position and so must be treated as parenthetical. As a repair strategy the argument slot of the verb must be filled by the referential pronoun *es* in the *Mittelfeld*.

[5]It should be noted that some speakers judge the absence of *es* in examples like (3d) and (4d) to be marginally acceptable, but there is general agreement that such sentences clearly contrast with the *sagen* class, where *es* must be absent in these constructions.

b. Was wurde (*es) gesagt, dass er gelesen hat?
what was it said that he read has
'What was it said that he read?'

c. *Wen beweist (es) deine Vorhersagen, dass er eingeladen
whom proves it your predications that he invited
hat?
has
'Who does (the fact) that he invited prove your predictions?'

d. Wen stört *(es) dich, dass sie liebt?
whom bothers it you that she loves
'Who does it bother you that she loves?'

(4) a. Gesagt, dass er krank ist, hat er (*es) nicht.
said that he sick is has he it not
'He did not say that he is sick.'

b. Gesagt, dass er krank ist, wurde (*es) nicht.
said that he sick is was it not
'It was not said that he is sick.'

c. *Bewiesen, dass er den Hans eingeladen hat, hat (es) deine
proved that he the Hans invited has has it your
Vorhersagen.
predictions
'That he invited Hans proved your predictions.'

d. Gestört, dass sie den Hans liebt, hat *(es) mich schon.
bothered that she the Hans loves has it me sure
'It sure bothered me that she loved Hans.'

Finally, if the embedded clause is topicalized by itself, *es* is always ungrammatical.

(5) a. Dass Hans krank ist, hat er (*es) gesagt.
that Hans sick is has he it said
'That Hans is sick, he said.'

b. Dass Hans krank ist, wurde (*es) gesagt.
that Hans sick is was it said
'That Hans is sick, was said.'

c. Dass er den Hans eingeladen hat, beweist (*es) deine
that he the Hans invited has proves it your
Vorhersagen.
predictions
'(The fact) that he invited Hans, proves your predictions.'

d. Dass sie den Hans liebt, stört (*es) mich.
that she the Hans loves bothers it me
'That she loves Hans, bothers me.'

## 8.2 Correlative *Es* as an Argument

Hoekstra (1983) proposed and Bennis (1986) developed the idea that the Dutch pronoun *het* ('it'), which like German *es* can occur in conjunction with a clause, is an argument, which is both case-marked and theta-marked and has to occur in an A-position. Consequently, the clause that occurs in conjunction with *het* cannot be an argument, but must be an adjunct, occupying an adjoined position (an A-bar-position). In the absence of *het*, however, the clause itself is assumed to be the argument, base-generated as the righthand sister of the verb.

As we have seen in chapter 4, Cardinaletti (1990) and Vikner (1995), following Hoekstra's and Bennis's treatment of *het*, assume that German *es* (when it occurs in conjunction with a clause) is likewise a thematic argument (Müller 1995b, p. 231 also endorses this view). That is, on their analyses *es* has the same grammatical status as *het*.

As will be shown in detail below, this analysis of *es* reduces the pattern with the *sagen* class to familiar argument/adjunct asymmetries, and the pattern with the *beweisen* class to independent constraints on SUBJ-clauses. This approach fails to predict the pattern with psych-verbs, however, since extraction and topicalization are grammatical only when *es* is present.

What this suggests is that the thematic status of *es* and its related clause is different with psych-verbs than with the other verb classes. We will show how, under this assumption, the relation between the a-structure and f-structure accounts for the full pattern of (co)occurrence of *es* and its related clause.

## 8.3 LFG-Analysis

### 8.3.1 Theoretical Preliminaries

The analysis is based on the following six assumptions which were already discussed in the previous chapters.

A. In German the syntactic functions of DPs are identified via case and agreement. Specifically, nominative case plus agreement with the finite verb determines that the DP functions as SUBJ, accusative determines the function of the DP as an OBJ, etc.
DP: $(\downarrow \text{CASE}) = \text{NOM} \wedge$ DP: $(\downarrow \text{AGR}) = (\uparrow \text{SUBJ AGR}) \Rightarrow (\uparrow \text{SUBJ}) = \downarrow$
DP: $(\downarrow \text{CASE}) = \text{ACC} \Rightarrow (\uparrow \text{OBJ}) = \downarrow$

Clauses, on the other hand, are neither case-marked nor do they show agreement with the finite verb. The functions of clauses thus cannot be determined by case and agreement.

B. Lexical case-assignment takes place prior to morpho-lexical operations, while default case-assignment takes place after these operations (cf. Zaenen, Maling, and Thrainsson 1985). In addition, it is assumed here that default case-assignment takes place before the mapping from thematic roles to grammatical functions.[6] Lexical case-assignment is an idiosyncratic property of certain lexical items. With default case-assignment the highest available thematic role is assigned nominative case, the next highest accusative.

C. The theme argument is underspecified [−r] in a-structure, which permits the theme in principle to be mapped either to the SUBJ [−r, −o] or the OBJ [−r, +o], in accordance with the Lexical Mapping Theory. Lexically case-marked thematic roles are obligatorily mapped onto $\text{OBJ}_\theta$ (in German) (cf. Zaenen, Maling, and Thrainsson 1985, p. 479).

D. German is a language that must satisfy the Subject Condition. In German this may also be satisfied by the verbal agreement morphology in default of a phonologically realized subject.

E. In the *Mittelfeld* both a thematic as well as a non-thematic *es* can occur. The non-thematic *es*, however, does not occupy a structurally given position; rather it must be subcategorized. Only certain classes of verbs subcategorize a non-thematic function.

F. A verb has the same argument structure regardless of the categorial realization of its arguments.[7] Consequently, on the level of f-structure argument clauses in German bear the same grammatical functions as DPs, e.g. OBJ or SUBJ.

For the three verb classes being considered, the following a-structures are assumed:

---

[6] Zaenen, Maling, and Thrainsson (1985, p. 465) assume that default case-assignment (which they also call 'functional case marking') applies after 'all association principles' to grammatical functions. However, as will be shown in section 8.3.3.1, there is evidence that case-assignment influences the mapping to grammatical functions.

[7] However, cf. Zaenen and Engdahl (1994), who assume the thematic role *proposition* with the intrinsic feature [−o].

| | | | |
|---|---|---|---|
| (6) | a. sagen | < agent | theme > |
| | | [−o] | [−r] |
| | b. beweisen | < $\theta$[8] | theme > |
| | | [−o] | [−r] |
| | c. stören[9] | < experiencer | theme > |
| | | [+o] | [−r] |

### 8.3.2 *Es* as a Thematic Argument

#### 8.3.2.1 OBJ-Clauses (*Sagen* Verbs)

The a-structure of verbs of the *sagen*-class has an agent which is intrinsically marked [−o] and a theme which is intrinsically marked [−r]. The two thematic roles are ordered within their argument structure in accordance with the universal hierarchy of thematic roles (cf. chapter 5, section 5.2.4). By the Lexical Mapping Theory, as formulated by Alsina and Mchombo (1993), the highest thematic role gets the default classification [−r] and is therefore mapped onto the SUBJ. The theme argument would be assigned [+r], but since the intrinsic value can't be changed it remains underspecified. Since the agent is already mapped onto SUBJ, the underspecified theme has to be mapped onto the OBJ. Due to the selectional properties of the verbs of this class, the OBJ can be realized by a DP or a CP.

| | | | |
|---|---|---|---|
| (7) | sagen | < agent | theme > |
| | | [−o] | [−r] |
| | | [−r] | |
| | | SUBJ | OBJ (DP/CP) |

Given the assumption (following Hoekstra, Vikner, etc.) that *es* is a thematic argument, the extraction pattern in (3a), repeated below in (8), is explained by the independently motivated assumption that extraction is possible out of an argument clause, but not out of an adjunct clause.

(8) Was hat er (*es) gesagt, dass er gelesen hat?
what has he it said that he read has
'What did he say that he read?'

If *es* is present, it will function as the OBJ and the clause will be an adjunct (ADJ), so extraction is ungrammatical. If *es* is not present, the clause itself will be the OBJ and extraction is fine. In the latter case, as was shown chapter 6, this can be captured either by the fact that the

[8] It is uncertain what theta-role the propositional subject of *beweisen* bears; for present purposes it is only important that it be [−o] and ranked higher than theme.

[9] On the argument structure of psych-verbs see e.g. Grimshaw (1990).

functional uncertainty path BODY is restricted to OBJ, or by the lexical entry of bridge verbs, which identifies the matrix DF only with the DF of their complement clause.

The VP-topicalization pattern in (4a), repeated below in (9), could be accounted for in purely structural terms if, following Bennis's implementation of Hoekstra's proposal, an argument clause is base-generated as the righthand sister of the verb (10), whereas an adjunct clause is adjoined to a V-projection (11); Bennis (1986, p. 105) gives the following structures (S′ corresponds to what we are calling CP):

(9) Gesagt, dass er krank ist, hat er (*es) nicht.
said that he sick is has he it not
'He did not say that he is sick.'

(10)

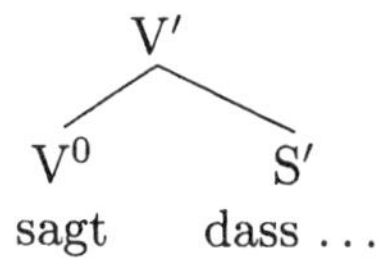


(11)

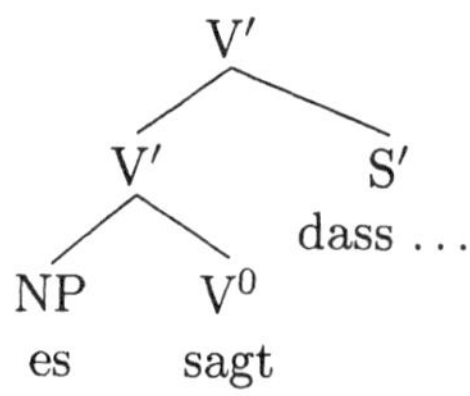


In (10) the verb and the S′ form a constituent, which can be topicalized. In (11), however, the verb and the S′ do not form a constituent and topicalization is not possible.[10]

There are several problems for this account. One is that, as we have seen in chapter 7, the order of extraposed argument and adjunct clauses is in general quite free in extraposed position. In addition, we have seen evidence in chapter 7 that the topicalized VP does not necessarily correspond to the VP in its base position. Furthermore, while analyzing the CP as an adjunct when it cooccurs with *es* captures the extraction and VP-topicalization paradigms of the *sagen* class, it does not account for the failure of topicalization of the CP alone in the presence of *es*, illustrated by (5a), repeated below in (12a). This is because in general

[10] Topicalization of the VP containing *es* and the CP is marginal:

(i) ? Es gesagt, dass der Hans krank ist, hat er nicht.
it said that the Hans ill ist has he not
'Say (lit. said it) that Hans is sick, he did not.'

This can be explained by the general prohibition against topicalizing an OBJ-*es* (cf. chapter 3, section 3.2.1). A topicalized OBJ has to receive phonological stress and since *es* cannot bear stress, topicalized OBJ-*es* is ungrammatical.

entire adjuncts can be topicalized, as (12b) illustrates: [11]

(12) a. Dass Hans krank ist, hat er (*es) gesagt.
that Hans sick is has he it said
'That Hans is sick, he said.'

b. Obwohl Hans krank ist, hat er ihm nichts gesagt.
although H. sick is, has he him-DAT nothing said
'Although Hans is sick, he didn't tell him anything.'

Vikner (1995, p. 239) suggests that there is an independent explanation for the ungrammaticality of cooccurrence in cases like (12a). He observes that the same effect arises with appositive DPs (Vikner 1995, p. 239, fn. 9):

(13) a. Heute habe ich $\text{Peter}_1$ getroffen, $[\text{meinen alten Freund}]_1$
Today have I Peter met my old friend
'Today I met Peter, my old friend.'

b. *$[\text{Meinen alten Freund}]_1$, habe ich $\text{Peter}_1$ heute getroffen.

Vikner therefore proposes to analyse the adjunct CP as a 'kind of apposition' which likewise prevents it from moving to CP-Spec (i.e. the *Vorfeld*).[12]

Vikner's observation can be formulated in LFG terms as a condition on the f-precedence relation:[13] An appositive element cannot f-precede the expression it is related to. This can be formalized as follows (APP stands for the f-structure element representing the apposition):

(14) For all f-structures $g$: $g <_f (g \text{ APP})$

Applying this to (12a), $g$, representing the f-structure of *es*, must f-precede ($g$ APP), i.e., the f-structure of *dass Hans krank ist*, but it doesn't, hence the sentence (with *es*) is correctly ruled out.

---

[11] I assume that adjunct clauses, unlike argument clauses, can appear in the *Vorfeld*, i.e., do not have to be left-dislocated. Evidence for that is (i) that in general adjunct clauses can also appear in the middle field and (ii) that not every adjunct clause has a corresponding resumptive pronoun—e.g. *obwohl*-clauses—which precludes left dislocation for such adjuncts.

[12] Vikner derives this fact about appositives from the assumption that A-bar-movement (of which topicalization is an instance) is only possible with maximal projections that are assigned both a theta-role and case. However, this explanation can't be right, since adjuncts are also assigned neither a theta-role nor case, but can nevertheless be topicalized, as we just saw in (12b).

[13] Cf. footnote 4 in chapter 5. That definition of f-precedence depends on the assumption that an apposition does not enter into an antecedent-gap relation; if it did, then in e.g. (13b), *Peter* would wrongly f-precede the apposition. This assumption is consistent with Bresnan's idea that traces are only needed for function specification.

Once this precedence condition is adopted, it can also be applied to the analysis of the VP-topicalization pattern, as in (9). In this case, too, the f-precedence condition is violated, since the appositive clause precedes the expression it is related to. So we can account for the VP-topicalization pattern without relying on the constituent structure assumptions of Hoekstra and Bennis given in (10) and (11) (Gereon Müller, p.c.).

### 8.3.2.2 SUBJ Clauses (*Beweisen* Verbs)

With the *beweisen* class, the higher theta-role bearing the intrinsic feature [−o] will be mapped onto the SUBJ, the theme onto the OBJ:

(15) beweisen < $\theta$ theme >
[−o] [−r]
[−r]
SUBJ OBJ

Thus if *es* is present and has the higher thematic role, it will be mapped onto the SUBJ.[14] Consequently, the related CP is an adjunct (i.e., an apposition). In this situation, the account of the cooccurrence pattern—cf. examples (3c)/(4c)/(5c), repeated below in (16)—is therefore the same as with the *sagen* class:

(16) a. *Wen beweist es deine Vorhersagen, dass er eingeladen
whom proves it your predications that he invited
hat?
has
'Who does (the fact) that he invited prove your predictions?'

b. *Bewiesen, dass er den Hans eingeladen hat, hat es deine
proved that he the Hans invited has has it your
Vorhersagen.
predictions
'That he invited Hans proved your predictions.'

c. *Dass er den Hans eingeladen hat, beweist es deine
that he the Hans invited has proves it your
Vorhersagen.
predictions
'(The fact) that he invited Hans, proves your predictions.'

---

[14]If *es* corresponds to the theme-argument as in (i), it is parallel to the *sagen*-class; i.e. *es* will be mapped on the OBJ and the clause is an apposition to *es*.

(i) Dieser Umstand beweist es, dass er lügt.
this circumstance proves it, that he lies.
'This circumstance proves that he is lying.'

That is, (16a) violates the general condition on extraction from an adjunct, and (16b-c) violate the f-precedence condition (14) on appositives.

When *es* is absent, the extraposed clause itself functions as SUBJ. In this case, however, in contrast to the *sagen* class, extraction and VP-topicalization remain ungrammatical (cf. (3c), (4c)). The examples are repeated in (17):

(17) a. *Wen beweist deine Vorhersagen, dass er eingeladen hat?
b. *Bewiesen, dass er den Hans eingeladen hat, hat deine Vorhersagen.

For the case of extraction, this is attributable to the general prohibition against extraction from a SUBJ-clause (see chapter 5 and Webelhuth 1984, p. 229). We have seen in chapter 7 that the ungrammaticality of (17b) indicates that VP-topicalization evidently is subject to an analogous constraint. Thus a clause which is a sister of the verb, as in the case of VP-topicalization (17b), will be identified as an OBJ. But then the subcategorization requirements of *beweisen* can't be satisfied.

The analysis of Hoekstra and others that *es* is the argument and the CP an adjunct (i.e. apposition) related to it essentially captures the cooccurrence patterns with the *sagen* and *beweisen* classes. As it stands, however, it cannot account for the pattern of the psych-verbs, since contrary to the predictions of this analysis extraction and VP-topicalization are only possible in the presence of *es*. In the next section it will be shown how the theory embodied by assumptions A-E accounts for the full range of cooccurrence patterns.

### 8.3.3 Psych-Verbs (*Stören* Class)

#### 8.3.3.1 A-Structure

The argument structure of psych-verbs implies that the theme argument, if clausal, can be either a SUBJ or OBJ. The reasoning goes as follows. Note first that both passivization[15] (cf. Fanselow 1987, p. 81; Fortmann 2001, p. 78) and Topic Drop (cf. Sternefeld 1985, p. 407) are ungrammatical with psych-verbs:

---

[15]As an anonymous reviewer of Berman (2001) noted, on an agentive reading of *stören* the passive is grammatical:

(i) ... weil ich vom Nachbarn gestört wurde.
because I from-the neighbour bothered was
'... because I was bothered by the neighbour.'

However, it seems plausible that the a-structure of the agentive *stören* is different from that of the purely experiencer reading, cf. Fortmann (2001, p. 78).

(18) a. ... weil mich der Fleck stört.
because me the stain bothers.
'... because the stain bothers me.'

b. ... *weil ich vom Fleck gestört wurde.
because I by-the stain bothered was
'... because I was bothered by the stain.'

(19) *(Mich) stört der Fleck.
me bothers the stain.
'The stain bothers me.'

These observations suggest that the experiencer, i.e., the higher thematic role, is not mapped onto an OBJ (which would permit Passive und Topic Drop).[16] Rather, it receives lexical case,[17] namely accusative, and in accordance with assumption (C), is mapped obligatorily onto $\text{OBJ}_\theta$.

Consequently, the highest thematic role to be assigned default case is the theme, which is thus case-marked nominative (assumption B). Although by the Lexical Mapping Theory (assumption C), the underspecified theme [−r] can in principle be mapped on the SUBJ or the OBJ, it is a property of German that nominative marked DPs can't be mapped on the OBJ and hence must be identified with the SUBJ (assumption A). But in the case of clausal realization (where syntactic function is not defined via case) the underspecification of the theme permits mapping to either the SUBJ or the OBJ, regardless of case-assignment.[18] These properties are encapsulated in the following mapping rule for psych-verbs:

(20) stören <experiencer theme>

| | experiencer | theme |
|---|---|---|
| | [+o]/[ACC] | [−r] |
| | | [NOM] |
| | $\text{OBJ}_\theta$ | SUBJ (DP) |
| | | SUBJ/OBJ (CP) |

Since the theme (as the highest argument which is not lexically case-marked) receives nominative case, it must, if it is a DP, be mapped on the SUBJ (cf. (18)). This is also the case for the nominative marked (thematic) DP *es*. However, if correlative *es* is mapped to the SUBJ,

[16]Cf. Fanselow (1987, p. 81), who remarks that, since psych-verbs with an accusative marked DP argument cannot be passivized, the DP is presumably not the direct object.

[17]This was suggested by Belletti and Rizzi (1988, p. 332f.) for Italian psych-verbs like *preoccupare* ('worry') and by Sternefeld (1985, p. 427) for similar German data.

[18]Note that in the case of *sagen* the underspecified theme, which is assigned accusative case, cannot be mapped onto the SUBJ, even if it is realized as a CP, since the agent, which is marked [−o], already fills that function (principle of functional uniqueness).

then on the above analysis the CP would have to be an adjunct, and the grammaticality of extraction and VP-topicalization in the presence of *es*—cf. (3d)/(4d), repeated in (21a/b)—would be unexplained.

(21) a. Wen stört *(es) dich, dass sie liebt?
whom bothers it you that she loves
'Who does it bother you that she loves?'

b. Gestört, dass sie den Hans liebt, hat *(es) mich schon.
bothered that she the Hans loves has it me sure
'It sure bothered me that she loved Hans.'

Hence there must be an alternative solution. Note that if the clausal theme argument can be mapped to the OBJ, then the extraction and VP-topicalization data could be explained.

This motivates the adoption of assumption E, that certain verbs—in particular, psych-verbs—subcategorize a non-thematic SUBJ. However, since the information at a-structure is semantically based, non-thematic functions, which are semantically empty, have no representation at a-structure (cf. Alsina 1996, p. 57f.). The non-thematic SUBJ is therefore not licensed by a mapping principle, but is a purely syntactic element.

### 8.3.3.2 Non-Thematic *Es*

If psych-verbs optionally subcategorize a non-thematic SUBJ and require that it be lexically filled by non-thematic *es*, then *es* satisfies the Subject Condition and the clausal argument can be mapped on the OBJ, as indicated in (22).

(22) a. Wen stört es-SUBJ dich, [dass sie liebt]-OBJ?

b. Gestört, [dass sie den Hans liebt]-OBJ, hat es-SUBJ mich schon.

This situation is encoded in the following lexical entry for *stören*:

(23) stören V PRED = 'stören $\langle(\uparrow \text{OBJ}_\theta)(\uparrow \text{OBJ})\rangle(\uparrow \text{SUBJ})$'
$(\uparrow \text{SUBJ FORM}) =_c \text{ES}$

Here is the lexical entry of non-thematic *es*:

(24) es N $(\uparrow \text{NUM}) = \text{SG}$
$(\uparrow \text{PERS}) = 3$
$(\uparrow \text{CASE}) = \text{NOM}$
$(\uparrow \text{FORM}) = \text{ES\_}$
$\sim (\uparrow \text{PRED})$

Non-thematic *es* does not have any PRED-feature, instead it is assumed that non-thematic elements have a FORM-feature (cf. Kaplan and Bresnan 1982, p. 213f.). The FORM-feature prevents the occurrence of more than one non-thematic *es* in c-structure. Since in German, the occurrence of a SUBJ or OBJ is not tied to structural positions, the occurrence of several DPs in c-structure which all could be unified under the same function must be excluded. In the case of thematic DPs this is done with the assumption that PRED-features, as instantiated symbols, can't be unified at all, even when they are identical (cf. Kaplan and Bresnan 1982, p. 225). In the case of non-thematic DPs this role is taken over by the FORM-feature, which, like PRED-features, has an instantiated symbol as its value (expressed by the underscore, following the notation of Kaplan and Maxwell 1996), and thus can't be unified (Jonas Kuhn, Gert Webelhuth, p.c.). This prevents sentences like (25):

(25) *... weil es es es mich stört, dass ...

The negative constraint '$\sim$ ($\uparrow$ PRED)' prevents unification with a thematic SUBJ (e.g., if the theme-argument of *stören* is mapped onto the SUBJ, as permitted by the alternative lexical entry in (30) below, non-thematic *es* is excluded). Thus the cooccurrence of *es* and another nominal SUBJ is correctly predicted to be ungrammatical:

(26) ... *weil es mich der Fleck stört.
because it me the stain bothers
'... because the stain bothers me.'

By contrast, the cooccurrence of non-thematic *es* and a clause, as in (2d), repeated below in (27), is grammatical, since the CP may, as we have seen, be mapped to the OBJ. Hence, the availability of non-thematic *es* with psych-verbs suffices to satisfy the Subject Condition in this case.

(27) ...weil es-SUBJ mich stört, [dass sie den Hans liebt]-OBJ/*SUBJ

The f-structure for (27), given in (28), shows how the Subject Condition is satisfied with psych-verbs with non-thematic *es*:

(28)
$$\left[\begin{array}{ll} \text{SUBJ} & \left[\begin{array}{ll}\text{PERS} & 3\\ \text{NUM} & \text{SG}\\ \text{CASE} & \text{NOM}\\ \text{FORM} & \text{ES}\end{array}\right]\\ \text{PRED} & \text{'stören } \langle(\uparrow \text{OBJ}_\theta)(\uparrow \text{OBJ})\rangle\ (\uparrow \text{SUBJ})\text{'}\\ \text{OBJ}_\theta & \left[\text{PRED}\quad \text{'mich'}\right]\\ \text{OBJ} & \left[\text{“dass sie den Hans liebt”}\right]\end{array}\right]$$

Since with psych-verbs the CP is still an argument—namely OBJ—even in the presence of *es*, this accounts for the grammaticality of extraction (2d)/(22a) and VP-topicalization (3d)/(22b). On the other hand, in the absence of *es* the clause itself must be mapped onto the SUBJ to satisfy the Subject Condition:

(29) ... weil mich stört, [dass sie den Hans liebt]-SUBJ

The alternative lexical entry is therefore:

(30) stören V PRED = 'stören $\langle(\uparrow \text{OBJ}_\theta)(\uparrow \text{SUBJ})\rangle$'

and the relevant part of the f-structure of (29) is the following:

(31)
$$\begin{bmatrix} \text{SUBJ} & \begin{bmatrix}\text{“dass sie den Hans liebt”}\end{bmatrix} \\ \text{PRED} & \text{‘stören } \langle(\uparrow \text{OBJ}_\theta)(\uparrow \text{SUBJ})\rangle\text{’} \\ \text{OBJ}_\theta & \begin{bmatrix}\text{PRED} & \text{‘mich’}\end{bmatrix} \end{bmatrix}$$

Thus, the ungrammaticality of extraction and VP-topicalization in this case—see (32)—is accounted for by the constraint on SUBJ clauses, just as with the *beweisen* class.[19]

(32) a. *Wen stört dich, [dass sie liebt]-SUBJ?
  b. *Gestört, [dass sie den Hans liebt]-SUBJ, hat mich schon.

As for topicalization of the CP alone in the presence of *es*, unlike extraction and VP-topicalization this is ungrammatical with psych-verbs, as with all other verb classes, as illustrated in (5d), repeated in (33).

(33) *Dass sie den Hans liebt, stört es mich.

But in contrast to the *sagen* and *beweisen* classes, in this case the ungrammaticality cannot be explained by a general prohibition against an appositive preceding the expression it is related to, since, as we have seen, with psych-verbs the clause is an argument, even in the presence of *es*.

The analysis of topicalization as left dislocation which was proposed in chapter 7 offers an explanation for the ungrammaticality. Recall that we argued that all finite argument clauses are obligatorily left-dislocated and can never occur in CP-Spec, which is instead occupied by a resumptive pronoun. The resumptive pronoun can be dropped in accordance with the conditions on Topic Drop in German (cf. Huang

[19] According to Bennis (1986, p. 135, ex. (78a-b)), the corresponding extraction sentences in Dutch have just the opposite behaviour from the German sentences: extraction out of the complement clause of a psych-verb is grammatical only if *het* is absent, ungrammatical if it is present. This indicates that the German pronoun *es* is not the exact pendant of the Dutch pronoun *het*, contrary to what Cardinaletti (1990) and Vikner (1995) assume.

1984, Sternefeld 1985, Oppenrieder 1991)—namely, only if the pronoun has the function SUBJ or OBJ. This analysis accounts for the failure of a "topicalized" clause (i.e., one in sentence-initial position) to cooccur with a correlative pronoun in the *Mittelfeld*. Since the argument is already filled by the (dropped) resumptive pronoun, the occurrence of the correlative pronoun in the *Mittelfeld* would violate the Coherence condition:

(34) Dass Hans krank ist, (das) hat er (*es) gesagt.

With *stören* the theme argument is assigned nominative case, so in the case of left dislocation the resumptive pronoun, being a nominal expression, must be realized as a SUBJ:

(35) Dass sie den Hans liebt, (das-SUBJ) stört mich.
that she the Hans loves that bothers me
'That she loves Hans, (that) bothers me.'

Non-thematic *es* cannot occur here, since it cannot be unified with a function containing a PRED-feature (see the lexical entry of the non-thematic *es* in (24) and example (26)):

(36) *Dass sie den Hans liebt, (das-SUBJ) stört es-SUBJ mich.

### 8.3.4 Passive of *sagen*

In light of the introduction of non-thematic *es*, it is necessary to consider how this interacts with the passive of *sagen*-class verbs. In this construction, the most prominent role in a-structure, the agent, is suppressed. Thus the underspecified theme argument, being the highest thematic role, is assigned nominative case. Hence, if it is realized as a DP it must be mapped onto the SUBJ, but if it is realized as a clause, it may also be mapped onto the OBJ:

(37) gesagt <agent theme>
[−o] [−r]
[NOM]
∅ SUBJ (DP)
SUBJ/OBJ (CP)

The possibility of mapping the theme argument to the OBJ, if clausal, provides an explanation of the extraction and VP-topicalization patterns in (3b)/(4b), repeated in (38):

(38) a. Was wurde gesagt, dass er gelesen hat?
what was said that he read has
'What was (it) said that he read?'

b. Gesagt, dass er krank ist, wurde nicht.
said that he sick is was not
'(It) was not said that he is sick.'

If the CP could only be mapped onto the SUBJ, then extraction and VP-topicalization would induce a violation, as with the *beweisen* class; but being mapped onto the OBJ, no violation arises.

However, non-thematic *es* cannot cooccur with the CP in these constructions to satisfy the Subject Condition, since *sagen* does not subcategorize for a non-thematic *es*, unlike *stören* (cf. (23)). But in this case the Subject Condition can be satisfied by the verbal agreement morphology, as discussed in chapter 4. Recall that the finite verb specifies a subject which contains only person and number information. Normally the subject specified by the verbal agreement morphology is unified with the structural subject to guarantee subject-verb agreement. But if the theme argument, the only argument of the passivized verb *sagen*, is mapped on the OBJ, the verbal agreement morphology introduces a non-thematic SUBJ into the f-structure and satisfies the Subject Condition.

The f-structure for (39) shows how the Subject Condition is satisfied with the passive of *sagen* taking a sentential OBJ:

(39) ... weil gesagt wurde, dass er das Buch gelesen hat.
because said was that he the book read has
'... because it was said that he read the book.'

$$\begin{bmatrix} \text{SUBJ} & \begin{bmatrix} \text{PERS} & 3 \\ \text{NUM} & \text{SG} \end{bmatrix} \\ \text{PRED} & \text{`sagen } \langle(\uparrow \text{OBJ})\rangle\text{'} \\ \text{PASSIVE} & + \\ \text{TENSE} & \text{PAST} \\ \text{OBJ} & \begin{bmatrix} \text{``dass er das Buch gelesen hat''} \end{bmatrix} \end{bmatrix}$$

Since the non-thematic subject is specified by the verbal agreement morphology, non-thematic *es* would violate Economy of Expression, since non-thematic *es* would require unnecessary syntactic nodes (cf. the discussion of impersonal passive in chapter 4).

In the case of psych-verbs, however, the verbal morphology cannot introduce a SUBJ, since the constraining equation in the lexical entry of psych-verbs requires that a non-thematic SUBJ must be lexically realized by *es* (cf. (23)). This is why in sentence (2d) with *es* absent, repeated below in (40), the embedded CP cannot be mapped onto OBJ, since then the Subject Condition would not be satisfied.

(40) ... weil mich stört, [dass sie den Hans liebt]-SUBJ/*OBJ
because me bothers that she the Hans loves
'... because (it) bothers me that she loves Hans.'

And being mapped onto the SUBJ results, as we have seen, in extraction and VP-topicalization being ungrammatical:

(41) a. *Wen stört dich, [dass sie liebt]-SUBJ?
b. *Gestört, [dass sie den Hans liebt]-SUBJ, hat mich schon.

With the passive of *sagen*, however, since this class does not subcategorize for a non-thematic *es*, *es* in conjunction with the clause must be a thematic SUBJ, with the CP therefore functioning as an apposition to *es*:

(42) ...weil es gesagt wurde, dass Hans krank ist.

$$\begin{bmatrix} \text{SUBJ} & \begin{bmatrix} \text{PRED} & \text{`pro'} \\ \text{PERS} & 3 \\ \text{NUM} & \text{SG} \\ \text{CASE} & \text{NOM} \\ \text{APP} & \begin{bmatrix}\text{``dass Hans krank ist''}\end{bmatrix} \end{bmatrix} \\ \text{PRED} & \text{`sagen } \langle(\uparrow \text{SUBJ})\rangle\text{'} \\ \text{TENSE} & \text{PAST} \\ \text{PASSIVE} & + \end{bmatrix}$$

Thus extraction and VP-topicalization are ungrammatical, cf. (2b) and (3b), repeated here:

(43) a. *Was wurde es gesagt, dass er gelesen hat?
what was it said that he read has
'What was it said that he read?'

b. *Gesagt, dass er krank ist, wurde es nicht.
said that he sick is was it not
'It was not said that he is sick.'

## 8.4 Summary

The cooccurrence patterns of correlative *es* and its related CP have been accounted for by independent principles of LFG, in particular those concerning the mapping from a-structure to f-structure, together with the additional assumption that German has not only a thematic *es*, but also a subcategorized non-thematic *es*. Thematic *es* functions as an argument, to which the CP is a kind of apposition (following Hoekstra, Bennis and Vikner). The extraction and VP-topicalization data confirm this analysis with verbs like *sagen* and *beweisen*. Non-thematic *es* does not fill a structurally given position in the c-structure, but must be governed by the verb. Non-thematic *es* is licensed by psych-verbs like *stören*. The a-structure of these verbs allows the CP to function as an OBJ, even when it cooccurs with *es*; this accounts for the different pattern with respect to extraction and VP-topicalization. With the passive of agentive transitive verbs, the clausal theme argument likewise can be mapped to the OBJ, but since these verbs do not subcategorize for non-thematic *es*, the verbal morphology serves by default to satisfy the Subject Condition.

# 9

# Conclusion

This work has investigated the clausal syntax of German in the framework of LFG. Analyses were provided for verb-second, so-called "subjectless" clauses, expletives and agreement, weak crossover, long distance dependencies, the distribution of subordinate clauses and the cooccurrence of correlative pronouns and embedded clauses. The focus of attention was on the proper c-structure representations of these phenomena and their interaction with the corresponding f-structures. The LFG principles and hypotheses that figure most prominently in this work are Extended Head, the Endocentricity principle, Economy of Expression, the Endocentric Mapping Principles, the Subject Condition, the Prominence Principle, and the Principle for Identifying Gaps. In applying these I have examined their effects and implications for German syntax in particular and LFG in general in a number of areas of theoretical interest. To conclude this investigation I recapitulate the principle claims and results, and then briefly touch some open questions raised by my research

## 9.1 Summary

The main positions argued for in this book are:

- German phrase structure has no distinct subject or object position. The grammatical functions are identifed by the morphology.
- In finite clauses without a lexically realized subject the Subject Condition is satisfied by the verbal agreement morphology.
- Local word order alternations do not involve an antecendent-gap configuration but non-local dependencies do.
- Finite clauses in sentence-initial position are obligatorily left-dislocated.
- Sentential arguments bear the same grammatical function as the corresponding nominal or prepositional arguments.

- In German there is a thematic as well as a non-thematic NP *es*.

Let us review these points.

German is a language with relatively free word order. I adopted Haider's position (e.g. Haider 1993a, Haider 1997) that German sentence structure has only one functional projection. The verb-second property of German is not accounted for by head-movement; rather, I showed that the verb in $C^0$ is the extended head of the VP and satisfies the Endocentricity principle. Based on the free distribution of subject and object and especially on the fact that the subject may be included in VP-topicalization, I argued that syntactic functions in German are not structurally encoded but identified by the morphology (Morphological Function Specification).

I showed that German is consistent with the Subject Condition, although there are finite clauses in German that lack a lexical subject, such as impersonal passives. This means that German is not a counterexample to the claim the Subject Condition is a universal. According to my analysis, the SUBJ function is introduced in f-structure by the verbal agreement morphology; this follows without further stipulations from the treatment of agreement in LFG. The SUBJ introduced by the agreement morphology in f-structure is not represented in c-structure by an empty category. Economy of Expression requires c-structure to have as few nodes as possible. C-structure nodes are only licensed if they add new information. Hence, in "subjectless" sentences like impersonal passives the representation of the SUBJ in c-structure by an empty category would violate Economy of Expression.

In terms of the analysis of weak crossover in Bresnan (2001), we saw that in German, weak crossover configurations arising from scrambling and local topicalization do not provide evidence for an antededent-gap structure, but those arising from non-local topicalization do provide such evidence. The fact that in German free word order is restricted to the local clause suggests that morphology identifies syntactic functions only locally. The claim was therefore that with non-local dependencies an empty category in the local domain of the predicate is necessary to guarantee the right predicate-argument relation. In this case the empty category is not ruled out by Economy of Expression, since it is needed for function specification. This is also the reason why I prefer Bresnan's analysis of weak crossover to the traceless approach of Dalrymple, Kaplan, and King (2001), although we found no empirical difference between them. Finally, it was shown that the analysis can also capture German weak crossover configurations involving adjuncts, double objects, complex sentences, long distances dependencies, and infinitives.

The relation between the antecedent and the empty category is captured by the Principle for Identfying gaps. We saw that the empty category can be related to its antecedent either by appealing to inside-out functional uncertainty or to inside-out function application. On the first approach the long distance dependency is reflected by means of indefinitely long attribute paths at f-structure. On the second approach, long distance dependencies are analyzed as lexically conditioned locally bounded dependencies which propagate cyclically. Non-local dependencies are subject to various restrictions. The architecture of LFG makes it possible to capture these restrictions on f-structure by means of off-path constraints, or by encoding them in lexical entries, without making c-structure unnecessarily complex and abstract.

Finally, I examined the distribution of sentential arguments, with detailed investigations of the conditions on (non)-topicalization of finite clauses and of the status of so-called correlative *es*, which cooccurs with extraposed clauses. The analyses are based on the assumption that sentential arguments have the same functions as nominal or prepositional arguments, namely SUBJ, OBJ, $\text{OBJ}_\theta$ or $\text{OBL}_\theta$ and not the distinct function COMP. Concerning (non)-topicalization, it was claimed that all finite clauses in sentence initial position are obligatorily left-dislocated. But in accordance with the conditions on Topic Drop in German, the resumptive pronoun in the topicalized position in the function of a SUBJ or an OBJ may be dropped. The cooccurrence pattern of correlative *es* and the clause it is related to was accounted for by a combination of independent principles of LFG and hypotheses defended in the preceding chapters; in particular, the principles concerning the mapping from a-structure to f-structure, and the claim that German obeys the Subject Condition, together with the additional assumption that German has not only a thematic but also a subcategorized non-thematic *es*.

## 9.2 Further research

In the course of my investigation of German clausal syntax, a number of questions arose that couldn't be addressed within the confines of the present book. I recapitulate the major ones here, to offer a springboard for further research.

The analysis of expletive subjects in chapter 4, according to which they can be introduced by the agreement morphology, could not account for the facts of Dutch. Dutch has subject-verb agreement, but contrary to the prediction of my analysis it also has phonetically realized expletive subjects:

(1) Misschien wordt *(er) gedanst.
perhaps is there danced
'Perhaps there was dancing.'

It would be interesting to see whether the Dutch data can be interpreted in a way compatible with my analysis, or whether it is possible to modify my analysis to account for Dutch while maintaining the core idea of expletives being introduced by agreement morphology. More generally, it would be interesting to apply my analysis to other languages to test its robustness.

We also saw in chapter 4 evidence that led Höhle to suggest that the controlled subject of infinitive clauses must be marked nominative, based on sentences like (78b), repeated here:

(2) Ich habe den Burschen geraten, im Abstand von wenigen
I have the boys-DAT advised in-the separation from few
Tagen einer nach dem anderen zu kündigen.
days one-NOM after the other to quit
'I advised the boys to quit one after the other within a few days.'

Since the phrase *einer nach dem anderen* ('one after the other') has to agree with its antecedent in gender and case, and in (2) it bears nominative case, this indicates that the c-structurally unrealized subject of the non-finite verb has to be marked nominative too. Now, as was also noted, this case pattern rules out an analysis in terms of functional control, since that requires the controller and controllee to share grammatical features, including case. So sentences like (2) raise the question whether there is functional control in German at all and if so, precisly what differences there are to anaphoric control.

In chapter 5, in the discussion of the traceless account of weak crossover by Dalrymple, Kaplan, and King (2001), I noted that both Bresnan's and Dalrymple *et al.*'s accounts implicitly assume that the extraction of the binder extends the binding domain. However, the empirical basis of this assumption still needs to be investigated. Some evidence might be provided by data like the following:

(3) [Welche Prüfung]$_i$ glaubte Otto, dass er bewältigt habe,
Which exam-ACC thought Otto-NOM that he passed has
nachdem sie$_i$ vorbei war?
after it over was
'Which test did Otto believe that he passed after it was finished?'

In this sentence the operator is extracted out of the complement clause and is able to bind a pronoun inside an adjunct clause of the matrix clause. This would indicate that the binding domain is extended.

However, the data are not clear. I have obtained contradictory grammaticality judgments from native speakers for sentences like the following, where the operator is inside the complement clause:

(4) Hans glaubte, dass er [jede Prüfung]$_1$ bestanden hat noch
Hans thinks that he every exam passed has even
bevor sie$_1$ vorbei war.
before it over was
'Hans thinks that he passed every exam before it was finished.'

A further unresolved problem concerning weak crossover is the case of VP-topicalization containing the operator:

(5) *Jeden$_i$ geliebt hat seine$_i$ Mutter.
everyone loved has his mother
'His mother loved everyone.'

Although in this case the pronoun neither precedes nor outranks the operator, nevertheless binding is ungrammatical. Perhaps the definition of the binding domain may also be relevant to account for the ungrammaticality in this case.

In short, further research is needed on the extent of the binding domain.

Both analyses of long distance dependencies discussed in chapter 6 were shown to be able to handle the same range of phenomena, including bridge verbs, extraction out of *dass*-clauses, and Split NPs. The account of Split NPs on the cyclic approach depends on there being an independent explanation for the distribution of the two nominal constituents, but we saw that this assumption is plausible. In contrast, the account of the first two phenomena on the inside-out functional uncertainty approach relies on features (LDD and DECL) used in the off-path constraints, whose independent motivation is open to question. Thus, the cyclic approach is currently preferable. Further research is needed to see whether there are other phenomena that clearly distinguish between the two approaches.

In chapter 7 it was claimed that sentential arguments have the same function as DP- or PP-arguments. However, it is still unclear how the function of clauses, which lack morphological marking, are identified. There is some evidence from VP-topicalization that the structural position may play a role, based on grammaticality contrasts like (78a-b), repeated here:

(6) a. Beweisen, dass er unschuldig ist (OBJ), könnte, dass er hier war.
prove that he innocent is could that he here was
'(The fact) that he was here could prove that he is innocent.'

b. *Beweisen, dass er hier war (SUBJ), könnte, dass er unschuldig ist.

This contrast indicates that with VP-topicalization the clause next to the verb cannot function as SUBJ. This in turn suggests that generally function specification of sentential arguments is structural. However, more research is required to either confirm or reject this hypothesis.

# References


Alsina, A. (1996). *The Role of Argument Structure in Grammar: Evidence from Romance.* Stanford, CA: CSLI Publications.

Alsina, A. and S. Mchombo (1993). Object asymmetries and the Chicheŵa applicative construction. In S. Mchombo (Ed.), *Theoretical Aspects of Bantu Grammar*, pp. 17–45. Stanford, CA: CSLI Publications.

Altmann, H. (1981). *Formen der "Herausstellung" im Deutschen: Rechtsversetzung, Linksversetzung, freies Thema und verwandte Konstruktionen.* Tübingen: Niemeyer.

Andrews, A. (1982). The representation of case in modern Icelandic. In J. Bresnan (Ed.), *The Mental Representation of Grammatical Relations*, pp. 427–503. Cambridge, MA: MIT Press.

Bader, M. (1996). *Sprachverstehen.* Opladen: Westdeutscher Verlag.

Baker, M. (1983). Objects, themes, and lexical rules in Italian. In L. Levin, M. Rappaport, and A. Zaenen (Eds.), *Papers in Lexical-Functional Grammar*, pp. 1–45. Bloomington: Indiana University Linguistics Club.

Bayer, J. (1994). Barriers for German. Technical Report 47, Universität Stuttgart. Arbeitspapiere des Sonderforschungsbereichs 340.

Bayer, J. and J. Kornfilt (1994). Against scrambling as an instance of move-alpha. In N. Corver and H. Riemsdijk (Eds.), *Studies on Scrambling*, pp. 17–60. Berlin: Mouton de Gruyter.

Bech, G. (1983). *Studien über das deutsche Verbum infinitum* (2 ed.). Tübingen: Niemeyer. Republication of the 1955/57 edition published by Munksgaard, Copenhagen.

Belletti, A. and L. Rizzi (1988). Psych-verbs and theta-theory. *Natural Language & Linguistic Theory* 6(3), 291–352.

Bennis, H. (1986). *Gaps and Dummies.* Dordrecht: Foris.

Berman, J. (1996). Topicalization vs. left dislocation of sentential arguments in German. In M. Butt and T. H. King (Eds.), *Proceedings of the LFG'96 Conference*, Grenoble. <http://www-csli.stanford.edu/publications/LFG/lfg1.html>.

Berman, J. (1997). Empty categories in LFG. In M. Butt and T. H. King (Eds.), *Proceedings of the LFG'97 Conference*, San Diego. <http://www-csli.stanford.edu/publications/LFG/2/lfg97.html>.

Berman, J. (1999). Does German satisfy the Subject Condition? In M. Butt and T. H. King (Eds.), *Proceedings of the LFG'99 Conference*, Manchester. <http://www-csli.stanford.edu/publications/LFG/4/lfg99.html>.

Berman, J. (2001). On the cooccurrence of *es* with a finite clause in German. In T. Kiss and D. Meurers (Eds.), *Constraint-Based Approaches to Germanic Syntax*, pp. 7–30. Stanford, CA: CSLI Publications.

Berman, J., S. Dipper, C. Fortmann, and J. Kuhn (1998). Argument clauses and correlative *es* in German – deriving discourse properties in a unification analysis. In M. Butt and T. H. King (Eds.), *Proceedings of the LFG '98 Conference*, Brisbane. <http://www-csli.stanford.edu/publications/LFG/3/lfg98.html>.

Berman, J. and A. Frank (1996). *Deutsche und französische Syntax im Formalismus der LFG*. Tübingen: Niemeyer.

Börjars, K. and C. Chapman (1998). Agreement and pro-drop in some dialects of English. *Linguistics 36*, 71–98.

Brandner, E. (1993). The projection of categories and the nature of agreement. In G. Fanselow (Ed.), *The parametrization of universal grammar*, pp. 73–121. Amsterdam: Benjamins.

Brandt, M., M. Reis, I. Rosengren, and I. Zimmermann (1992). Satztyp & Satzmodus & Illokution. In I. Rosengren (Ed.), *Satz und Illokution*, pp. 1–90. Tübingen: Niemeyer.

Breindl, E. (1989). *Präpositionalobjekte und Präpositionalobjektsätze im Deutschen*. Tübingen: Niemeyer.

Bresnan, J. (1977). Transformations and categories in syntax. In R. Butts and J. Hintikka (Eds.), *Basic problems in methodology and linguistics*, Part Three of the Proceedings of the Fifth International Congress of Logic, Methodology and Philosophy of Science, pp. 261–282. Dordrecht: Reidel.

Bresnan, J. (1982). Control and complementation. *Linguistic Inquiry 13*, 343–434.

Bresnan, J. (1994). Locative inversion and the architecture of universal grammar. *Language 70*, 72–131.

Bresnan, J. (1995a). Category mismatches. In A. Akinlabi (Ed.), *Theoretical Approaches to African Languages*, pp. 19–46. Trenton, N.J.: African World Press.

Bresnan, J. (1995b). Linear order, syntactic rank, and empty categories: On weak crossover. In M. Dalrymple, A. Zaenen, J. Maxwell, and R. M. Kaplan (Eds.), *Formal Issues in Lexical-Functional Grammar*, pp. 241–274. Stanford, CA: CSLI Publications.

Bresnan, J. (1998). Morphology competes with syntax: Explaining typological variation in weak crossover effects. In P. Barbosa, D. Fox, P. Hagstrom, M. McGinnis, and D. Pesetsky (Eds.), *Is the Best Good Enough? Optimality and Competition in Syntax*, pp. 52–92. Cambridge, MA: MIT Press.

Bresnan, J. (2001). *Lexical-Functional Syntax*. Oxford: Blackwell.

Bresnan, J. and J. Kanerva (1989). Locative inversion in Chicheŵa: A case study of factorization in grammar. *Linguistic Inquiry 20*, 1–50.

Bresnan, J. and S. Mchombo (1987). Topic, pronoun, and agreement in Chicheŵa. *Language 63*, 741–782.

Bresnan, J. and L. Moshi (1990). Object asymmetries in comparative Bantu syntax. *Linguistic Inquiry 21*(2), 147–185.

Bresnan, J. and A. Zaenen (1990). Deep unaccusativity in LFG. In K. Dziwirek, P. Farrell, and E. Mejías-Bikandi (Eds.), *Grammatical Relations: A Cross-Theoretical Perspective*, pp. 45–57. Stanford, CA: CSLI Publications.

Büring, D. (1995). On the base position of embedded clauses in German. *Linguistische Berichte 159*, 370–380.

Büring, D. (1997). *The Meaning of Topic and Focus. The 59th Street Bridge Accent.* London: Routledge.

Büring, D. and K. Hartmann (1995). All right! In U. Lutz and J. Pafel (Eds.), *On Extraction and Extraposition in German*, pp. 179–211. Amsterdam: Benjamins.

Butt, M. (1998). Constraining argument merger through aspect. In E. Hinrichs, A. Kathol, and T. Nakazawa (Eds.), *Complex Predicates in Nonderivational Syntax*, Volume 30 of *Syntax and Semantics*, pp. 73–113. San Diego: Academic Press.

Butt, M., M. Dalrymple, and A. Frank (1997). An architecture for linking theory in LFG. In M. Butt and T. H. King (Eds.),

*Proceedings of the LFG97 Conference*, San Diego. http://www-csli.stanford.edu/publications/LFG/2/lfg97.html.

Cardinaletti, A. (1990). *Impersonal constructions and sentential arguments in German.* Padua: Unipress.

Choi, H.-W. (1995). Weak crossover in scrambling languages: Precedence, rank, and discourse. Paper presented at the 1995 Annual Meeting of the Linguistic Society of America, New Orleans.

Choi, H.-W. (1999). *Optimizing Structure in Context: Scrambling and Information Structure.* Stanford, CA: CSLI Publications.

Chomsky, N. (1982). *Some Concepts and Consequences of the Theory of Government and Binding.* Cambridge, MA: MIT Press.

Dalrymple, M. (1993). *The Syntax of Anaphoric Binding.* Stanford, CA: CSLI Publications.

Dalrymple, M. (2001). *Lexical Functional Grammar*, Volume 34 of *Syntax and Semantics.* New York: Academic Press.

Dalrymple, M. and R. Kaplan (1997). A set-based approach to feature resolution. In M. Butt and T. H. King (Eds.), *Proceedings of the LFG97 Conference*, San Diego. <http://www-csli.stanford.edu/publications/LFG/2/lfg97.html>.

Dalrymple, M., R. Kaplan, and T. H. King (2001). Weak crossover and the absence of traces. In M. Butt and T. H. King (Eds.), *Proceedings of the LFG'01 Conference*, Hong Kong. <http://www-csli.stanford.edu/publications/LFG/6/lfg01.html>.

Dalrymple, M. and H. Lodrup (2000). The grammatical functions of complement clauses. In M. Butt and T. H. King (Eds.), *Proceedings of the LFG'00 Conference*, Berkeley. <http://www-csli.stanford.edu/publications/LFG/5/lfg00.html>.

d'Avis, F.-J., S. Beck, U. Lutz, J. Pafel, and S. Trissler (1993). Extraktion im Deutschen. Technical Report 34, Universität Tübingen. Arbeitspapiere des Sonderforschungsbereichs 340.

Dowty, D. (1991). Thematic proto-roles and argument selection. *Language 67*, 547–619.

Eisenberg, P. (1999). *Grundriß der deutschen Grammatik*, Volume 2: Der Satz. Stuttgart: Metzler.

Erdmann, O. (1886). *Grundzüge der deutschen Syntax nach ihrer geschichtlichen Entwicklung. Erste Abteilung.* Stuttgart: Cotta.

Falk, C. (1987). Subjectless clauses in Swedish. *Working Papers in Scandinavian Syntax 32*, 1–26.

Falk, Y. N. (2001). *Lexical-Functional Grammar.* Stanford, CA: CSLI Publications.

Fanselow, G. (1987). *Konfigurationalität - Untersuchungen zur Universalgrammatik am Beispiel des Deutschen.* Tübingen: Narr.

Fanselow, G. (1991). Minimale Syntax. *Groninger Arbeiten zur Germanistischen Linguistik 32.*

Féry, C. (1992). Focus, topic and intonation in German. Technical Report 20, Universität Tübingen. Arbeitspapiere des Sonderforschungsbereichs 340.

Féry, C. (1993). *German Intonational Patterns.* Tübingen: Niemeyer.

Fortmann, C. (2001). Defizitäre Argumente – Bedingungen der thematischen Lizensierung. Habilitationsschrift, Universität Stuttgart.

Frank, R., Y.-S. Lee, and O. Rambow (1992). Scrambling as nonoperator movement and the special status of subjects. In S. Barbiers, M. den Dikken, and C. Levelt (Eds.), *Proceedings of the Third Leiden Conference for Junior Linguists*, pp. 135–154.

Frey, W. (1993). *Syntaktische Bedingungen für die semantische Interpretation.* Berlin: Akademie Verlag.

Frey, W. and H. T. Tappe (1991). Zur Interpretation der X-bar Theorie und zur Syntax des Mittelfelds. Ms., Universität Stuttgart.

Grewendorf, G. (1988). *Aspekte der deutschen Syntax: eine Rektions-Bindungs-Analyse.* Tübingen: Narr.

Grewendorf, G. (1989). *Ergativity in German.* Dordrecht: Foris.

Grimshaw, J. (1982). Subcategorization and grammatical relations. In A. Zaenen (Ed.), *Subjects and other Subjects: Proceedings of the Harvard Conference on the Representation of Grammatical Relations*, Bloomington, pp. 35–55. Indiana University Linguistics Club.

Grimshaw, J. (1990). *Argument Structure.* Cambridge, MA: MIT Press.

Haider, H. (1987). Deutsche Syntax – generativ: Parameter der deutschen Syntax. Habilitationsschrift Teil II, Universität Wien.

Haider, H. (1990a). PRO-BLEME. In G. Fanselow and S. Felix (Eds.), *Strukturen und Merkmale syntaktischer Kategorien*, pp. 121–143. Tübingen: Narr.

Haider, H. (1990b). Topicalization and other puzzles of German syntax. In G. Grewendorf and W. Sternefeld (Eds.), *Scrambling and Barriers*, pp. 93–112. Amsterdam: Benjamins.

Haider, H. (1991a). Fakultativ kohärente Infinitkonstruktionen im Deutschen. Technical Report 17, Universität Stuttgart. Arbeitspapiere des Sonderforschungsbereichs 340.

Haider, H. (1991b). Null subjects and expletives in Romance and Germanic languages. In W. Abraham, E. Kosmeijer, and E. Reuland (Eds.), *Issues in Germanic Syntax*, pp. 49–66. Berlin: Mouton de Gruyter.

Haider, H. (1993a). *Deutsche Syntax – Generativ. Vorstudien zur Theorie einer projektiven Grammatik.* Tübingen: Narr.

Haider, H. (1993b). ECP-Etüden: Anmerkungen zur Extraktion aus eingebetteten Verb-Zweit-Sätzen. *Linguistische Berichte 145*, 185–203.

Haider, H. (1995a). Downright down to the right. In U. Lutz and J. Pafel (Eds.), *On Extraction and Extraposition in German*, pp. 245–271. Amsterdam: Benjamins.

Haider, H. (1995b). Studies on phrase structure and economy. Technical Report 70, Universität Stuttgart. Arbeitspapiere des Sonderforschungsbereichs 340.

Haider, H. (1997). Projective economy: On the minimal functional structure of the German clause. In W. Abraham (Ed.), *German: Syntactic Problems – Problematic Syntax*, pp. 83–103. Tübingen: Niemeyer.

Halvorsen, P.-K. and R. M. Kaplan (1988). Projections and semantic description in Lexical-Functional Grammar. In *Proceedings of the International Conference on Fifth Generation Computer Systems (FGCS-88)*, Tokyo, Japan, pp. 1116–1122. Reprinted in M. Dalrymple *et al.* (Eds.), *Formal Issues in Lexical-Functional Grammar*, 279–292. Stanford: CSLI Publications. 1995.

Hoekstra, T. (1983). The distribution of sentential complements. In H. Bennis and W. van Lessen Kloeke (Eds.), *Linguistics in the Netherlands*, pp. 93–103. Dordrecht: Foris.

Höhle, T. (1982). Explikationen für 'normale Betonung' und 'normale Wortstellung'. In W. Abraham (Ed.), *Satzglieder im Deutschen*, pp. 75–153. Tübingen: Narr.

Höhle, T. (1983). Topologische Felder. Ms., Universität Köln.

Höhle, T. (1986). Der Begriff "Mittelfeld". Anmerkungen über die Theorie der topologischen Felder. In A. Schöne (Ed.), *Kontroversen alte und neue: Akten des 7. Internationalen Germanisten-Kongresses, Göttingen 1985*, Volume 3, pp. 329–340. Tübingen: Niemeyer.

Huang, C.-T. J. (1984). On the distribution and references of empty pronouns. *Linguistic Inquiry 15*, 531–574.

Jackendoff, R. (1990). On Larson's treatment of double object construction. *Linguistic Inquiry 21*, 427–456.

Kaplan, R. (1995). The formal architecture of Lexical-Functional Grammar. In M. Dalrymple et al. (Eds.), *Formal Issues in Lexical-Functional Grammar*, pp. 7–27. Stanford, CA: CSLI Publications.

Kaplan, R. and J. Bresnan (1982). Lexical-Functional Grammar: A formal system for grammatical representation. In J. Bresnan (Ed.), *The Mental Representation of Grammatical Relations*, pp. 173–281. Cambridge MA: MIT Press. Reprinted in M. Dalrymple *et al.* (eds.), *Formal Issues in Lexical-Functional Grammar*, 29–130. Stanford, CA: CSLI Publications. 1995.

Kaplan, R. and J. T. Maxwell (1988). An algorithm for functional uncertainty. In *Proceedings of COLING-88*, Budapest, pp. 297–302.

Kaplan, R. and J. T. Maxwell (1996). LFG grammar writer's workbench. Technical report, Xerox Palo Alto Research Center. <ftp://parcftp.xerox.com/pub/lfg/lfgmanual.ps>.

Kaplan, R. M. and A. Zaenen (1989). Long-distance dependencies, constituent structure, and functional uncertainty. In M. Baltin and A. Kroch (Eds.), *Alternative Conceptions of Phrase Structure*, pp. 17–42. Chicago: Chicago University Press. Reprinted in M. Dalrymple *et al.* (Eds.), *Formal Issues in Lexical-Functional Grammar*, 137–165. Stanford: CSLI Publications. 1995.

Kathol, A. (2000). *Linear Syntax.* Oxford: Oxford University Press.

King, T. H. (1995). *Configuring Topic and Focus in Russian.* Stanford, CA: CSLI Publications.

Kiparsky, P. and C. Kiparsky (1970). Fact. In M. Bierwisch and K. Heidolph (Eds.), *Progress in Linguistics. A Collection of Papers*, pp. 143–173.

Kiss, T. (1995). *Infinitive Komplementation: Neue Studien zum deutschen Verbum infinitum.* Tübingen: Niemeyer.

Köhler, K.-H. (1976). Zum Problem der Korrelate in Gliedsätzen. In H. Schumacher (Ed.), *Untersuchungen zur Verbvalenz*, pp. 174–239. Tübingen: Narr.

Koster, J. (1978). Why subject sentences don't exist. In S. J. Keyser (Ed.), *Recent Transformational Studies in European Languages*, pp. 53–64. Cambridge, MA: MIT Press.

Kratzer, A. (1984). On deriving differences between English and German. Ms., TU Berlin.

Kroeger, P. (1993). *Phrase Structure and Grammatical Relations in Tagalog.* Stanford, CA: CSLI Publications.

Kuhn, J. (2001). Resource sensitivity in the syntax-semantics interface: Evidence from the German split NP construction. In T. Kiss and D. Meurers (Eds.), *Constraint-Based Approaches to Germanic Syntax*, pp. 177–215. Stanford, CA: CSLI Publications.

Lehmann, C. (1982). Nominalisierung: Typisierung von Propositionen. In H. Seiler and C. Lehmann (Eds.), *Apprehension. Das sprachliche Erfassen von Gegenständen*, Volume I, pp. 66–84. Tübingen: Narr.

Mahajan, A. (1990). *The A/A-BAR Distinction and Movement Theory.* Ph. D. thesis, MIT, Cambridge, MA.

Meier, J. (1994). Zur Syntax des Verbalkomplexes im Deutschen. Technical Report 55, Universität Stuttgart. Arbeitspapiere des Sonderforschungsbereichs 340.

Mereu, L. (1997). For a lexical-functional representation of agreement affixes and clitics. In M. Butt and T. H. King (Eds.), *Proceedings of the LFG'97 Conference*, San Diego. <http://www-csli.stanford.edu/publications/LFG/2/lfg97.html>.

Meurers, W. D. (1999). Raising spirits (and assigning them case). *Groninger Arbeiten zur Germanistischen Linguistik 43*, 173–226.

Mohanan, T. (1994). *Argument Structure in Hindi.* Stanford, CA: CSLI Publications.

Müller, G. (1995a). *A-bar syntax: a study in movement types.* Berlin: Mouton de Gruyter.

Müller, G. (1995b). On extraposition & successive cyclicity. In U. Lutz and J. Pafel (Eds.), *On Extraction and Extraposition in German*, pp. 213–243. Amsterdam: Benjamins.

Müller, S. (1999). *Deutsche Syntax deklarativ. Head-Driven Phrase Structure Grammar für das Deutsche.* Tübingen: Niemeyer.

Müller, S. (2001). Case in German — towards an HPSG analysis. In T. Kiss and D. Meurers (Eds.), *Constraint-Based Approaches to Germanic Syntax*, pp. 217–255. Stanford, CA: CSLI Publications.

Neidle, C. (1994). Lexical Functional Grammar. In *Encyclopedia of Language and Linguistics*, pp. 2147–2153. New York: Pergamon Press.

Netter, K. (1988). Nonlocal-dependencies and infinitival constructions in German. In U. Reyle and C. Rohrer (Eds.), *Natural Language Parsing and Linguistic Theories*, pp. 356–410. Dordrecht: D. Reidel.

Netter, K. and C. Rohrer (1987). Syntactic analysis in Lexical Functional Grammar: The example of German prepositional phrases.

*T. A. Informations, Revue International du Traitement Automatique du Langage (Numéro spéciale 'Linguistique et Informatique en République Fédérale Allemande') 28*, 71–95.

Nichols, J. (1986). Head-marking and dependent-marking grammar. *Language 62*, 56–119.

Nordlinger, R. (1998). *Constructive Case: Evidence From Australian Languages*. Stanford, CA: CSLI Publications.

Oppenrieder, W. (1991). *Von Subjekten, Sätzen und Subjektsätzen*. Tübingen: Niemeyer.

Pittner, K. (1995). The case of German relatives. *The Linguistic Review 12*, 197–231.

Raposo, E. (1987). Case theory and INFL-to-COMP. *Linguistic Inquiry 18*(1), 85–109.

Reis, M. (1977). *Präsuppositionen und Syntax*. Tübingen: Niemeyer.

Reis, M. (1982). Zum Subjektbegriff im Deutschen. In W. Abraham (Ed.), *Satzglieder im Deutschen*, pp. 171–211. Tübingen: Narr.

Reis, M. (1995). *Wer glaubst du hat recht?* On so-called extractions from verb-second clauses and verb-first parenthetical constructions in German. *Sprache und Pragmatik* (36), 27–83.

Rohrbacher, B. (1999). *Morphology-driven syntax: a theory of V to I raising and pro-drop*. Amsterdam: Benjamins.

Sadler, L. (1996). New developments in LFG. In K. Brown and J. Miller (Eds.), *Concise Encyclopedia of Syntactic Theories*. Oxford: Elsevier Science.

Sadler, L. (1997). Welsh clitics and the structure-function mapping. In M. Butt and T. H. King (Eds.), *Proceedings of the LFG'97 Conference*, San Diego. http://www-csli.stanford.edu/publications/LFG/2/lfg97.html.

Safir, K. (1985). *Syntactic Chains*. Cambridge, MA: University Press.

Schwarz, B. and S. Vikner (1996). The verb always leaves IP in V2 clauses. In A. Belletti and L. Rizzi (Eds.), *Parameters and Functional Heads*, pp. 11–62. Oxford: Oxford University Press.

Sells, P. (1998). Optimality and economy of expression in Japanese and Korean. In N. Akatsuka et al. (Eds.), *Japanese/Korean Linguistics*, Volume 7, pp. 499–514. Stanford, CA: CSLI Publications.

Sells, P. (1999). Japanese postposing involves no movement. Paper Presented at the meeting of the Linguistics Association of Great Britain.

Sells, P. (2000). Raising and the order of clausal constituents in the Philippine languages. In I. Paul, V. Phillips, and L. Travis (Eds.), *Formal Issues in Austronesian Linguistics*, pp. 117–143. Dordrecht: Kluwer Academic Publishers.

Staudacher, P. (1990). Long movements from verb-second-complements in German. In G. Grewendorf and W. Sternefeld (Eds.), *Scrambling and Barriers*, pp. 319–339. Amsterdam: Benjamins.

Stechow, A. v. and W. Sternefeld (1988). *Bausteine syntaktischen Wissens.* Opladen: Westdeutscher Verlag.

Sternefeld, W. (1985). Deutsch ohne grammatische Funktionen: Ein Beitrag zur Rektions- und Bindungstheorie. *Linguistische Berichte 99*, 394–439.

Stowell, T. (1981). *Origins of Phrase Structure.* Ph. D. thesis, MIT.

Travis, L. (1984). *Parameters and Effects of Word Order Variation.* Ph. D. thesis, MIT.

Vikner, S. (1995). *Verb Movement and Expletive Subjects in the Germanic Languages.* Oxford: Oxford University Press.

Vikner, S. (1997). $V^o$-to-$I^o$ movement and inflection for person in all tenses. In L. Haegeman (Ed.), *The New Comparative Syntax*, pp. 189–213. London: Longman.

Webelhuth, G. (1984). German is configurational. *The Linguistic Review 4*, 203–246.

Webelhuth, G. (1992). *Principles and Parameter of Syntactic Saturation.* Oxford: Oxford University Press.

Zaenen, A. and E. Engdahl (1994). Descriptive and theoretical syntax in the lexicon. In B. Atkins and A. Zambolli (Eds.), *Computational Approaches to the Lexicon*, pp. 181–212. Oxford: Oxford University Press.

Zaenen, A., J. Maling, and H. Thrainsson (1985). Case and grammatical functions: The Icelandic passive. *Natural Language Linguistic Theory 3*, 441–483.

# Index

a-structure, 7, 19–21, 59, 78, 79, 83, 152, 157–159, 162, 164, 165
  and weak crossover, 84
  of *beweisen*-verbs, 156
  of *sagen*-verbs, 153
  of psych-verbs, 157
adjoined positions, 37, 44, 75, 81, 98, 140, 151
adjunct, 11, 12, 16, 36, 37, 82, 102, 104, 155n, 159
  clause, 26, 104, 142, 153, 154
adverbials, 25, 30n
agreement, 56
  subject-verb, 13, 52, 53, 55, 57, 59, 61, 163
  verbal morphology, 52, 56, 57, 59, 61–63, 64n, 67, 68, 70, 74, 152, 163
apposition, 155–157, 164
  f-precede condition on, 155–157, 161
argument clause, 26, 142, 144, 153, 154
argument function
  canonical position of, 75, 76, 81, 82, 87, 96–98, 100
argument-structure, *see* a-structure
asymmetries
  argument/adjunct, 151
  subject/object, 35
attribute-value pairs, 10

binding domain, 77, 80, 82, 84–90, 92, 171
  extended, 86, 92, 93, 170
bridge verbs, 113–116, 118, 154

c-command, 42, 43
c-structure, 7–9, 13, 16, 29, 30, 41, 53, 71, 78, 79, 84, 92, 98, 99, 110, 114, 165
case
  accusative, 30, 47, 49, 50, 151, 158
  dative, 51
  default, 158
  lexical, 50, 51, 158
  nominative, 30, 47–50, 106, 151, 158, 162
    in non-finite clauses, 72–74
case-assignment
  default, 49, 50, 152
  lexical, 49, 152
  nominative, 72
CAT-operator, 110
categorial features, 8, 16
categorial restriction, 110
categories, 7
  empty, *see* empty category
  functional, 8, 16, 107, 140
  levels of, 8
  lexical, 8, 16, 41, 76
  types of, 8

Chicheŵa, 53, 54, 56, 79
coarguments, 90, 92
Coherence, 12, 58, 59, 64, 99, 162
coherent infinitives, 89, 132
COMP, 11, 91, 98, 101, 103, 104, 108–110, 116, 123–126, 129, 130, 133–137
complement, 8, 16, 17, 30, 31
  clause, 24, 91, 93, 103, 107, 113, 116, 125, 126
complementizer, 24, 26, 27, 29, 118, 141
  declarative, 118
Completeness, 11, 12, 57, 64, 68, 76, 87, 94, 99, 106, 108, 112
configurational languages, 8, 98
configurational structure, 10, 19, 33
constituent-structure, *see* c-structure
constraining equation, 61, 67, 72, 163
control
  anaphoric, 68–72, 74, 170
  arbitrary, 68, 73
  functional, 68, 73, 170
control equation, 68, 71, 74
coordination, 134, 136
CP, 29, 30, 81, 101, 110, 125, 126, 128, 131, 140, 148, 153, 154, 159, 160, 163

Danish, 52, 58n, 59
declarative clause, 23, 65
dependent-marking, 17, 18, 47
DF, *see* discourse function
discourse function, 29, 30, 60, 75, 81, 96, 106–109, 111–113, 137, 140
dominance, 8, 42
Dutch, 52, 61n, 151, 161n

Economy of Expression, 10, 38, 42, 62–64, 67, 71, 72, 75–77, 87, 94, 98, 108n, 163
empty category, 3, 62, 71, 75–77, 81, 82, 86, 88–90, 93, 98, 99, 101, 103, 106, 108, 110, 112, 115
  annotation on, 100, 104, 108
endocentric complement, 16
Endocentric Mapping Principles, 15, 16, 29, 41, 75, 81, 94, 97–99, 107
endocentric phrases, 8, 15, 29, 40
Endocentricity, 41–44
English, 8, 17, 58n, 60, 61, 62n, 72, 75, 76, 79n, 81, 82, 93, 97, 99, 103, 124, 130, 134, 141n
ergative verb, 35, 46, 48, 62
*es*
  as personal pronoun, 30
  as placeholder, 65
  as thematic argument, 153–157
  correlative, 148–164
  in *Mittelfeld*, 65–67
  in *Vorfeld*, 65
  in control constructions, 66
  non-thematic, 67, 159–162
    subcategorization of, 152, 159, 163
exocentric category S, 9, 10, 19, 33
Extended Coherence, 12, 108, 112
extended head, 40–44
Extended Projection Principle, 62
extraction, 96, 99, 101–103, 106, 107, 110, 114, 116, 149, 153, 154, 157, 159, 161, 162, 164
  of binder, 92, 93
  out of adjunct, 102, 115, 157
  out of object clause, 102
  out of subject clause, 102, 157
  out of *dass*-clause, 118–120
extraction islands, 133
extraposed clauses, 26, 39, 141–144, 148, 157

f-precedence, 78, 91n, 155, 156

f-structure, 7, 8, 10–15, 54, 57, 77–79, 90
  co-heads, 17, 30, 41
  head, 30n, 52
  path, 94, 96, 97, 106, 110, 111, 154
FOC, 30, 80, 96
FORM-feature, 159, 160
free relatives, 140
function application, 17n, 97
  inside-out, 99, 100, 111
function specification, 33
  lexocentric, 37, 44, 81, 89, *see* function specification, morphological
  morphological, 17–19, 47, 75, 77, 94, 106, 142
    restricted to local clause, 86, 87, 93
  of sentential arguments, 144
  structural, 62, 93, 98, 100
functional annotations, 7, 13, 14
functional hierarchy, 21, 78, 80n, 82n, 90, 91
functional projection, 29, 33, 36
functional uncertainty, 98
  inside-out, 96, 99–110, 119, 125n
  outside-in, 97–98, 125n
functional-structure, *see* f-structure

gap, 101, 155n, *see* empty category
German sentence structure, 23, 27, 33, 34, 107
grammatical functions, 10, 11, 15, 17, 19, 20, 36, 59, 123
  of complement clauses, 4, 131, 133–137, 144

head-marking, 17, 18, 47, 52, 53
Hindi, 46, 79, 86, 88

Icelandic, 31, 32, 50n, 58, 60
incoherent infinitives, 89, 132n
instantiated symbols, 54, 160
IP, 31, 32, 38, 75, 97

left dislocation, 29, 127, 137, 138, 142
Lexical Integrity, 10, 32
Lexical Mapping Theory, 7, 19, 21, 46, 152, 153, 158
lexocentricity, 17
linear order, 78, 87, 89, 142
linear prominence, 91–93
long distance dependencies, 86, 87, 91, 95–120
  as cyclic locally bounded dependencies, 111–120

mapping function $\phi$, 13, 45
  inverse mapping $\phi^{-1}$, 42
*Mittelfeld*, 27, 30, 65, 140, 141, 152
  unacceptability of finite clauses in, 136

*Nachfeld*, 27, 140, 141, 148
negative constraint, 119, 160
non-bridge verbs, 114
non-configurational languages, 9
non-configurational structure, 17
non-finite clauses, 67–74, 89
Norwegian, 52, 58, 59

$\text{OBJ}_\theta$, 57, 58, 64, 83, 152, 158
object
  accusative, 84, 126n, 127, 138
  clause, 142, 143, 153–156
  dative, 84, 126n, 138
  genitive, 126n, 127, 128, 137, 138
  non-thematic, 48n
  prepositional, 126n, 127, 130, 132n, 137, 141
off-path constraints, 107–110, 116, 120
operator binding, 77, 79–82, 84, 86, 89, 90, *see* weak crossover

passive, 46, 48–51, 62, 70, 135, 136, 157
  impersonal, 51, 52, 61, 63, 70
  of *sagen*-verbs, 162–164
PRED-feature, 11, 54, 56, 58, 70, 95, 140, 159, 162
Principle for Identifying Gaps, 95, 100, 108, 113
PRO, 71
*pro*, 62, 63
pro-drop, 53, 54, 56
proform, 133, 134, 138
Prominence Principle, 77–79, 86, 91, 93
pronoun incorporation, 54–56
psych-verbs, 84, 149n, 157, 159, 161, 163
  mapping rule for, 158

quasi-argument, 65–67

referential index, 70
relative clauses, 26
resumptive pronoun, 137, 140, 142, 161
  deletion of, 138
Russian, 35n, 75, 76

*Satzklammer*, 27, 30, 37
scrambling, 34, 34, 35n, 79–81, 86–88
semi-pro-drop, 62
sentential argument
  distribution of, 123–145
  extraposition of, *see* extraposed clauses
  infinitival, 140, 141
  proform of, 130, 136
  topicalization of, *see* topicalization
Split NP construction, 117–118
SUBJ, *see* subject
subject
  as discourse function, 30
  clause, 115, 127, 142, 143, 157, 161
  expletive, 52, 57–59, 61–63, 65, 68, 70, 72
    phonetically unrealized, 62
  in non-finite clauses, 67–74
  position of, 33, 36
Subject Condition, 2, 21, 45, 46, 48–51, 57, 59, 67, 68, 71, 152, 159–161, 163, 164
subject-verb agreement, *see* agreement, subject-verb
Swedish, 52, 58, 59, 134
syntactic phrase structure nodes, 8, 10, 16, 38
syntactic rank, 78

thematic hierarchy, 19, 20, 83, 153
thematic prominence, 78
thematic role, 7, 20, 36, 49–51, 152, 153, 158
third construction, 90
TOP, 30, 80, 95, 96, 99–101, 140
Topic Drop, 137, 138, 157, 161
topicalization, 35n, 77, 80–82, 97, 99, 117, 132, 144, 154, 161
  as left dislocation, 137–140, 161
  English vs. Russian, 75
  of adjuncts, 155
  of sentential arguments in English, 123–125
  of sentential arguments in German, 125–140
  of VP, *see* VP-topicalization
topological model, 27, 28
trace, 3, 40, 81, 88, 128, *see* empty category

unification, 13, 52–54, 57, 63, 160
Uniqueness Condition, 13, 54

V-to-I-movement, 31
V2, *see* verb-second
verb-second, 23, 27, 28, 30, 33, 40–42, 44, 65, 102n, 103
  embedded, 24, 120

verbal (agreement) morphology,
  *see* agreement, verbal
  morphology
verbal affix, 52, 53, 60, 69n, 72
verbal complex, 37–39
*Vorfeld*, 27, 30, 65, 137, 140–142,
  148
*Vorvorfeld*, 27
VP-topicalization, 33, 35, 39, 43,
  85n, 144, 149, 154, 156, 157,
  159, 161, 162, 164

Walpiri, 9
weak crossover, 75, 77–94
  between objects, 83–84
  with adjuncts, 82
  with complex sentences, 84
  with infinitives, 89
  with long distance
    dependencies, 86–89
  with scrambling, 79
  with topicalization, 80–82
  without traces, 90–93
wellformedness conditions, 10,
  11, 46, 58
wh-clause
  embedded, 107
word order, 24
  canonical, 33, 35
  of extraposed clauses, 154

X-bar, 8

yes/no-questions, 26
Yiddish, 31, 32, 60